BUSINESS HACKS

◆

A Guide for Start-ups and Entrepreneurs

Jamie Rice and Andrew Leong

Contents

vi

INTRODUCTION

Are you looking to start your own business? Does the whole concept overwhelm you? Are you unsure where to start or how to get your business up and running? Maybe you're involved with a start-up, but you're feeling a bit lost? Are you confused as to how you would actually take your customers' payments? Does selling and marketing your business seem terrifying? Have you read several business-related books, but still feel none the wiser? If your answer to any of these questions is "yes" then we want you to know you're not alone. Everyone feels like this when they start.

This book was written for you and for anyone who's found that many of the business books available tell you what you need to do, but don't tell you how to actually do it. How do you sell your product or services? What do you say to persuade people to buy from you? How do you set up a website and do it without spending lots of money? How do you set up your business bank accounts? How do you come up with creative ideas? How do you do marketing? Where do you go to get a logo created?

We decided to write a business book that breaks the mould in giving readers step-by-step instructions on how to create a business. We've done this by breaking down and explaining the functions of a business with easy to follow instructions and examples.

We've also created a library of online resources that you can download for free. At times the book will refer to these resources, because some things are best experienced first-hand rather than read about. Whilst we'll demonstrate many topics in detail, we'll touch on others, such as technology, only lightly, simply because detailed instructions will quickly become out-of-date as technology advances.

Whilst this book tells you step-by-step what to do, it won't work unless you actually follow these steps. It's a bit like reading about climbing a mountain: you've still got to get up and climb the mountain to reach the top. We'll tell you where to put your hands and feet for the climb, but be prepared, it'll still be hard physical work and you'll occasionally slip.

You'll notice that there's some repetition within the book. This is not only because certain subjects crossover naturally, but also to reinforce and help you embed the learning. You can read this book from cover-to-cover, but it's also designed in such a way that you can dip into any chapter to help you tackle the problem you're facing.

In fact, while you can read this book from start to finish, it'll be difficult to absorb and retain the rich information within. Some of the content you won't be able to relate to until you're at that particular stage of your business and faced with that specific problem. Therefore, we recommend that you keep this book with you as a guide, so that when you face specific problems, whether it's website development or sales, you can simply refer back to the book.

DON'T TRY TO BOIL THE OCEAN

When many people think of becoming entrepreneurs they think of starting large billion pound companies. This is fantastic, and we want you to keep this dream. However, companies like this are at the mature stage of their business life. They didn't start like this. Their business founders learnt to crawl before they could run. That's what we recommend to you. Therefore, rather than trying to build a billion pound business overnight, at first build a company that generates £500 a month.

By building a business that generates £500 a month you'll learn how to create a product, how to sell and market it, how to distribute it, and how to get customers. You'll learn how to build a business.

This will have some very powerful psychological effects. Trying to build a billion pound business will seem so unattainable that most people will give up before they even start. However, building a £500 a month business is realistic and achievable. It takes the pressure off and the fear of failure out of the equation. Once you hit £500 a month your confidence will start to grow and you'll start to feel self-sufficient. You can then aim for £1000 a month. At this point your brain will start looking for ways to cut costs, operate better and increase sales in order to reach your £1000 target. You'll be thinking and acting like an entrepreneur.

PART 1

SET UP

Business Idea Generation

In this chapter we'll look at creative ways to come up with new businesses, products and services. You may already know or have an idea of what product or service your business is going to be providing. In this case you can use this chapter to question your idea, or improve it. You might want to start a business, but you haven't got an idea for a product or service yet. In this particular case you can use the techniques and tools in this chapter to help you create a product or service. For simplicity, for the rest of this chapter we'll use the term "product" to mean either a product or a service.

Firstly, we want to stress the importance of only opening a business in something you're passionate about. If you're new to business you're going to make a lot of mistakes, you're going to be working late nights and you're going to be learning an extraordinary amount. If you're not passionate about your business you just won't have the energy or motivation to make it a success.

For example, if you're passionate about fashion you might decide to open up a business in:

- clothing, shoes, bags or jewellery
- physical or online fashion magazine
- freelance fashion designing

- fashion events
- modelling agency
- fashion advice
- fashion retail store
- tailors or alterations

As you can see the range of businesses for one industry is vast and this is just a sample, but whatever you do you should be *passionate* about it.

Before we delve into product development it's important to know that there are two central ways of being competitive:

1. Selling products at a lower price than your competition. Good examples of this include: Poundland, Aldi, Home Bargains and Primark.

2. Offering your customers a different product from your competitors. Therefore, enabling you to sell at a higher price. A good example of this is Apple in the technology industry.

If you produce a product that can't be competitive in price or offer something different then you'll have difficulty selling your product. This is especially true as a new company that customers or clients won't immediately trust or recognise. Don't let this obstacle put you off, instead let it motivate you to innovate and create ideas that disrupt the market place.

"Being the richest man in the cemetery doesn't matter to me. Going to bed at night saying we've done something wonderful... that's what matters to me." - Steve Jobs.

New product development is simply the process of creating a new product that offers benefits to the customer. It can be a completely new product or it can be the modification of an existing product that enhances and improves it. The customer will benefit from lower costs or better functionality.

Your natural tendency will be to ask customers what they want and then provide them with this service. While this offers some benefit, top business people and inventors know that customers don't always know what they want. You have to show them what they want. Henry Ford, who developed and manufactured the first automobile, once famously said:

> *"If I had asked people what they wanted, they would have said faster horses."*

Steve Jobs also famously said:

> *"People don't know what they want until you show it to them."*

You may notice we refer to Steve Jobs and Apple several times in this chapter. From a business perspective you can't talk about product development and innovation without referring to one of the most innovative individuals of our time.

Now at this stage you might be panicking and thinking that you're not creative. You might be worried that you don't have the engineering or computer programming skills to create new products. This isn't true, you *are* creative, and this section of the book will help you tap into your creative ability. Firstly, many people confuse art with creativity. Artists are creative, but not all creative people are artists. Creativity can be as simple as connecting things and making something simpler. For example, people used do their food shopping by going to the bakery for bread, the butchers for meat and the greengrocer for fruit. Then someone had the idea of a supermarket, which combined all these individual shops under one roof. This creative idea was ingenious and didn't necessitate any technical skills. You too can create such innovate ideas.

You might have come up with a product that requires technical skills that you don't have. This isn't a problem and many entrepreneurs come up with inventions beyond their ability. In fact without doubt you'll face many aspects of your business that you don't have the skills to deal with. Being an entrepreneur means solving problems and leading the way. Entrepreneurs use even more intelligent people to solve their problems and create the things they need. We'll discuss this more later in the book. Just to prove this point though, if you do a bit of research you'll find that many entrepreneurs are university dropouts or school dropouts. However, their employees are all highly educated with MBAs or other professional qualifications and degrees. Now we understand that you're a start-up and you might not have the money to hire people; honestly, don't worry about this. We'll introduce you to the beauty of outsourcing later in the book. Just to give you a quick example, take this book for instance. We wrote it, but we hired people to design the book cover, edit the book and then we used publishers to create the book and then someone else's platform to distribute it. Our skills were in writing the book and bringing together the right people to bring it to life.

We'll now introduce you to creative tools used by creative experts to solve problems and invent new and better products. We don't care how old you are or who you are, when using these tools you have full permission to be as imaginative and creative as possible. There are no silly ideas or silly questions and you should remove all limiting beliefs.

CREATIVE TOOLS
This section discusses the creative tools that are available to you.

Seeing a Gap in the Market

This isn't strictly a tool, but we'll place it here for the flow of the book. One of the best ways to identify a potential new product is when you need it, but it isn't available to buy. For example, you might be gardening one day and you find that if you had a certain piece of equipment it would make your life so much easier. This piece of equipment would save you backache, time and effort. You search for such a product on the Internet and by visiting garden centres. To your amazement no such product exists. You've now identified something that could potentially be a product and a business idea.

Let's take another example; let's say you want to learn a particular skill or take a particular course, for instance, public speaking classes. However, you find that there are no public speaking classes in your area. Instead you would have to travel to another city. This is an opportunity for you to take that course and learn the skills. Then bring those skills back with you and run your own public speaking courses in your area.

Brainstorming

You'll have likely heard of brainstorming, but we'll cover this topic in case you haven't, or haven't done it before. Brainstorming is literally a brain dump of ideas around a central topic. It works well in a group because people can build on each other's ideas. If you're setting up your business as a team or a partnership then you should do this together. Even if you're setting up your business alone you can still use brainstorming and we encourage that you do.

The first thing to do is get your team together, or just yourself if you're a sole trader. Then write your topic heading on a flipchart, whiteboard or some other easily-visible platform. Ensure your topic is well-defined and clear as this will lead to a better brainstorming session. Allow the participants to ask any clarifying questions to ensure they understand the topic.

You then move forward in two ways. The first way is to have everyone shout out their ideas and to have one person note them down in free-flow. The second way is to work in silence and have everyone write their own ideas down. They can then share these ideas and build on them. Brainstorming sessions can be noisy and manic, with strong characters often dominating the session. You don't necessarily want this to happen, so silent brainstorming can prevent this problem occurring. In fact, research shows that individual brainstorming is far more effective at producing both quality and quantity of ideas.

You need lots of ideas so encourage quantity and also encourage freewheeling. You want to come up with crazy and bizarre ideas, so ensure no ideas are censored or criticised as this will kill the creative spirit. An idea might not be useful in itself, but it could inspire the next idea, so promote building on ideas too. Avoid analysing any of the ideas during the session as this will prevent the flow of new ideas.

At the end of the session, conclude and establish what the next steps are. You may have identified a particular avenue you want to explore or an area within which you need to conduct some research.

Reverse Brainstorming

Reverse brainstorming is conducted in exactly the same way as classic brainstorming, which is discussed above. However, instead of trying to solve a problem or central topic, you brainstorm how to cause it. For example, you might be looking at the problem: How to speed up trains. In reverse brainstorming you reverse the problem, so it would become: How to slow down trains. You would then brain dump all your ideas about how to slow down trains instead.

This enables you to look at a problem in another way and the results can be phenomenal. By finding ways to cause the problem you can find ways to solve the problem that you might not have considered otherwise. The next step, once you've exhausted ideas on how to cause the problem, is to use these ideas to create ways to prevent the problem.

Challenge Assumptions

As we get older and gain life experience we start to form assumptions and beliefs about everything. Many of these beliefs can be limiting and block our progress. For example, in 1876 William Orton, the president of Western Union, turned down the patent to the telephone. Western Union was already a communications giant with its telegraph monopoly, so Orton felt it was unnecessary to take any risks. Orton assumed the telephone lacked "commercial possibilities" due to it resembling an "electrical toy." This assumption caused him to miss out.

A customer leaves a shop after purchasing a product. On their departure they notice the assistant serving them had given them the wrong amount of change. The customer re-enters the shop and tells the assistant, who grumpily replies, "All change must be counted before leaving the shop, so I can't help you." The customer says "No problem, thank you for the extra £5."

Challenging assumptions causes you to look at the problem with a new perspective. For example:
Problem: We need to build an ecommerce website.
Assumption: It'll be expensive.
Challenge: It might not - let's get quotes, and if it is, we'll make it ourselves.
Assumption: We don't have the technical skills.
Challenge: No one was born with technical skills, we can learn.
Assumption: It won't be as good as a professional.
Challenge: There may be software that is easy to use with a professional, finished look.
Assumption: This will be expensive.

Challenge: We'll look to see if there is any open source (free) software available.

By the way, if you're thinking of opening up an ecommerce store, there are free and inexpensive software tools available to you, which we'll discuss later in the book. You don't need to be a programming expert to set up an ecommerce store with these tools.

Let's look at another example:

Problem: I want to start a business but I feel I'm too old.
Assumption: I'm too old to start a business.
Challenge: I've got more life experience, more contacts, and many more positives.
Assumption: I won't have the energy to keep up.
Challenge: If I'm passionate about my business I'll have the energy; I'll plan better and work smarter.
Assumption: People won't want to work with me because I'm not young.
Challenge: People will take me more seriously because I'm older.
Assumption: Young people are more innovative.
Challenge: Youth is no guarantee of innovation, and I can learn creative techniques and tools.

Challenge each of your assumptions and you'll be pleasantly surprised with what you can come up with.

Connect the Unconnected

Connecting random objects and words to your problem is a powerful tool for creative thinking. There are several ways of doing this.

One method is to use a random word. Using a dictionary, close your eyes and open the dictionary at any page. With your eyes still closed select a point on the page. The selected word is then used as a starting point for your creative thinking as you try to connect the word with your problem. This exercise stimulates your brain by forcing you to make associations. It doesn't have to be a dictionary, you can do this with any book or magazine. You can also use pictures or other physical items.

Rewording the Problem

Rewording the problem is similar to reverse brainstorming and challenge assumptions, as it forces you to look at a problem in a different way. Rewording the problem is simply stating the problem using different phrases. "What is stopping consumers buying?", "How do I access consumers?", "How can I make it easier for consumers to buy?", "Where do my consumers hang out?", "Who has influence over my consumers?" etc.

Questions are extremely powerful. We're taught in school to answer questions and then we're rewarded for answering them correctly. This is one potentially massive flaw in education. Answering questions on topics you know requires very little brainpower as it only takes memory recall. Thinking of inquisitive questions requires brainpower. Entrepreneurs question things, and it's questions that solve problems. Einstein came up with the theory of relativity by asking the question of what it would be like to ride on a beam of light.

Rephrasing your problem switches your brain into problem-solving mode and you may just come up with new ideas.

SCAMPER

SCAMPER was developed by Bob Eberle and it's a toolbox or checklist to help you create new products or enhance existing products. You can use the elements of SCAMPER in any combination or individually.

The seven elements of SCAMPER are: Substitute, Combine, Adapt, Modify, Put, Eliminate and Reverse. We'll discuss each in turn.

Substitute: Put something else in place of another. This can be components, materials, people etc. A good example of this is Apple's iPhone when it was first released: It was one of the first phones to replace a mobile telephone keypad with a touch screen system. Remember, we said use your imagination, so don't hold back.

Combine: Mix different things together. Let your imagination go wild, but if you're struggling, use the "connect the unconnected" dictionary method to help you generate new ideas. One product that did this well is vitaminwater. Selling water isn't a unique concept, but by adding vitamins to the water they made a completely new product that differed from their competitors'. Another example is simply combining a suitcase with wheels, which made life easier for travellers. Combinations don't have to be physical items, for example combine holidays with yoga and you have yoga holidays.

Adapt: Alter, modify, change the function or use another element of the product. Apple did this with the iPad. The computer screen contained the keyboard and all the other hardware, making a smart, simple-to-use tablet computer.

Modify: Increase or reduce a feature, change its shape or colour, or alter any other aspect of the product. You'll see this happen often in the automotive industry. Automotive companies will produce newer editions of cars by modifying the body of the car and its engineering.

Put: Put the product to another use; for example, converting your garage into a small one-bedroom apartment to rent out. You'll be amazed at what you can do with products when you put them to another use. Did you know you can use Coca-Cola to unblock drains? Did you know you can take an elastic band, wrap it around a paint tub so that it cuts across the opening, and then use it to wipe your paint brush to prevent the paint going on the rim of the tub?

Eliminate: Remove, simplify and reduce elements of your product and see what the outcome is. When mobile phones first came onto the market they were large with extendable aerials. Over time, the aerials have become hidden within the handset and they have reduced in size dramatically. Again, experiment with this and don't hold back. What if you removed the buttons from lifts and instead spoke which floor you wanted? James Dyson pioneered the vacuum cleaner by removing the need for bags and he completely disrupted the market.

Reverse/Rearrange: Turn the product inside out and upside down, reverse the order or sequence and try doing the exact opposite. For example, instead of an item of clothing used to keep you warm, what about an item of clothing that made you cooler, which might be useful in sports.

Reframing Matrix

The Reframing Matrix was created by Michael Morgan in 1993 and published in his book *Creating Workforce Innovation*. When you look at objects from different angles you see different things. For example, you would see completely different features of a car if you were to look at one for the first time from only one side. When you look at problems from only one angle you suffer the same limitations. Therefore, a disruptive way of thinking that enables you to see a problem from different perspectives can help you identify solutions. The reframing matrix helps you do exactly this.

You can visit our website at www.businesshacks.tips to see examples of the reframing matrix, but we'll also explain the process here.

Draw a rectangle in the middle of a page which contains your problem. Draw a four-box grid around this central problem, so that your problem sits in the middle of a four-box matrix. The four boxes around your problem are where you put your different perspectives.

There are two ways to approach the reframing matrix: the 4Ps approach and the professional approach.

The 4Ps approach is as follows, and you would put each section into one of the four boxes in your matrix:

- Product perspective - Are there any problems with the product? Is it priced accurately? How well does it serve the target market? Is it reliable to the consumer?
- Planning perspective - Are the business, marketing, and sales plans appropriate. Do we have the right strategy? How could we improve these?
- Potential perspective - How would we increase sales of the product? If we were to increase our targets, how would we achieve this and what would happen?
- People perspective - What impacts do people have on the problem? Who are the people involved? What do people involved with the problem think? Why are customers not using or buying the product? Why are people choosing one product over another?

The above questions are just examples and they can be easily tailored to your product.

The second approach to the reframing matrix is to look at the problem from the perspective of different professionals. A builder would look at the problem differently to a sales professional. This would also be true of an engineer or a teacher. Therefore, instead of using the 4Ps you could have four professionals in each box, and write down the questions they would ask.

Once you've created your four-box matrix either using the 4Ps or the professional method, you can then populate the sections with questions and answers using brainstorming. At the end of the exercise your completed matrix will help you better understand your problem and situation, so that you can generate solutions.

Biomimicry

Biomimetics or biomimicry is the imitation of nature for the purpose of solving human problems. For example, Swiss engineer Georges de Mestral invented Velcro after going out with his dog. When he came back he noticed his pants and his dog were covered in burrs from the burdock plant. He examined the burrs under a microscope and identified that they had very tiny hooks which enabled them to hook on to things like fabrics. Another example is solar panels that mimic the folds and creases in leaves to make them much more efficient.

Look at the product you're developing and look towards nature to see if nature is doing something similar and better. As another example, living organisms adapt to their environment. We sweat when we're hot and we shiver when we're cold. Our eyes widen in the darkness and contract in the light. Companies look towards producing products that can adapt to their environment, such as car headlights that automatically turn on in a certain level of darkness, or windscreen wipers that automatically turn on when it rains.

Attribute Listing

Attribute listing is a good technique for finding new combinations of products and examining different aspects of a problem. In attribute listing you break the product down into smaller bits and explore what you discover during the process.

The steps are as follows:

List attributes - For the product under examination list all the attributes: colour, material, weight, shape, price, size and so on. As you break the product down, look at the attributes of each individual part. For example, if you break down a chair the legs may be made of plastic and the cushion made of leather.

Consider the value of the attributes - For each attribute ask what value or benefit it gives. The attributes may even have negative values. The leather cushioning of the chair, whilst reducing the possibility of stains, may alienate vegans and passionate animal campaigners.

Modify the attributes - Look at ways to modify the attributes you've identified, potentially increasing the value and decreasing the negative value, or creating something new. You could modify the leather on the chair to use a more animal-friendly material. Using another example, if you wanted to develop a new shoe you might just concentrate on the attributes of the heel. You could raise the heel, put springs in the heel, put lights in the heel, change the material, remove the heel, change the shape, or add an air bubble into the heel, and so on.

Look Beyond the Product

Another way to improve or develop a product is to look at things associated with the product but not actually the product itself. For example, supplements in the form of tablets bought online or through a catalogue used to be contained within a cylindrical shape. The problem was these cylindrical containers could not be posted through the letterbox, causing delivery problems. As a result, some creative person enhanced the container from a cylindrical shape into a flat, rectangular container enabling them to be posted through a letterbox. Notice that this wasn't a development of the tablet, but the packaging.

Mixing Cultures

You may look towards other cultures and countries to see what they're doing, and what you could possibly implement in your own country. For example, Simon Woodroffe developed the restaurant 'Yo! Sushi' after a Japanese friend of his suggested he set up the UK's first conveyor-belt sushi restaurant.

Mixing Old and New

You can look towards old products to develop new products. While camera companies were developing sharper more powerful cameras to create highly detailed photographic images, Kevin Systrom and Mike Krieger developed 'Instagram', a mobile phone photo-sharing social network that enabled users to modify their pictures to look old and retro. Julie Deane founded the 'Cambridge Satchel Company' after Julie found that no one made these satchels anymore and decided to supply them herself.

CREATIVE TOOLS SUMMARY

Don't fool yourself that these tools won't work. They're very powerful, but you must stop any limiting beliefs that you're not creative, and stop any self-punishment for bizarre or whacky ideas. It's whacky to believe that we can fly across the sky in a piece of metal at 529mph. Thank you to the Wright brothers for challenging these assumptions and building the world's first successful aeroplane.

To make these tools work, you have to *use* them, not just read about them. People can fall into the trap of reading about brainstorming and believing that's the same as brainstorming. That's like reading about bodybuilding and expecting to build muscle. You have to actually participate. You may at first struggle, especially if you haven't tapped into your creative brain for a while. Don't worry about it. The more you do it the more creative you'll become.

PROTOTYPING

If you've come up with your idea and you want to take it further, what do you do? You'll now need to create a prototype or run a pilot. A prototype is an example model and a test concept to act as the thing to be replicated or learned from. It won't have the full functionality of the finished product, but it'll serve as an example. In this section, we'll discuss ways to bring your idea to life so that you can demonstrate your idea, get it produced, raise finance and sell it.

Before approaching anyone to make your prototype, you'll want to consider several things:

- Ability - Can you make the prototype yourself or will you need a professional?
- A nondisclosure agreement - This is a contract through which you and the other party agree not to disclose information covered in the agreement. It creates a confidential relationship between you both to protect any type of confidential information.
- Budget - You'll need to work out your budget for your prototype. Prototyping can be expensive, so you should agree fees at the start so you and the prototype maker are clear.
- Details - Provide the prototype maker with as much detail as

possible through homemade prototypes, drawings, detailed explanations and face-to-face meetings. Keep in regular contact so that you can stop them going off track at any stage.

PHYSICAL PRODUCT PROTOTYPE

If you're creating a new type of physical product that you wish to mass produce, firstly you'll have to get a prototype made so that manufactures know what it is. It'll also serve as an example if you're trying to pitch for finance or you're discussing your needs with suppliers. So how do you actually make a prototype? Well this depends on exactly what your idea is. If your idea is a simple product you can easily make yourself, try some of the suggestions below:

Polymorph - You can purchase a material called 'polymorph' from the Internet or your local hardware store. Polymorph comes in a tube of small white plastic granules that melt at 62°C. Once you heat the granules in hot water the pellets melt together to form a transparent, flexible substance, allowing you to form the plastic by hand into unique shapes. To learn how to do this, we recommend going online to find some videos. (Please be careful when handling hot water.) With Polymorph you'll be able to create a physical model. It might not work exactly how you want and it'll have limited functionality, but that's fine, it's just a prototype. The idea is to give people a visual guide and understanding.

Sugru - Another suggestion is to use 'Sugru', which is mouldable glue that turns into rubber, bonds to anything, is waterproof, flexible and electrically insulated. You could make your prototype out of Sugru, or you could make a mould out of Sugru and use the mould to make your prototype using something else, such as Polymorph.

Sculpey/Fimo - 'Sculpey' and 'Fimo' are clays that you could use to make your prototype, or to create the moulds to cast your prototype.

Another option you can explore when making prototypes is to visit local hardware and craft stores to see what materials you could use, such as wood, piping, ball bearings, paper, card etc. (Tara, n.d).

Useful links:

- www.sugru.com
- www.sculpey.com

You could also try finding local 'fabrication laboratories', which are small-scale workshops offering personal digital fabrication, which make almost anything. You could also try your local universities. If you can't find any local fabrication laboratories you could try an online one such as www.ponoko.com, or online 3D printers such as www.shapeways.com (Tara, n.d).

If you want to use the skills of a professional engineer, developer, handyman or designer you can find ones using Yellow Pages or doing an online search. You might find www.thomasnet.com useful.

SOFTWARE/APP PROTOTYPE

If you're creating a software package or a mobile phone application and you're not a programmer you'll still need to create a prototype so that software developers understand what you're trying to achieve.

You could do this using a number of methods. You could use software such as Microsoft PowerPoint and have clickable links to show how functions would work. If you wanted to go further, and we recommend that you do, there are free and paid websites and tools available that enable you to make prototype apps without the need for code. These will give your prototype apps a more realistic and professional feel. Use a search engine to find a tool that meets your requirements.

SERVICE PROTOTYPE

If you're developing a service-based business such as a training business, you can still create a pilot to test your idea first. For example, you could put together your training course, hire a very low cost hotel meeting room and offer your course for a very low fee, or even free of charge. From this pilot you can gather feedback to improve your service and at the same time get some testimonials.

PROTOTYPING SUMMARY

This section has given you some ways to bring your ideas to life through the process of prototyping. They may not all be suitable for your particular idea, but you can certainly use the ideas above to identify how you can make a prototype, or use them as creative inspiration to remove any obstacle in getting your ideas created.

LOCATION, UTILITIES AND EQUIPMENT

One of the most important elements of your business is your location, and it's one of the things many rookie entrepreneurs get wrong when opening their first business. As a very crude example, imagine your business idea is a bar that sells trendy cosmopolitan cocktails created in a unique way that entertains your customers. Your target market is young professionals. If you then open the bar in a remote rural area where the demographic consists of retired pensioners your business is likely to fail. No matter how fantastic the service is or the drinks are, your target market doesn't exist in that area. This example may seem silly and extreme, but it happens. In this chapter we'll look at how to find the perfect location for your business.

HOME-BASED BUSINESS

Many successful businesses have started in their owner's kitchen or bedroom. About 70 percent of businesses start from home, and at the time of writing there are 2.9 million home-based businesses in the UK contributing £300 billion to the economy, (www.gov.uk, 2014). The benefit of opening a business from your home is that you don't have the added costs of running a facility; you can test out your idea, and if it doesn't take off then you can shut it down without any hassle or being tied into any contracts.

Some examples of businesses you can start successfully from your home include: an online business, consulting, recruitment, marketing services, bookkeeping, credit control services, coaching and many more. It's not uncommon that people turn their kitchens into food manufacturing plants or their kitchen tables into manufacturing workshops, or their bedrooms into offices. These days with technology such as 3D printers, broadband, the Internet, forums, social media and online video communication software, it's easier than ever to build a business from your home and reach your target market.

As your business matures you may continue to run your business from your home, and this is especially true for those of you who only see their business as a side income, or want to keep that work life balance. Depending on how you want to scale your business, at some point, when it meets a level of maturity and you need to hold more stock or recruit staff, a physical location will be needed. However, for this section we'll concentrate on home-based businesses, especially when starting up.

Consumers can become suspicious of businesses that use a home addresses, and clients in business-to-business (B2B) may be turned off by your small size and unprofessional feel. In other words, your professional business appearance matters. For example, you may use the services of a babysitter but you wouldn't expect them to have a prestigious city centre office. However, if you wanted to use the services of a strategic management consultancy you probably *would* expect them to have that prestigious address. If they didn't, you might question their ability and be likely to think, consciously or subconsciously, that if they're not doing well enough to grow their own business then they're unlikely to help you grow yours.

Now we know what you're thinking, that you're just starting up so logically you can't afford a prestigious office. Don't worry about it, that's why you've bought this book.

Virtual Office - If you're running a "professional" business from home you can create the perception that you work from an office using a 'virtual office'. A virtual office is when you pay a company to use their address but you don't actually work from that location. Instead you continue to work from home, but your customers or clients are none the wiser. The benefit of a virtual office is that they are cheap because you don't pay the expense of running an office, but your business is presented as professional, large and successful. If your business provides professional services such as consultancy then we highly recommend using a virtual office.

For a basic package you'll be looking at between £15 and £50 a month depending on your local rates. Extra options will also be available at a surcharge, including mail forwarding and the use of the office's land line phone number with a receptionist who can take messages for you. This can be good if you don't get many calls, but ideally you want customers to contact you directly. We'll discuss this in more detail shortly.

Similar to a virtual office is a Post Office Box address, more commonly known as a P.O. Box address. A P.O. Box address is an alternative address to receive your mail, which will be held at a post office. Prices vary, but they can go for as little as £20 per month. If you want the professional look, find and use a virtual office address. However, if you want to find out more about P.O. Box addresses and you're based in the UK you can visit www.royalmail.com.

You might be setting up a business in an industry or with a target market that see it as trendy, even rebellious, to be working from your home. Remember, Apple began in Steve Wozniak's bedroom and then later moved into Steve Jobs' garage. However, be careful not to actually advertise your home address, because you're potentially advertising that you have a lot of stock at your home. Even if you're an eBay seller and an eBay member requested your details, which any eBay member can do, eBay would give the address listed (home address) immediately. Therefore, you should consider always using a virtual address, P.O. Box address or another alternative address.

Telephone Line - Working from home has another potential pitfall, your business telephone number. Not having a telephone number is a big turn-off for customers. There are lots of statistics available showing percentages of customers who click away from a website when there isn't a phone number. Customers want to know that they can interact with a business and if something goes wrong they can pick up the telephone and contact you. Depending on your country, having a telephone number on your website can be a legal requirement.

As with the office address you have options. You can put down your home number, but you'll need to answer every phone call in a pro-fessional manner. This means saying the name of your company and introducing yourself to the caller. Customers won't like it when you answer the phone with just a "Hello" instead of a professional busi-ness opening line. Alternatively, you could have a separate land line installed into your home address which is a dedicated business line. You could just use a mobile number, but this creates a low value per-ception of your business. Customers will see a company with only a mobile number as either untrustworthy, unsuccessful, or a one-per-son company. Another option is to use a 'virtual telephone num-ber' also known as 'call forwarding', which is a professional looking number that the customer dials, but it diverts to your mobile phone. Just ensure that you answer every unknown telephone call profes-sionally, or use a separate mobile phone for your business. You can purchase a very cheap mobile phone for this purpose.

With call forwarding you get to choose a phone number such as; 0800, 0845, 0300, 0161. This number is then assigned to you and redirects to your mobile phone. We honestly believe this to be invaluable to people running a business alone or from home.

As mentioned earlier we recommend using a separate mobile phone. A basic mobile phone is all that you'll need which can be bought very cheaply. There's no need to purchase the most expensive mobile phone on the market because all you'll be doing with it is taking calls. Now you'll know when the phone rings that it's business-related. Make sure that you have a professional voicemail message e.g. *"You've reached the answering service of <your company name>, unfortunately all our staff are busy taking other calls, if you leave a message we will get straight back to you"*. When you do answer the phone, again, ensure that you do so in a professional manner, as we mentioned above "Hello" doesn't cut it; portray yourself as a professional company. When you answer say: *"<company name>, <your name> speaking."*

Insurance - Depending on your business, even though it's run from home you'll need to purchase insurance, or inform your home insurance company. If you're storing your valuable product at home, incidents can happen - such as floods, fires and thefts. If you've purchased thousands of pounds of goods and this happens without insurance you'll lose money. If you're a service business you'll need to consider 'professional indemnity insurance', which covers you in the event that you give faulty advice that causes financial loss to a client. If you employ people, even in your own home, you're legally obliged to take out employers' liability insurance. Not doing this could lead to a large fine. Make sure you read your policy documents carefully and that you understand any exclusions that apply. Do your research and find out what level of professional indemnity insurance your clients might expect before you make a purchase. If your customers or clients are visiting your home, you'll also need to get 'public liability insurance'. This type of insurance covers your business if someone is injured in some way by your business.

Now not everyone owns their own home and you may be a tenant. At the time of writing the laws are changing and an updated planning guidance will make it clear that planning permission should not normally be needed to run a business from your home. Additionally, in most circumstances, home-based businesses will not attract business rates.

Working from home always sounds great, but there are several operational pitfalls you need to be aware of:

- Cabin fever and isolation - Working from home by yourself can get very lonely and boring once the novelty wears off. Unlike the office you can't bounce ideas off colleagues or interact with anyone. These simple things are necessary for healthy human interaction. Even introverts need to be around other people even if you're not conversing. You can help reduce or prevent this by attending networking meetings, or working from a different location from time to time such as a library.
- Work life balance - If you're working from home you'll probably think that you'll have an excellent work life balance. Actually the opposite can happen, and you can become so obsessed with your business that you'll find it difficult to switch off. Make sure you have a cut-off period. Logically it makes sense to continually work nonstop, as this will create a greater output. This couldn't be further from the truth. There is something called the "law of diminishing returns". This means that every hour that passes, your tiredness causes your productivity levels to drop, so while you're working longer your actual output is decreasing. Switch off, you're allowed to rest.

• Procrastination and distractions - Another pitfall is procrastinating and distractions such as the fridge, television, cleaning, gardening, social media and everything else. To solve this, define your working hours and stick to them. Create a dedicated area for your business and when you sit in this area it's work time.

RETAIL - PHYSICAL LOCATION

If your business requires a physical location for customers such as a clothing store, restaurant, a bar or an estate agents then your location will be one of the main factors for your success.

Parking - Consumers are generally lazy and any inconvenience will deter them. Therefore, if your business doesn't have accessible parking this will impact your sales. Your parking doesn't necessarily have to be onsite, but you should at least be close to parking spaces and car parks.

Competition is healthy - Common sense says that the less competition the more successful your business will be. This is true for some businesses and less so for others. For example, if you open up a good sandwich shop in an area with many hungry workers, and you're the only sandwich shop in the area, you'll reap the rewards for being the only supplier. However, consumer behaviour changes depending on the product. For example, when people like to go to bars and nightclubs they generally like to visit several different venues in one night. Therefore, if you decide to open up a bar that is completely remote and out the way for the customer, while you won't have any competition you also won't have any customers. Instead you would be better opening close to your competitors so that customers can leave one bar and enter yours during their night out. In this case the way to attract customers is to be better and more unique than the other bars, rather than geographically solo. However, if there are too many bars in the area then you may have difficulty making sufficient profits as the customer has too much choice. You may find that in one area several bars open up and they thrive, but their success attracts other entrepreneurs causing an influx of other bars which saturate the market. What you might not realise is that many bars in the same area are owned by the same company. They understand that customers want a choice, so by opening several differentiated bars they provide this choice while at the same time reducing the competition.

When looking for a location, consider who else is doing business in the area. Are there already many businesses with the same idea as yours? Is the area thriving or full of empty shops? Successful businesses attract other successful businesses.

Size - Size matters and depending on your business space can fill up quickly. This is especially true for companies such as restaurants as they need a kitchen, tables, seats, a counter and other equipment. If it's a retail store and you're holding stock is there room to store your stock? If you're opening a gym with free weights, studios and machines you're going to need a lot of space. Do your measurements.

Visibility - In business-to-consumer (B2C) your business must be highly visible with lots of passing customers either by foot or vehicle. Making your business highly visible to the public is great advertising as it reminds them that your business exists and that they should come in. Although we must make you aware that if the premises is highly visible to passing traffic, but it isn't easy to park or access then you'll be inaccessible to customers. The only way around this would be to sell predominantly through a website. Make sure you open up in an area that is easily accessible with lots of passing customers.

Reputation - Some locations, especially in the restaurant or bar industry, seem to host failed business after failed business. Usually this is because a previous and similar business offered a bad service or a poor product, so customers associate the place and consequently any business with those negative feelings.

Impulsive purchase - While you'll want your customers to make impulse buys, you don't want to make impulse purchases on something major as a property. It can happen, as you walk into the building and you get that feeling it can be very powerful and exciting. It's fine to use your gut feelings and we encourage you to do so, but always do your research.

Times - Visit the area at different times of the day and on different days. The area might be extremely busy on a Saturday, but empty on every other day. It might be very busy in the evenings, but quiet during the day.

Demographics - Take a look at the demographics of the people in the area. Are they wealthy or are they struggling? There's no point opening an expensive furniture shop in an area where people can't afford these products.

Supplier access points - Your suppliers might arrive in large vehicles and your business might create a large amount of waste that needs to be professionally removed by big trucks. You'll need to consider this if it's applicable to your business

PROFESSIONAL SERVICES-BASED BUSINESS LOCATION

Not all businesses require a shop front and this is generally when your customers or clients tend not to visit you to make a purchase. For example, if you're opening up a bookkeeping business, it wouldn't make sense to open in a prime city centre shopping spot. While there would be high footfall, it's not your target market and the premium rates you'd be paying would be a waste of money.

With a service-based business there are several more suitable options and in some cases a shop front might be necessary, but its location requires a different chain of thought. Let's start at the bottom and work our way up.

Home-based - Previously in this chapter we went into detail about working from home and using a virtual office as a professional front. This should be your first option when opening up a service-based business.

Business incubators - They provide start-ups with a location to develop and grow their business. They usually offer advice and support to help you with your start-up. They're all run slightly differently and some may have state of the art laboratories and technology while others might just provide easy cost-effective premises. If you're a graduate, or a student your university will most probably have a business service that offers business incubators. If you're a particular type of business, for example a technology start-up, you might want to find a business incubator that houses similar industry-related businesses for shared learning and mentoring.

Serviced office - As you set up your business you'll realise that virtually everything is a business. Some people's business is to buy or lease large spaces or buildings, and then divide these up into smaller offices to rent out to other businesses. In other words, you rent an office space to run your business from. These usually come with receptionists and a reception area. Some come with break out rooms for informal meetings, private meeting rooms and pods, as well as conferencing facilities. They might have a range of offers which include a phone line and broadband. Not every offering will be the same so you'll need to identify what you need, what your target market expects and what your serviced office can offer. One of the benefits of serviced offices is that contracts can be for a short period, allowing you to test your business. Serviced offices can be in technology parks, business parks or in the city centre. Don't forget to consider security, location, size, facilities, parking, other businesses in the building and anything else that matters to your business. Always look at the bigger picture. You may have found cheap offices, but if they have no car park and you have to pay an obscene amount to park nearby then they're not really so cheap after all.

STORAGE, WAREHOUSING AND OPERATIONS

Warehousing is a place you store your products. This can be your house, garage, a storage centre or an actual warehouse. Depending on the size of your home it can become uncomfortable and impractical to store your product there, especially as the business grows. In such a case you may want to consider using a self-storage company to store your product while you run your back office (sales, finance etc.) from home, or move both your stock and back office to a self-storage company.

You'll need to think commercially and logistically when using a self-storage company. The cheapest price won't necessarily mean cost savings. For example, if you manage your back office from home, you'll need to travel to the storage facility to fulfil orders. If you've picked the cheapest option, but the storage unit is many miles away the travel costs will affect your operating costs. You'll also want to consider opening hours and days, because if you run your business after 5pm but the storage company closes at 5pm then you won't be able to fulfil orders. The same is true of weekend availability.

Using a self-storage company comes with numerous benefits, and many online businesses are now running their whole operations from self-storage units. Entrepreneurs are attracted by the flexibility, the short-notice periods and low overheads. You don't need to pay council tax, because it's all included in the rent. It gives you flexibility, because if the business isn't performing you can give one month's notice and move on, or you can reduce your space; it gives you options. Businesses using self-storage also do not have to pay business rates, which are the taxes usually paid on commercial properties. This is because the burden falls on the self-storage company who is assessed as a warehouse, so the operator of the self-storage facility will generally be liable for the payment of business rates rather than its customers. Using self-storage will also give you peace of mind because you won't have to worry about break-ins to your house or domestic disasters. This is because self-storage companies use secure facilities with CCTV and security.

So with self-storage, depending on the company, generally there are no business rates, service charges or utilities charges for security and lighting. Additionally, there are no long term storage leases or complicated contracts to sign. You just pay one all-inclusive price and they look after everything.

When looking for a local storage company don't just look at the first page of Google or any other search engine, look through at least four pages and ask anyone you know if they can recommend a company. Do not use a self-storage company for the sake of using a self-storage company. For example, if you're only holding £500 worth of stock, it wouldn't be commercially sensible to use self-storage.

MANUFACTURING SITE

Manufacturing is simply the mass production of your product. To begin with, your production line might be you in your kitchen, bedroom or garage. With technology becoming more advanced and less expensive, your manufacturing can potentially be done in your home with 3D printers, sewing machines, your home oven etc. depending on your business and product. If your business is still at this stage then, please, refer to the section about home-based businesses earlier in this chapter. At present you might not have the in-house capability to produce your product, so you'll need to consider outsourcing your manufacturing.

At some point when your business becomes large enough you may want to consider bringing all or some of your manufacturing in-house on a much larger scale. When you've reached the stage of needing to manufacture in-house with large machines, to be honest your business must have become successful enough by this point that you'll need to hire specialists to help you locate and set up a manufacturing facility.

However, part of success is having an understanding of where you want to go. Your business can quickly scale up from your kitchen table to outsourcing and then to an in-house manufacturing site if successful. As we mentioned earlier, at such a level you have reached beyond the scope of this book, and the subject of setting up a manufacturing site would be a book within itself. Nonetheless, it's useful to understand where you want your business to go.

Countries are generally divided up into areas and these areas have their own economies. For example, in England, London has a different economy from the North West and they both have a different economy from the North East. Then the cities within these different areas also have their own economies. With these different economies come different skills, different levels of employment, access routes, productivity levels, suppliers etc.

All of these are vitally important. If you open up your manufacturing site in an area far away from your suppliers this may cause supplier issues, and you may struggle to keep production up with demand. Therefore, in such a case you would need to stockpile raw material which would cost you more, and cause you to raise the price of your product to meet costs. This price increase wouldn't benefit your profit line, but it would make you less competitive and potentially turn customers away. If you open up in an area where there's a skills shortage or high levels of employment then you will struggle to find staff to operate your business. All these factors need to be considered when bringing manufacturing in-house or scaling upwards. If your business model is mainly exports then setting up near a port may reduce distribution costs.

You might look and decide the country you are in doesn't have the skills, tax laws, or correctly located suppliers. In this case you may benefit from looking towards other countries for your manufacturing site where more benefits are offered and costs are lower.

LEASE AND LANDLORDS

If you're leasing your property remember to negotiate and ask the landlord to bring the price down. Negotiation depends on leverage, so if the area is thriving and most of the locations are occupied you'll have less leverage to negotiate. However, if the location has been vacant for several months, the landlord will be more flexible and open to negotiation. When you negotiate, you can even try asking for a very cheap first year, or even not paying any rent for the first year. This may sound shocking, but if you don't ask you don't get. You're probably asking why any landlord would give away a year's free rent. While it's not ideal for the landlord they'll look at the bigger picture. If your business is going to do well and you want to stay in their property for many years, one year's free rent is insignificant. We know a large and well-known retail company that gets all their new store locations with one year's free rent for that exact reason. When negotiating you may want to ask for some of the following:

- Lower rent
- One year's free rent
- A rent holiday while you prepare your premises
- Lower rent on the first year

When communicating with the landlord, Steve Parks in his book *Start Your Business Week by Week* (2005) covers some great questions you'll want to ask, including:

- How much is the property to rent?
- Are there extra costs on top of the rent?
- Are utilities covered in the rent (gas, water)? (unlikely in a shop premises)
- Who currently provides the utilities to the premises?
- Who is responsible for maintenance of the internal and external structure? (most likely you in a shop premises)
- Are the premises available now, if not when?
- What's the minimum rental period?
- What's the notice period?
- When is the rent reviewed and how is it reviewed?
- What restrictions are there on the use of the premises? (some landlords may object to fast food businesses, especially if they have tenants living in a flat above)
- What uses has the local planning authority approved the property for?
- Has the premises ever been vandalised or broken into?
- What businesses have been there in the past?
- Why are the premises vacant?

UTILITIES

The location and nature of your business will determine your utility usage. Some business incubators and serviced offices will provide all or some of the facilities that your business will need.

Telephone - If you're working from home and you don't expect to be making a lot of telephone calls you might like to consider a virtual telephone number combined with a cheap mobile phone for incoming calls. This was discussed in detail earlier in this chapter. However, if your business requires a greater amount of telephone usage you'll want to consider a more appropriate option. Ask yourself the following questions:

- Will I be using the telephone a lot? Both inbound and out bound calls.
- If I'm working from home would a separate line be best?
- Will I be making international calls?
- Could I get a limitless call package?
- What's the cheapest deal I can get?
- Could I also use free online video chat software for special occasions?
- Do I need a fax line?
- Will I need an additional line for credit card processing terminals?

Electricity - If your premises don't come with electricity included you'll need to find an electricity supplier, or review the supplier if the premises are already connected. Electricity companies will be able to give you an estimated use of energy if you explain to them the nature of your business. Not all businesses use the same amount of electricity, for example a newsagent will use less electricity than a tanning shop, or one that requires lots of computers.

Gas - Go through the same process as you would for electricity.

Water and sewage - You'll need to go through the same process for water and sewage as you did for electricity. You might want to consider a water meter. A water meter measures the exact amount of water you use, rather than relying on estimates based on rateable values. Depending on your location and business, a metered water approach could save you money on your water bills.

Saving money on utilities - We can imagine, at this point, you probably feel after reading the above that your business is leaking money. This is why it's important to plan your business and work out the finances first, or at least get an estimate. Depending on what utilities and resources your business requires you can do some simple things to save money:

- Shop around for the best prices.
- Negotiate on prices.
- Switch off electrical equipment when taking a break or fin- ishing for the day.
- Insulate your premises, whether that's your home, office or shop.
- Keep your thermostat low and wear a jumper (this is good for home-based businesses, but less so for retail shops where customers appreciate the warmth.)
- Don't fill the kettle to the top and instead just use the correct amount of water.
- Use energy-efficient light bulbs.

EQUIPMENT AND RESOURCES

You'll need to sit down and identify what resources and equipment you'll need. For example, if your business is going to be an ecom- merce store then you're going to need a computer, desk, broadband, a printer, a telephone, storage facilities, packaging etc.

If you're setting up a retail store your equipment list might include: tills, counters, racks, wall displays, credit card terminals, lighting, air-conditioning, heaters, a shop sign etc.

If you're setting up a restaurant your equipment list might include:

tables, chairs, a bar, fridges, cookers, ovens, utensils, glasses, cups, uniforms etc.

If you're setting up an office or have a back office in your store then your equipment list might include: desks, computers, chairs, filing cabinets, whiteboards, printers, telephones, lights, stationery cupboards, stationery etc.

What vehicles will your business need, such as a car, or a van?

You'll need an email address so that clients or customers can contact you. You often see small businesses with a public email address. These are fantastic services and they're free too. We use them, but we use them for our personal email addresses not for our business. Using a public email facility will make you look amateurish. Instead what you should use is an email address that's associated with your website 'domain name', which would look something like 'name@ yourcompany.com'. This looks far more professional, trustworthy and credible. As your email address is connected to your website's domain name we'll discuss how to set up an email address in the chapter: Setting Up a Company Email Address.

Depending on your business you may also need specialist software to send out mass emails, or store customer details. We'll discuss more about these types of software later in the book, and how you can acquire them for free.

Saving Money on Equipment

Not everyone's budget is the same and not everyone's business is the same, but one of the universal rules of business is not to waste money on unnecessary things. One of the reasons for the first dot-com crash was because businesses were wasting money on fancy offices, first-class flights and other unnecessary expenses. If your business is a luxury high-end market business then yes you'll need to buy more extravagant things. However, that doesn't mean you can't shop around for the best suppliers. Use the Internet to search for suppliers and compare prices.

If you're working from home can you use your personal computer to run your ecommerce store until you've made enough to buy another PC?

Look for second-hand equipment, look on eBay or put a message on www.gumtree.com to say you'll happily take away any unwanted chairs and tables from people. This might not make sense to you because you're an entrepreneur, but people will throw out old goods that they don't want rather than take the time to sell them. Therefore, they'll be more than happy if you come and collect it from them as it'll save them the trip to the skip.

We'll give you one good tip from experience. If you're working in an office situation (desk and chair), make sure you get a comfortable desk and chair combination. You must try these out rather than just purchase them over the Internet. You don't want a bad back and you don't want the hassle of disassembling the equipment and sending it back if it's not right for you.

BUSINESS RATES AND INSURANCE

Business rates - You'll need to pay business rates, which are taxes on business properties. The tax is set by the government and the business rates are collected by local authorities. The money is then used to help pay for the services the local authority provides. Business rates are charged on most non-domestic properties, for example shops, offices, pubs, warehouses, factories etc. If you're working from home, in most circumstances home-based businesses will not attract business rates. If you're based in the UK you can check if your home-based business requires business rates by contacting the Valuation Office Agency by visiting www.voa.gov.uk. Not all home-based businesses are the same, for example an online ecommerce store is not the same as converting your garage into a hairdressers.

Business insurance - We touched on business insurance earlier in this chapter, but what *is* business insurance? Business insurance is a broad term used for several insurance policies a business may need. It's unlikely you'll need all of them as a start-up working from home, but you'll need to research what insurance you need for your particular type of business, especially if you're opening up shop. Opening up a retail business where you hire staff and customers visit you onsite will require more insurance than a home-based business with no staff.

Why do you need business insurance? Great question. Let us paint a picture for you. If your customers visit your home, or premises, or you visit their premises, and you cause them to suffer injury or damage to themselves or their property, they could make a claim against you. Similarly, if a product you design, manufacture or sell injures a customer or causes damage, you could face legal and compensation costs if you're found responsible. If, as a business owner, you're considered to be personally responsible, you could even face criminal charges if found negligent. For example, if your business is making delicious cupcakes and one of these cakes makes your customers sick, then they may take legal action against you.

Having business insurance also affects your chances of winning work if you're B2B. For example, if you're an advisory, training or consulting business you'll need a business insurance called 'professional indemnity insurance'. This protects both you and the client should they follow your advice and it causes them substantial financial loss. How will this affect winning work from a client? When a client looks for a supplier, they'll want to ensure that you have this insurance to reduce their risk. If you don't have it they'll simply not give you the work.

If you're hiring staff then you'll need 'employers' liability insurance'. This sounds scary and expensive, but don't let it put you off. If you're running an online business from your home as a side income then you're not going to need all these different insurance policies. However, do identify which policies you need for your business and shop around for different quotes.

Tax relief - What is tax relief? Tax relief is an amount that can be deducted from your annual income to reduce the amount on which tax is paid. For example, let's say your business income is £50,000 for the year, after going through your expenses your tax will be calculated on a reduced amount and not the full £50,000. In simple terms, you pay less tax due to the expenses you've paid out on your business.

If you're not starting up an accounting or tax-specialist business then this is likely to be a subject that won't excite you, so we won't go into detail. The topic is complex and it's also constantly changing. In case you didn't know, you can also claim tax relief if you work from home. Our advice here is to keep every receipt of every purchase you make, and find a good accountant to assist you. Also, ensure you use a business bank account rather than a personal current account to control your money, which we'll discuss later in the book in the Finance chapter. For more information about tax, visit: www.hmrc.gov.uk.

IMPORTANT LINKS
www.bigyellow.co.uk - Example of a self-storage Company
www.voa.gov.uk - Information about business rates
www.hmrc.gov.uk - Information about taxes and tax relief
www.royalmail.com - P.O. Box address
www.gov.uk/browse/business - Information about setting up, tax, business rates and other useful information.

RAISING CAPITAL

One of the biggest problems for new entrepreneurs is raising enough money to start their business. They may come up with a range of business ideas, but not know how to raise the capital to make those ideas a reality. In this chapter we'll look at different ways to raise money for your business. Not all these will be suitable for every business, so it's important to understand the differences between each of these methods. When it comes to raising money from investors we'll talk you through how to approach an investor and how to pitch them your business.

SELF-FUNDING
Self-funding includes:

- Salary
- Savings
- Credit card
- Family
- Friends

It's a fact that you'll have to spend some money to start a business, but depending on your business you don't necessarily need a lot of money. There are many successful multimillion pound businesses that started with very little money. It's even easier today with modern technology and the Internet, as you have access to a global market and free easy-to-learn tools. However, you'll have to be creative and you'll have to roll up your sleeves.

We're going to talk you through a fictional example so you can visualise it, but this fictional example is mirrored by several successful entrepreneurs.

Lisa works fulltime as a marketing executive and she enjoys her job, but her dream is to become an entrepreneur and run her own business. She's passionate about fashion, particularly vintage clothes. Lisa isn't overly impressed with the current offering of online vintage clothing stores and thinks she can do a better job. She decides to put some money aside from her salary each month and invest this in a business. Her philosophy is that the money is an investment whatever happens, because even if she loses money the learning experience will be valuable. She calculates how much money she wants to put away for her business as £150 a month. What she doesn't spend will simply accumulate on to next month's savings. She realises that she'll have to sacrifice some of life's luxuries, such as the Friday night takeaway or a new pair of shoes, to reach her savings target.

Lisa sets up an eBay store, which can be a low-cost option and gets your products seen around the world on a platform that is known and trusted. The monthly fee at the time of writing was just below £20 and a 9.9% fee is taken when an item is sold. She's not a technical person so she has to take time learning eBay through free online video tutorials, free online documents and visiting her local library.

Once her eBay store is set up she needs vintage clothes to sell. She spends her weekends looking through charity shops for vintage clothing, spending between £5 and £20 per item. Sometimes the clothes are damaged, so she uses this advantage to negotiate the price down by always asking for ten percent off. She then patches the clothes up or makes slight alterations to make them suitable for sale.

Lisa uses the camera on her phone to take pictures of vintage clothes and even gets her friends to model the clothes. She uses Pixlr, (https://pixlr.com) a free online image editing and effects website, to edit the pictures.

She uses these pictures to build a Facebook page and a Twitter page. She then spends her time connecting with young women who wear vintage clothing. She goes through the lists of friends and followers of her competitors, fashion magazines, musicians, certain brands or it-girls to follow all their followers. Soon she has a following of thousands of people and she posts information to drive them to her eBay auctions. This is all free marketing.

Her one-off items combined with her marketing activities mean that bidders drive up selling prices of her items from £10 to £600.

Lisa uses the money to reinvest back into the business by saving it and buying more stock, also known as bootstrapping. She constantly analyses her stock, seeing what sold and what didn't. She buys more of the type of items that sell and stops buying items that don't.

After a year Lisa has built up such a following and customer base that she decides to open up her first ecommerce website. By now Lisa can afford to have her website built, but she has fallen in love with being self-sufficient and decides to learn how to do it herself. She feels that learning HTML would be too technical and time consuming, so she instead learns how to use WordPress. WordPress is a free and open source tool used to create blogs, websites and ecommerce websites. She uses free online tutorials and documents to learn how to do this, see chapter 'Website Creation' on how to build websites.

The above example is an adaptation of the story of entrepreneur Sophia Amoruso, the CEO of Nasty Gal. Her book *#girlboss* is a fantastic read.

Let's look at another example in a different situation to give you a diverse range. Jackie lost her job as an administrator and is struggling to find a new job. Jackie isn't happy with her situation and has decided to set up her own business. Jackie, like many successful entrepreneurs, doesn't have any qualifications and doesn't have much money to start buying and selling items. She decides to open up a house-cleaning business. This is ideal for Jackie, because it's a service business, which means no expensive stock.

Jackie gets 1000 leaflets made with her contact details on for £16.99 and posts these through people's doors in affluent areas. She also purchases a bucket, some cleaning products and protective clothing for less than £20. She figures that any expensive items, such as a Hoover, will be available at her clients' houses. Jackie gets her first client from one of her leaflets and with excitement and passion she starts to work on this house one day a week. Jackie does a great job so her client spreads the word among friends winning her more clients. Jackie purchases more leaflets and continues to post these through people's doors winning her more clients. One of her clients is a business owner and he is so pleased with her services he asks her if she would also clean his offices. Jackie agrees and realises that many of her other clients are likely to be business owners too. She makes her other clients aware that she now cleans commercial properties and they provide her with more work.

We hope these examples help you to visualise and understand that to begin with you don't need a lot of money to get started. In these cases you can use a percentage of your salary or your savings to finance your business. You're likely to make many mistakes and have many failures. Therefore, learning to start businesses with very little money will mean you can set up and close businesses without financial ruin. You may find the book *$100 Startup* by Chris Guillebeau an interesting read.

We've noted that you can use friends, family and credit cards to raise money for your business. Personally these are not options that we would recommend. Starting a business is notoriously risky and losing your family's or your friends' money is just going to make your life awkward. As for starting a business on a credit card, this is very risky. We've known people to use this option for financing their start-up only for their business to fail leaving them heavily in debt for years to come. There's nothing wrong in your business failing, but like riding a bike you want to be able to get back on straight away. There are exceptions to every rule and you may have read an inspiring story about a company that started on borrowed money from friends or maxed-out credit cards such as Alibaba or Snapchat. However, to every successful story like this there are hundreds, if not thousands, of disaster stories. These are not mathematical probabilities you want to play with. Risk is good, but recklessness isn't. If you decide to ignore this advice and finance your start-up using a credit card, please, at least read the fine print of your terms and conditions and plan appropriately. If the worst happened ask yourself if you'd be able to keep up the repayments if your business was no longer operating.

ECOSYSTEM FINANCING

Ecosystem financing refers to a type of organisation or government entity that provides grants or loans to help start-ups. Their goal is to support businesses as this will provide jobs and increase trade, which helps the local community and the wider economy.

Some examples of ecosystem financing include:

- Business plan competitions
- Government grants

Business Plan Competitions

Business plan competitions are competitions for you to pitch your business to a friendly panel of judges to win money for your start-up. They may also offer business support alongside the money. Please, forget what you've seen on TV where judges on a show belittle entrepreneurs. That's just for television and not what a business plan competition is like. Even if you don't win the competition the business exposure, experience, feedback and learning will help you with your business. You'll also meet potential investors and business partners.

To enter you'll likely have to complete a submission form for the competition, create a business plan and do a presentation. Don't rely on the strength of your business idea. A great business idea is nothing without a sharp entrepreneur, so you'll need to demonstrate this through a powerful presentation. Remember, practice makes perfect. Predict any questions they may ask you about your company finances, competition, your background, your growth plan, your strategy and anything else. Then prepare answers to these questions, so you're not put on the spot. You may even want to practice your pitch on family and friends. It's also a good idea to film yourself doing the pitch, that way you'll be able to pick up on any bad habits you have and improve your delivery.

A quick online search will help you find some business plan competitions, but to give you a flavour here are some examples:

- Profitunity! by Ernst & Young
- L'Oreal Brandstorm
- Social Enterprise Day competition
- Shell LiveWire Awards
- Investors' Circle
- MIT IDEAS Competition
- BiD Network
- Harvard Social Enterprise Club Pitch for Change Competition
- Lloyds TSB Enterprise awards
- Digital Entrepreneur Awards
- O2 Think Big

Government Grants

Government grants and other types of business grants are amounts of money given to a business usually for a specific project or purpose. The advantages of grants are that you won't have to pay it back or pay any interest. You'll also get to keep full control of your business.

The disadvantages of grants are that there is lots of competition for them; you may be expected to match the funds you're given, for example the grant may cover half of the project but you'll have to cover the other half. They tend to be awarded for proposed projects rather than ones already started and the application process can be slow.

You can find out more about grants by visiting:

- Government grants:

https://www.gov.uk/business-finance-support-finder

- Private grants http://www.betterbusinessfinance.co.uk/

COMMERCIAL FINANCE

We now move from self-funding and ecosystem financing towards the more money-driven end of the scale. Commercial finance is about borrowing money from a bank. A bank will loan you money with the expectation that you pay back the loan plus the interest, which makes the bank money.

Some examples of commercial financing include:

- Home equity loan - also known as 'homeowner loans' or a 'second mortgage'
- Small business loans / commercial loans

Home Equity Loan

If you own your own home then a home equity loan enables you to borrow money against the value (equity) you have in your home. How does this work? If your home is valued at £200,000 and you have £50,000 outstanding on your mortgage then the equity in your home would be £150,000 (75%). If you had completely paid off your mortgage then your equity would be £200,000 (100%). In other words the equity is the saleable value of your house minus the money borrowed against it such as your mortgage.

There are two types of home equity loans: a 'fixed-rate loan' and a 'home equity lines of credit' (HELOC). The fixed-rate loan provides you with a single lump sum, which you repay over a period of time at an agreed rate of interest. A HELOC allows you to borrow smaller sums of money. You'll be pre-approved for a certain spending limit and can withdraw the money when you need. Monthly payments vary based on the amount of money borrowed and the current interest rate.

A home equity loan isn't specific to business, so you can use this money for any purpose such as renovating your house or buying a new car. However, it's an option that you can use to acquire money for your start-up. Remember to think carefully before securing debts against your home. Your home may be repossessed if you do not keep up repayments.

Small Business Loan

A small business loan or a commercial loan is a loan you take out specifically for business purposes. Again, like all loans from a bank, you'll need to pay back the principle (the amount borrowed) and the interest. Businesses are risky investments for banks due to their high failure rate, so the rules for getting a business loan are a lot stricter. You'll also need collateral to secure the loan. Collateral is a term used to describe assets that the bank can take from you should you fail to make repayments. Assets can be physical things such as property, vehicles or equipment, so if you fail to make payments the bank can repossess these assets and make money by selling them.

Before the banks can make a lending decision they'll need a thorough understanding of what your business does. The information required by the bank will vary according to your business and what you want, but it'll usually involve some or all of the following:

- Business plan - so they can understand what your business is.
- Personal budget planner - so they can assess the level of withdrawals you'll need.
- Personal asset statement - so they can identify the collateral you possess.
- Up-to-date trading accounts - balance sheet, profit and loss accounts.
- Profit and loss and cash flow forecasts - for the coming 12 months.
- Costs breakdown - specific to your lending request, for example if you need money for a vehicle your cost breakdown should include insurance costs and road tax.

Small business loans are usually, at the time of writing, available between £1,000 and £25,000 with repayment terms between one and ten years. The individual options and benefits will vary between banks so it's a good idea to compare rather than pick the first one you see. Review them online and also arrange face-to-face meetings with your local branch so you can ask questions. You'll also want to work with a business manager you like and trust, which you'll be able to identify at a face-to-face meeting. You're not expected to know everything about business loans, so there is nothing wrong in being honest and asking them for their advice and guidance. However, they'll be carefully assessing you as a person. They'll want to see if you've got what it takes; how professional you are; if you know your business field inside and out; if you've got the experience and the confidence. This will come across by being fully prepared, dressing appropriately and asking the right questions. Put yourself in the business manager's shoes and imagine if someone asked you to lend them money for a business. What would you expect them to be like? What would you expect them to know? How would you expect them to behave?

If you take out a business loan do take the time to build a relationship with your business manager. This'll give you the best chance of the bank maintaining and increasing its support, but it'll also minimise the drawbacks in the event that your business goes through difficulty. To build rapport with your bank manger open good channels of communication by having face-to-face meetings, telephone calls and communicating via email. Don't give your banker nasty surprises or try to hide anything, so be open and honest about your situation. If need be, involve your accountant as bankers will appreciate that you have a trusted and professional advisor. When negotiating, create win-win situations, so both you and your bank manager are happy. It's not uncommon for banks to change their business managers, which means you'll have to start again with the relationship-building process. Do take the time to build a relationship with any new business managers. Another option for you if you have a strong relationship with your business manager and they change banks is to switch banks with them.

What if the business manager isn't keen to loan you money? Welcome to entrepreneurship, where rejection is part of your daily life. If your bank manager isn't keen on lending you money, don't take this to heart, especially if after a great deal of research your business is a good one. Banks are very strict when it comes to lending money to businesses, and after the 2008 crash unsurprisingly banks tightened up their lending processes even more. You're going to have to be what entrepreneurs are: creative, persistent and resilient, because you might be rejected by 20 different banks before you get a yes. However, be aware that every time you apply for a loan it goes on your credit history and may affect your credit rating. Ask your business manager for more details before you apply for a business loan.

If your business manager isn't keen to lend you money because you don't have enough collateral then ask them about Enterprise Finance Guarantee (EFG). EFG is a loan guarantee scheme, which allows banks and other lenders to offer small businesses which lack security or a proven track record, a normal secured commercial loan (gov.uk, 2014). The EFG means that the lender doesn't bear all the risk because the risk is shared with the government. At the time of writing, there are currently 42 lenders in the scheme, including:

- all main UK high street banks
- smaller specialist banks
- invoice finance providers
- community development finance institutions (CDFIs)

INVESTORS
In today's world when entrepreneurs think of raising money for their

start-up they tend to think of investors and jump straight to this end of the scale first. This is probably due to all the glamorous stories about tech start-ups like Facebook, Twitter, Snapchat and others who have raised millions of dollars to grow their business. However, there are only certain types of businesses that are appropriate for these types of investors and it's important to understand this.

Investors tend to be successful people and not always business people who want to invest in the next generation of entrepreneurs. This is because they find it interesting and fun and they can get a bigger return on investment if their investment business is success-ful rather than leaving the money in a bank.

Some examples of investors include:

- Angel investors
- Crowdfunding
- Venture Capitalists

Angel Investors

Angel investors are people who have an interest in financing small companies and start-ups. They are not the same as a venture cap-italist as the money they invest is their own. They can play either hands-off or hands-on roles for the company that they invest in. A hands-on role would mean your business has more skills and expe-rience to utilise. Therefore, it's important to understand what level of interest the angel investor(s) has in your company. Is it purely for money or are they interested in the business and want to help out? How does this match with what you're looking for in an angel investor? Are you looking for just money, or are you looking for an angel investor who can also fill the holes in your team?

Angel investors can come as an individual or as a group, so typically investments can vary between £10k and £1m+.

What's the difference between a business loan and an angel investor? A business loan is a loan that you pay back with interest, so you still have a hundred percent ownership of your business. However, with an angel investor you're selling equity (ownership) in return for money and they'll typically take between 20% and 50%+ of your business. Be aware that if you chose an angel investor who has both a financial and an operational role it can cause complications, because they have the power to change the operations and hire and fire employees.

How do angel investors make their money from investing in your business? Let's say an angel investor invests £50k in your company and the rest of your company is worth £50k, so your total company worth is £100k. In this case the angel investor owns half of your company. As the company grows and becomes successful the angel investor might decide to sell their equity in your company. For example, if the company is now worth £500k and they sell their half they'll make £250K from an initial investment of £50K.

How easy is it to get money from an angel investor? Again put yourself in the investor's shoes. If you're a computer programmer who's studied at Harvard University, worked at Google for a couple of years and you and a couple of colleagues want to raise money to build an app, investors are probably going to get pretty excited about you even if you haven't even started the company yet. However, if you're let's say 21 years old, straight out of university with no work experience you're going to find it extremely difficult to find an investor based solely on an idea. In this case they'd want to see the business taking off, processes in place, orders to buy etc. You're probably asking why you would need an angel investor if your business is already set up and you have customers. Remember at the beginning of the chapter we said not all these ways of raising finance are suitable for every business. You may have started your business from your savings, but you've now reached a point where you have more customers and orders than you can manage. In order to fulfil these orders you need more machinery and more employees. However you don't have the money to buy this machinery or hire more employees. Therefore, you would go to an angel investor to raise the money. Some people get confused at this point as they think if you're getting orders why don't you have the money? Remember an order isn't money. If we order your product but you don't have the capacity to fulfil the order, you won't get our money.

How do I get an angel investor? Angel investors are just people and like all people they're driven by different things. For example, if the angel investor you're pitching to comes from an accounting or engineering background they may be more likely to warm to information they can analyse such as order quantities, revenue and exit strategies. While other angel investors may be more motivated by the problem you're trying to solve and their passion for you and your business. However, angel investing is a very emotionally driven business and if you're excited and passionate about your business they're likely to become excited and passionate about your business too. It's also not just about your business it's about you as a person. Do they like you? Would they go for coffee with you? Do you have what it takes?

How do you find an angel investor? The first thing you can do is let everyone know you're looking for an angel investor, so that's your friends, family, your dentist, and everyone in your network - except your boss or your work colleagues if you're still in work. While you're not trying to raise money from these people it's possible they may know someone who is an angel investor, or wants to become one. For example, one of Andrew's old work colleagues became Managing Director of an angel-backed business and he put Andrew in touch with his investors. Being introduced to an angel investor through someone you know is always best, because if this person is trusted by the angel investor it'll stand you in more favour.

While meeting an angel investor is always best through a mutual connection, it's not the only route, so don't worry. There are now an increasing number of angel investor workshops and events that you can attend to meet people. It's probably best to attend these workshops and events regardless so that you can be around angel investors. That way you'll get to understand them as people, the language that they use and what they look for in entrepreneurs. An Internet search should provide you with a list of workshops and events you can attend.

You can also get connected to angel investors online. A quick Internet search will provide you with websites that connect you with investors such as:

- www.angelinvestmentnetwork.co.uk
- www.ukbusinessangelsassociation.org.uk
- www.angelcofund.co.uk
- www.angelcapitalassociation.or

You can also use websites like LinkedIn to find angel investors.

How do you introduce yourself to an angel investor? How you introduce yourself to an angel investor will depend on the method you choose above. If you only have a name and an email address you'll at first have to send them an introductory email. Basically you're going in cold. Lots of people do this so don't worry about it. Please note that we recommend you reread this section on angel investors, if that's what you're aiming for, after you've read the chapter on sales. Having a better understanding of sales and rapport-building will help you sell to investors.

The idea of the introductory email isn't to sell them your business idea, but to sell them a face-to-face meeting. Therefore, you'll want to avoid the mistake that many people make and that's bombarding them with massive amounts of information. This will just bore the investor and they're likely to delete the email before even reading it.

Instead you'll want to create interest and curiosity. To do this your email should have the following elements:

- Strong subject line
- Personal connection
- Elevator pitch
- Traction
- Team
- Social proof
- The close

Just like you, angel investors get lots of email, some legitimate and some junk. If they don't open your email you'll have failed at the first hurdle. An example of a bad subject line is something like: "*Great Investment Opportunity*", which is bland and obvious. Whereas a good subject line would be: "*Delta One Power - founded by ex-Dyson engineer*".

You'll want to establish a personal connection to show that you're a legitimate person. To do this your opening paragraph should address the investor by their first name, reference someone you both know and reference the investor's background. For example:

"Hi Jamie,

Our mutual contact, Joe West from somebusiness.com, suggested I contact you. I'm currently launching a business called Delta One Power, which provides an alternative, cheaper and environmentally friendly power source to cars. I understand that you have an interest in the energy industry and have helped fund several solar power businesses."

The next element of your email is the elevator pitch. When you read the chapter about sales, you'll understand the power of three. We're going to apply this here and use three pieces of key information to hook your investor's interest. Don't worry about this being short, that's the idea. Long drawn-out heavily information-based pitches are a turn-off. The concept of an elevator pitch is born out of the idea that if you were in the lift with an investor and you only had 30 second to sell them your idea, what would you say? We're applying this well-known concept here in the email. An example might be:

> *"Delta One Power will help 30 million drivers in the UK save £2,000 a year by providing them with an alternative, cheaper and environmentally friendly power source for their cars."*

After the elevator pitch follows your business traction, which explains how far your business has come and where it's going. Examples could include:

> *"Our pre-orders have totalled 25,000 units and we're taking pre-orders of 100 a day."*

Or

> *"Our website traffic has increased to 20,000 views a month and this is increasing every month by 30 percent."*

The next element is your team because behind every successful business are great people. The angel investor will be looking at how qualified and experienced your team is in your particular industry. In the case of Delta One Power, a good example would be:

> *"Our team includes the former marketing director of BMW and the former head of distribution from BP."*

The next element of your email is your social proof, which is how credible you are. For example, if you're Mark Zuckerberg (founder of Facebook) and you want to launch a new social media app for mobile phones, you'll probably find it extremely easy to raise the finance due to your social proof. Not that Zuckerberg would need to raise finance, but you get our point. So how do you show you have social proof? There are several ways such as winning a competition, having a large amount of pre-orders or having someone else with social proof investing in your business. For example:

"My Delta One Power unit has recently won invention of the year."

Or

"James Dyson, founder of Dyson Ltd, has invested £100k in Delta One Power."

The last element of your email is the close, which is where you ask for the amount you need and a time to meet. Get straight to the point with this one, for example:

"We're raising £100,000 to help with production to meet the growing demand. We're keen to discuss this with you and wondered when you'd be available for a quick meeting? Just drop me a quick email back and we can coordinate diaries."

Now if you joined all these sections up to form the email it would likely be fewer than 200 words. Yet it tells the angel investor what your company does, how credible you and your team are, and that the business is already taking pre-orders.

If your email is successful then the angel investor will want to meet with you. However, and it's likely, you'll get many rejections just at the email stage. Don't let this knock you off course, but do take note. It's possible you're getting rejected because your email isn't hitting the right notes. Change and adapt your email making it better and more appealing. There are lots of good resources available on the Internet to help you with this such as: www.invstor.com/funding-101. If you can't get all the elements in your email, then that's a sign that you have more work to do before you become appealing to angel investors. If you're joining an angel investment website it'll probably require you to submit a proposal for investors to read. The elements will remain the same to spark that initial interest.

So now you've found an angel investor, you've emailed them and they want to meet you. What happens next? Next is your pitch, but you must realise that after a successful pitch is another stage in the process, which is due diligence. That means you still don't get the money yet. A due diligence is basically a review of your company to establish its assets, liabilities and assess its potential. The format in which you meet and pitch to your angel investor will vary. Some angel investors will meet you over a coffee while others might prefer a more formal presentation-style pitch. Regardless, the underlying rules remain the same. When you meet your potential angel investor, we'll state again, many entrepreneurs bombard them with too much data and information. You want to inspire them and excite them. Imagine you were the person who invented the iPhone and you pitched it as follows:

"Height: 4.87 inches, GSM model A1428, assisted GPS, retina display, 4-inch diagonal widescreen, multi-touch display with video recording, HD (1080p) up to 30 frames per second with audio..."

You're likely to put your angel investor to sleep and not raise any finance. To structure your pitch we're going follow and discuss Guy Kawasaki's the '10/20/30 pitch rule'. For those of you who don't know who Guy Kawasaki is, "Kawasaki is the chief evangelist of

Canva, an online graphic design tool. Formerly, he was an advisor to the Motorola business unit of Google and chief evangelist of Apple. He is also the author of *APE, What the Plus!, Enchantment,* and nine other books. Kawasaki has a BA from Stanford University and an MBA from UCLA as well as an honorary doctorate from Babson College." - This was taken and quoted from Kawasaki's LinkedIn profile.

The 10/20/30 Pitch Rule

The '10' part of the rule is that 10 is the optimum number of slides your presentation should have. This will ensure your presentation doesn't bombard your angel investor, but instead only provides them with relevant information. In other words, less is more. Remember that the purpose of your pitch is to progress onto the next stage, which is the due diligence stage. No angel investor is going to give you money at the end of a pitch, no matter how successful your pitch is. Kawasaki states that the ten slides could be as follows:

- Title
- Problem
- Solution
- Business model
- Underlying magic
- Marketing and sales
- Competition
- Team
- Projections
- Status and timeline

You don't have to stick exactly to 10 slides, but you shouldn't be presenting a 50 slide presentation, so try to keep it to around ten.

The '20' part of the rule refers to the amount of time your presentation should last, which is 20 minutes. Even if you have a 60-minute appointment booked, your presentation should still stay around 20 minutes.

The '30' part of the rule refers to the font size, which should be a 30-point font. Using a font size of 30 will force you to put only the key points on your slides and prevent you from writing paragraphs. One of the worst things you can do is write big paragraphs in a small font, then read it to the audience. They'll have read it before you finish speaking, if they can see it, and they'll know that you don't know your business well enough.

Watch Kawasaki walk you through the 10/20/30 rule on YouTube. Search for "Guy Kawasaki the 10/20/30 pitch rule". The 10/20/30 pitch rule might not be for everyone, and pitching is not an exact science, so you may tailor it to your situation. However, if you've never pitched before, it's a good starting point for you to follow.

When pitching your business always show them prototypes or any examples of your product. A prototype is an early model or sample of your product or idea. The production and use of a prototype makes the product feel more real and will enable the angel investor to see it and touch it rather than for it be purely theoretical. The prototype doesn't need to be a fully-functional product, but it does need to provide a good idea of what you're trying to achieve. A prototype also doesn't need to be a physical object, for example if your business idea is a mobile phone app then creating a mock-up app that has some functionality will make it far more real for the angel investor. For more information on prototyping refer to the chapter: 'Prototyping'.

Which angel investor should you chose? Don't assume all angel investors are good or good for your particular business, and don't have the mentality that they're doing you a favour. If your business is good, which we assume you think it is, then realise it's an opportunity for them. You need to do as much of a due diligence on them as they will do on you. You'll want to ask them questions about their successes as an angel investor. You'll want to ask for references and speak to other entrepreneurs who took money from them. This way you'll be able to know if there's synergy.

Crowdfunding

In recent years, 'crowdfunding' websites have become popular. Traditionally, raising money for your business involved a small number of investors investing large sums of money. However, crowdfunding flips this model on its head and is used to raise money from thousands or millions of people via the Internet. People offer money from as low as £5 up to thousands of pounds.

How do investors make money from crowdfunding? There are officially three forms of crowdfunding: donation crowdfunding, debt crowdfunding and equity crowdfunding.

Donation crowdfunding - When people donate their money and expect no financial return. Instead they'll probably receive rewards such as acknowledgements, free tickets to an event, a tour of the business or some other type of free gift. People's motivation for donating money is usually social or personal to feel good about being involved in something they enjoy (Andrew, 2013). Some websites include:

- www.banktothefuture.com
- www.buzzbnk.org
- www.crowdbnk.com
- www.peoplefund.it
- www.gambitious.com

Debt crowdfunding - When people loan money for a financial reward, so investors will receive their money back with interest.

With the 2008 crash when banks became stricter about loaning their money debt crowdfunding became a popular alternative for entrepreneurs to fund their businesses. This is also known as peer-to-peer lending (Andrew, 2013). Some websites include:

- www.abundancegeneration.com
- www.banktothefuture.com
- www.buzzbnk.org
- www.trillionfund.com

Equity crowdfunding - When people exchange money for shares in your business (Andrew, 2013). Some websites include:

- www.banktothefuture.com
- www.crowdbnk.com
- www.crowdcube.com
- www.gambitious.com
- www.microgenius.org.uk
- www.crowdmission.com
- www.seedrs.com

Simply joining these websites won't guarantee that you raise finance for your business. You'll still have to dazzle your investors with an interesting pitch usually in the form of a video and a project overview. You'll also have to market your proposal and spread the word to make people aware that you're seeking money. We recommend that you review successful projects where people have raised their required amount of money. This way you'll be able to analyse, copy and improve how these people raised the money from crowdfunding investors. Even better would be to contact them and ask them for direct advice.

Venture Capitalists
Another way to fund your business is through the use of venture

capitalists (VCs). However, it must be noted that VCs tend to have very little interest in early-stage businesses, unless under exceptional circumstances such as a "tech business" with successful owners.

There are several differences between VCs and angel investors. Firstly, angel investors can be an individual investor whereas a VC is an investment company. That is, their business is to invest in other businesses. The VC will usually have a pot of money from around £25m to around £150m and their aim is to increase this money by investing in different businesses. They'll typically invest starting amounts of £1m+, so they invest a much larger amount than angel investors. VCs also tend to invest additional money in your business over the lifetime of their investment. They do this to maintain their ownership percentage as your company grows, or even to increase their ownership percentage. These are known as investment rounds with the 'A round' being the initial investment.

A VC will have money invested in many businesses and they'll sit on the board of these companies. As well as providing capital and sitting on the board of a company a VC will also provide guidance, access to experts, a wealth of experience, useful contacts and media exposure. However, not all VCs are as good as each other, so you need to do your due diligence on them too. They'll usually invest for around seven to nine years, which is when they sell their shares for a financial return. They'll expect this return to be around 10 times the amount they've invested.

As you can see not every business idea is suitable for funding from a VC. If you're opening up a single restaurant or a sideline business from your bedroom then a VC isn't an appropriate investment strategy. This book is for people who are starting up these types of small businesses and the subject of VCs is quite expansive. Therefore, we won't go into detail about VCs. However, there may be a point when your bedroom business significantly grows and you may need the funding of a VC.

RAISING CAPITAL SUMMARY

In this chapter we've discussed a variety of ways of raising money to fund your business from self-funding across to using investors. The type of business you're setting up will determine your capital raising strategy, because not all methods will be relevant. One of the most important skills of an entrepreneur is the ability to raise money.

BRANDING

When you think of corporate brands like McDonalds, you know wherever you are in the world the food will taste the same and you'll get the same level of customer service. If you take the time to consider more brands, you'll realise that some you'll perceive as trustworthy, for example the National Health Service (NHS) and Johnson & Johnson who produce healthcare products. Some brands you'll think are fun, such as Old Spice through their use of humorous online adverts; others you'll see as luxury and prestigious such as Rolex. Corporations market their brand in such a way as to appeal to their target audience. They'll even have specialist Brand Managers working full-time on their brand to ensure it is constantly aligned with their vision, mission and values. In this chapter we'll look at branding and how you can brand your company so it's aligned with your goals and customers.

WHAT IS YOUR BRAND?

When most people hear the word brand or when asked what a brand is they'll usually think of a logo. A company logo, while it's a big part of branding, is only one aspect. Imagine a company had the best logo in the world, but they had a terrible website. Would you continue with your purchase? Probably not. Imagine a company had the best logo in the world, but their customer service team were rude to you. Would you shop with them again? Probably not. Imagine a company sold a great product, but they donated money towards terrorist organisations. Would you shop with them or even work for them? Probably not. Basically, a brand is everything that the customer sees, touches, smells, hears and tastes; so your brand includes:

- Website
- Quality of product or service
- Packaging
- Social media
- The way you and your employees dress and speak (personality)
- Your adverts and marketing material
- Any descriptions, writing and copy that comes from your company
- Location
- Partners
- Your client or customer base
- Processes
- Charities you donate money to
- Celebrities chosen to endorse your company
- Design work
- Price
- Service
- Colour
- Pictures used
- Vision, mission and values
- Logo
- Company name
- Product labels

Basically all the points of your company the customer touches must reflect your brand, and if they don't, then your brand isn't aligned.

CREATING YOUR BRAND

The first thing many new entrepreneurs do is hire a graphic designer to produce a logo without any real thought. They're so hungry to get started that they rush this stage and never really understand the true value of getting the brand right. Time invested in getting the right brand will be returned with greater sales.

In this section we'll gather the right information and identify what your company is trying to achieve. From this we'll be able to create a brand that your customers can relate to and fall in love with.

Who Are Your Customers?

The first thing you should do is look at what you're selling and who your target market is. Are you selling cheap high-volume goods to young consumers who are tight for cash? Are you selling prestigious items to the high-end market? Are you selling marketing services to small and medium-sized enterprises (SME's)? Are you selling high-end consultancy services to large organisations? This is extremely important to know, because knowing what you sell and who your customers are shapes your brand.

We've worked with an established consulting company who sold high-end consultancy services to medium and large-sized organisations. However, over time their brand became dated. Therefore, their brand didn't match the prices they charged and the services they delivered, which affected their new business development. There was a complete misalignment between what the organisation thought they were and what clients saw. This meant winning new clients was significantly harder and recruiting the best talent was also difficult. The reasons for this were that they hadn't defined what type of consultancy services they were offering and who their customers were. The first thing we did with this company was to establish what consultancy services they should specialise in, which then led to who

73

their customers were. Once you understand who your customers are you'll start to formulate a picture of how your brand should be.

Remember, your brand isn't just about selling to customers it's also about attracting the best talent, partners and suppliers too.

Who Do Our Customers Want Us To Be?

Once you've established your target audience you'll need to understand your target audience better so that you can identify what they want you to be. As a crude example, if your target market is children then an expensive and prestigious looking luxury brand is likely to be unattractive while a more fun, colourful and vibrant brand is likely to be more appealing. Some questions to ask yourself include:

- What causes my target market to buy what I'm selling? (pain, pleasure, time, convenience, pride, fun, health, envy, career advancement, self-improvement, money, popularity, security, comfort, to make something better.)
- What do they look for in a company of this type? (fun, trust, prestige, speed, intelligence, safety, security.)
- From whom do they currently buy these products or services?

Some of this will be common sense, for example if your start up is selling products for children, then you can imagine safety and trust would be high on a customer's (parent's) list. You may need to do some desk research, which involves reading literature and searching the Internet. You could also do field research which would involve speaking directly to your target market.

Who Are My Competitors?

Now that you understand who your target market is and you have an idea of what they want from a company in your industry, it's time to look at your competitors.

There are likely to be lots of competitors, so to prevent information overload pick the top three or four competitors and analyse them. Look at everything including: logo, website, social media, shops, marketing material, advertising media, colours, language used, pictures, customer reviews and everything else. You may even test their services by making a purchase. Analyse what you like and what you don't like about your competitor's brand, and what they could do better.

Once you've identified your target market, discovered what your target market looks for in a company and recognised your competitors, you'll have some idea of how your company should be branded. Don't worry if you don't know exactly how your brand should be yet. However, it's highly likely you'll start to have some idea even if you can't materialise it.

Vision, Mission and Values

A company's vision, mission and values (VMVs) can seem fluffy and theoretical to many people. They'll throw them together because they feel a company should have them for the sake of it, without any real meaning or strategy behind their creation.

If you need to get to a specific place by a certain time that requires long travel, would you plan your route or leave and hope for the best? Obviously you'd have a plan and a strategy for getting there. This topic is expansive and a book in itself. However, as this book is for start-ups we won't need to go into great detail, but just enough for you to get started.

A company's VMVs are important to the success of achieving its strategic goals. Successful organisations spend a great deal of time getting their VMVs right, often hiring consultants and conduct-ing both internal and external market research. Organisations who have VMVs that have been thrown together by one person or a few senior people in isolation will find that their brand is misaligned both internally and externally. In other words their business and operations will suffer. This is because while that one person or a few senior people have created the VMVs, the other people in the organisation may have completely different values and missions. To create successful VMVs most people in the organisation to a degree need to be involved.

If your start-up is just you then you're fine to create VMVs alone, but if you have partners or employees then you'll need to come up with them together. In fact it's at this stage you might find that your partners or employees are not right for you. If you want your company to be the best in the industry, but your partners or employees have different ambitions then there is a mismatch. In this case these differences would have come out in your branding and your customers would have been confused about your brand identity.

How do VMVs impact your branding? Remember your branding isn't just a logo it's everything, including your behaviours. Your VMVs affect how your company, you and your employees behave. If your company is selling online payment protection and your brand is all about security and safety, which are reflected in your values, then it wouldn't look great if hackers broke into your systems and stole customer details. If your mission is to provide the best customer service ever known then everything you do will revolve around this mission and your brand will be known for this.

Vision Statement

A vision statement explains "where" you want your company to be, so it explains the future state. Here are some examples:

Disney - To make people happy

Oxfam - A just world without poverty

Ikea - To create a better everyday life for the many people

Microsoft - A computer on every desk and in every home; all running Microsoft software

Nike - To be the number one athletic company in the world

Toys 'R' Us - Our vision is to put joy in kids' hearts and a smile on parents' faces

Amazon - To build a place where people can come to find and discover anything they might want to buy online

Avon - To be the company that best understands and satisfies the product, service and self-fulfilment needs of women - globally

Starbucks - To establish Starbucks as the most recognized and respected brand in the world

Notice how many of the vision statements start with "to build", "to be", "to create" and "to make" as it describes the future state.

What's your vision? Where is it that you want your company to be?

Mission Statement

A mission statement explains "how" you'll get to where you want to be by explaining what you do today. Here are some examples:

> **Apple** - Apple designs Macs, the best personal computers in the world, along with OS X, iLife, iWork and professional software. Apple leads the digital music revolution with its iPods and iTunes online store. Apple has reinvented the mobile phone with its revolutionary iPhone and App Store, and is defining the future of mobile media and computing devices with iPad.

> **Pfizer** - We dedicate ourselves to humanity's quest for longer,

healthier, happier, lives through innovation in pharmaceutical, consumer and animal health products.

Unilever - Our mission is to add vitality to life. We meet everyday needs for nutrition, hygiene and personal care with brands that help people look good, feel good and get more out of life.

So you have your vision, but how are you going to get there? What's your mission?

Company Values

Values are beliefs that you, your partners and your employees hold and adhere to no matter what you face. Your values are part of your strategic foundation and they guide the conduct, activities, behaviours and goals of your company.

As an example, Coca-Cola's values are (at the time of writing):

- Leadership
- Passion
- Integrity
- Accountability
- Collaboration
- Diversity
- Quality

As another example, Kellogg's values are (at the time of writing):

- Integrity
- Accountability
- Passion
- Humility
- Simplicity

- Results

A company called Zappos is famous for its company culture and values, which are (at the time of writing):

- Deliver WOW Through Service
- Embrace and Drive Change
- Create Fun and A Little Weirdness
- Be Adventurous, Creative, and Open-Minded
- Pursue Growth and Learning
- Build Open and Honest Relationships With Communication
- Build a Positive Team and Family Spirit
- Do More With Less
- Be Passionate and Determined
- Be Humble

The above values are not simply lists of words and phrases. These values are at the heart of everything these companies do. They help drive the strategy of these companies and make their brand. They'll even specifically recruit people who match these values and only work with suppliers who are similar.

Take the time to really think what your values should be by looking at what industry you're in, what you're trying to achieve and who you are.

Company Colours

Colours have a powerful effect on people. Stop and think about this. Have you ever been to a hospital with its dull, clinical white colours? How did you feel? Did you know when we see the colour red it increases our heart rate? Colours are powerful.

In this section we'll discuss more about colours. We won't tell you which colour you should use for your brand, but we'll give you enough information for you to make an educated decision based on your research.

- **Red:** is associated with danger, heat, aggression, love and passion. It's often used by restaurants because the colour red increases appetite. You'll notice McDonalds, Heinz, Coca-Cola and Kellogg have red as their corporate colours. Some other companies that use red as their company colour include: Netflix, YouTube, H&M, Nintendo, Lego and Virgin.
- **Blue:** is associated with the sky, the sea, trustworthiness, cleanliness and calmness. Blue is also mostly preferred by males. Blue is a cold colour and the downside to this is that it can make your company feel cold. Some well-known companies that use blue include: Oral B, Dell, LinkedIn, Ford, Facebook, Twitter and Oreo.
- **Orange:** is associated with warmth, sunshine, tropics and caution. Orange also promotes people to carry out actions such as to buy, sell or subscribe. You'll notice if you shop on Amazon or have made a purchase through PayPal, their payment buttons are orange. This is not a coincidence. Research has shown orange buttons have a higher rate of clicks. Some companies that use orange as their brand colour include: Harley-Davidson, Fanta, Orange, Firefox and Amazon.
- **Green:** is associated with nature, the environment, health, growth, money and jealousy. Some companies that use green in their branding include: Starbucks Coffee, BP, Xbox, Land Rover, Holiday Inn and Green Peace.
- **Purple:** is associated with luxury, spirituality, religion, mystery and royalty. Many cosmetic and anti-aging brands use the colour purple. Some companies that use purple in their branding include: Yahoo, Wonka, Hallmark, Cadbury's and Ralph Lauren,
- **Yellow:** is associated with sunshine, energy and optimism. Yellow is very eye-catching, which is why it's often used in

shop windows and in "For Sale" signs. Some companies that use yellow in their branding include: McDonalds, Ferrari, Caterpillar, Ikea, DHL, Shell and Hertz.

- **Black:** is associated with luxury, boldness, mystery and seriousness. It's probably not a good colour to be used for a services business and works best to represent a product business. Some companies that use black include: Nike, Guinness, BlackBerry, Tiffany & Co, Giorgio Armani, Jack Daniels and the BBC.
- **Brown:** is associated with earth, dependability, the outdoors, stability and being approachable. However, it can be associated with dirt and lack of sophistication. Some companies that use the colour brown in their brand include: UPS, M&Ms and Louis Vuitton.

Creating a Branding Brief

At this stage of the process you should know who your target audience is, what your competitors' branding is like, have your vision, mission and values and know what colour you want. This information will have given you an idea of what your brand should look like, but unless you're a graphic designer or an artist you probably won't be able to put all these together to make your brand logo.

However, what we're going to do at this stage is put all this information into a something called a design brief, which a graphic designer can use to create your brand and logo. A design brief is simply a document which explains to a designer what you want your brand to look like.

A design brief should have the following:

- **Your brand and business:** a one to two sentence overview of your business.
- **Target audience:** here, you might say something like, "Women

aged between 25 and 35, who have luxury taste in fashionable shoes."

- **Values to communicate with your design:** discuss your company values and how you want these to be reflected in the design.
- **Style:** how you want the logo to look. Do you want an animal in your logo, something bold, strong or sophisticated? Point the designer in the right direction.
- **Colours:** have you decided what colours suit your target audience? Discuss these here.
- **Example images:** as you can imagine graphic designers are visual people and a picture paints a thousand words. Provide designers with example logos that you like. However, you'll want to differentiate your logo from competitors.
- **Anything else?** If you have any special requests or comments add this information here.

Materialising Your Brand

Once you've got your design brief, you'll need to find a graphic designer. You can do this in several ways. If you know any graphic designers personally you could approach them and ask them to do it for free. If you don't know any graphic designers you're going to have to outsource it.

- **Open contests:** there are websites available where you offer prize money for graphic designers to create your logo. You only pay for the winning logo.
- **Outsourcing websites:** are websites where you can hire people such as graphic designers to create you a logo. Please, be aware that if you're paying for example £30 for a logo you're not going to get a 100% bespoke logo. They're likely to use stock images, which may be used in another company's logo. When a graphic designer provides you with a logo, it's important that you do an image search to ensure that it's not being

used by any other company or is a copyrighted image. You can simply do this by using 'Google's Inside Search' engine which allows you to search by image. Simply drag and drop your logo into the search engine and see what comes up.

- **Professional illustrator:** another alternative is to use a professional illustrator. Use Google or another search engine to find one. Depending on what you're looking for, professional illustrators can be very expensive. However, their work will be original. Nonetheless, it's always worth doing a 'Google Inside Search' on the image to ensure it is.
- **Branding / creative agency:** you can use a branding or creative agency to create your brand and logo. You'll still need to provide them with a design brief. However, this option can be expensive and might not be necessary if your start-up is a small business.

How much should a logo cost? This depends on your budget and what your company is selling. Here are some examples of what companies have spent on their logos:

- British Petroleum (BP): $211,000,000
- ANZ: $15,000,000
- BBC: $1,800,000
- Accenture: $100,000,000
- Pepsi: $1,000,000
- Twitter: $15
- Nike: $35
- Google: $0
- Coca-Cola: $0

When your designer provides you with samples you don't have to accept any of these if they're not what you're looking for. Provide the designer with constructive feedback so that they can go away and make alterations until it's perfect for you.

Remember your logo is going to be a different size on your business card than it is on your website. Ensure your logo isn't so detailed that it's not scalable to different sizes. You need to be able to manipulate your logo.

When you're happy with the logo and you make the purchase, make sure you get the illustrator files too. Ensure that you're fully purchasing the logo and have full rights to it. What you don't want to find is several years later you're running a successful business and the graphic designer actually owns the copyright to the logo.

Once you have your desired logo, you may want to have your designer start looking after other branded material such as letter heads, business cards, presentations, thank-you slips, packaging, or whatever else you need. Negotiate a better rate if the designer does all of your design work, but pay a fair amount so the designer isn't disgruntled and still wants to do a good job for you. You could shop around to have different designers do different pieces for you, but take into account that you'll be managing different people and the end result may not be uniform.

This chapter has covered branding at a very high level. If you're just starting your business or your business is relatively new, or even relatively old, you should have a good foundation for developing your brand.

WEBSITE CREATION

Whatever business you own, or are setting up, you'll need a website. A business without a website is seen as unacceptable and strange in the eyes of the customer. Not only will you need a website, it'll need to be a good website. There are several ways to get a website for your business such as hiring a web developer or purchasing an 'off the shelf' package or building a website yourself. There are advantages and disadvantages to all these options. However, in this chapter were going to discuss how you can build your very own website, without the need for a degree in computer science.

Why would you want to build your own website? Your website is likely to need updating constantly, whether it's new content such as blogs or news, changes to products, fixing mistakes such as typos and other reasons. If you're paying for a web developer to change your website you're not in control, which means these changes won't happen instantly and you'll also be leaking money. Being able to create your own website also means you can set up, test and close businesses with ease and virtually no financial loss. If you're paying £500 per website you simply couldn't do this. Being able to build and maintain your own website is an extremely powerful and liberating skill.

DOMAIN NAME

Before getting started with creating a website we need to look at purchasing your domain name if you haven't done so already. The domain you're looking for probably won't be available with a .com or .co.uk - unless you have a really unique or long name. If your domain is not available it'll already be in use or it may be a 'parked domain'. A parked domain means that it has been purchased and not used, so the owner is waiting for someone like you to come along and buy it from them. This can be a very frustrating situation as a number of people ask for hundreds, sometimes even thousands of pounds to give you the domain, which should only cost a couple of pounds.

If your domain isn't available then it becomes your task to create a variation of your domain name that *is* available. If you wanted www.examplewebsite.com but it wasn't available you could look at variations such as:

www.example-website.com
www.theexamplewebsite.com

Just make sure you don't create too much of a variation so that the domain name doesn't represent your business name. We advise not using too many dashes, for example: www.the-example-website.com. We also advise against using one of the lesser-known or lesser-used .com variations (unless applicable):

- .com - originally stood for 'commercial' but is now the most sought after and used for a wide variety of websites.
- .edu - educational establishments
- .info - informational websites
- .net - originally intended for network infrastructures but now unrestricted
- .org - originally for organisations but again now unrestricted

The list goes on; most countries have their own variation, as .co. uk stands for the United Kingdom .de stands for Germany. Make sure you think about which is correct for your website, or if you think more than one might be applicable it can be a good idea to purchase both. Purchasing a number of variations of your domain name can stop competitors from taking it. For example, if you only purchased the .co.uk of your business name the .com could still be available and could be purchased by a competitor.

To get things started visit an Internet domain registrar such as www.123-reg.com, www.godaddy.com, or www.x10premium.com to begin a search to see if your domain name is available. If it is, you should expect to pay in the region of £7 to £15 a year to own the domain name. To ensure you keep your domain we suggest selecting 'auto renew' when purchasing the domain (or afterwards in the settings), meaning that when your domain ownership is coming to an end it automatically renews for another year, incurring another charge of around £7-£15 for that year.

WEBSITE HOSTING

After securing your domain name you'll need to purchase a hosting package to hold your website on. A hosting company houses your website for a fee. We won't get too technical; just think of hosting costs as the equivalent of paying rent for a property. Thankfully though, hosting is very cheap; we use x10premium.com, an American company who for around £4-£5 a month provides us with hosting for a large number of websites, company email addresses and more. We recommend starting here, but feel free to shop around, there are many companies out there offering website hosting for a wide range of prices, from free to thousands of pounds a month depending on the needs of your website. Usually these companies offer both domain name registration and hosting.

There are some options available for free website hosting but it can be a bad idea. A number of companies will offer website own-ers free hosting, but in return the website will contain advertising placed there by the hosting company. For personal websites this is fine, but for a business it can give a poor first impression to a potential customer. With hosting costing just a few pounds a month, it's worth the investment.

When you purchase a hosting package you'll be given login details to access your own 'admin area'. Within the admin area you can do a number of things, such as creating email addresses on your domain (e.g. contact@examplewebsite.com), assigning a blog to your website and much more. Each hosting company will have a slightly different 'admin area' so our advice is to do a YouTube search for an instructional video on your chosen hosting company. Some of the videos available are absolutely fantastic, step-by-step guides showing you exactly what to do and where things are. It can be a good idea to make sure there are a good number of YouTube instructional videos before choosing a hosting company to go with.

Personally, we recommend using a web hosting service that uses 'cPanel'. cPanel is a hosting control panel that makes your website development extremely easy. It also provides you with free email addresses that you can create and control.

CONTENT MANAGEMENT SYSTEMS (WEBSITES)

Don't be put off by technical terms, a content management system (CMS) is simply the software which holds your website's content and allows you to edit and add to it. There are a wide range of CMSs that you can install on your domain name.

Due to the large number available we're going to choose one to cover: WordPress. WordPress started in 2003 and has grown into the largest self-hosted blogging tool in the world, used on millions of websites around the world. As with anything, WordPress has its critics, many cite that as it is primarily intended to be used as a blog it should not be used for anything else. Against this though there are some absolutely fantastic websites out there created on WordPress; it is also very straightforward and simple to use without any need for technical coding knowledge.

Again there are a huge amount of videos available on the topic of WordPress. There are instructional videos and articles that take you through the very basics of how to get started right up to how to solve problems that crop up. We advise watching a few of these videos before you get started yourself as you'll get to actually see the admin area in action.

From your hosting admin area there is usually a very simple one-click installation process which puts WordPress onto your domain name. If you're not sure what to do either contact your hosting company for support or search YouTube for an instructional that will show you how to do it. When installing WordPress you will need to set a username and password, we cannot emphasise strongly enough how important it is to have a very secure password. Use at least eight characters with a combination of numbers, letters and punctuation marks.

Logging in for the first time might be a bit daunting if you're not confident with your computer skills, but our advice is to just start playing around, making changes and seeing what everything does. We have always found it to be the best way to learn. Don't be worried about breaking things, that's how we learn, by breaking something and then putting it back together.

What we love about WordPress is the themes that are available to install on your website. A theme is literally a designed website, a template, with filler information and images which you simply replace with your own. There are a great deal of free WordPress themes available which can look really good but may not be enough for your business site; if this is the case you need to look at paid themes. A WordPress theme can cost from a few pounds to really expensive depending on what you're looking for. You can normally find a good theme for around £50. Remember, that's relatively inexpensive compared to paying a web developer to build your website.

We always use Themeforest.net when searching for a new theme if we're looking for a high quality template. This is because it has a huge stock of theme templates, an excellent feedback system, which means you can read how others found the theme you're thinking about buying and great support from the theme owners should you encounter any difficulties. Before you purchase a theme read through the comments and feedback, not just so you don't waste a few pounds but more importantly so you don't waste hours, maybe days with a really complex theme which has people pulling their hair out. We always look for feedback with things like "*Great support, straightforward to use*" etc. Really look into the feedback though, don't just buy after you see one or two people say it was simple to use, as they might be coding experts. Look right through to see if anyone has found it confusing, too complex or simply frustrating to use. To take it a step further, we also like to ask the theme owner a question about it and see how quickly they reply (if at all), a good theme owner will reply in under 24-hours on a working day, if it takes longer than this then alarm bells start to ring. Remember that if you run into a problem when working on the theme, the theme owner will be the person who will help, so you need to know if they're someone who actually replies to messages.

When you have decided on a theme and purchased it you'll be given access to the file you need to download. Download it and then install the folder into WordPress. This is done by entering your

WordPress admin area, going to Appearance - Themes - Add New - Upload, select the file, click upload and your theme will go live. Again if you're not confident, search for an instructional video, there are dozens covering this topic.

Now that your theme has been activated it's time to start replacing the 'demo content' with your own words and images. The vast majority of the content will be held in the sections 'Posts' and 'Pages'. A 'Post' is traditionally used for a blog update whilst a 'Page' is used for the pages within a website such as the homepage, contact us page etc. Replacing the content can sometimes be a case of trial and error, seeing the content on the website and then finding that content in the admin area and making the change.

Following the above isn't very difficult but you can run into frustrating problems that can consume quite a bit of time if you let it. If you run into a problem doing any of the above, first search for an instructional video to solve the problem, if that doesn't work contact the theme owner, explain the issue and ask for the solution. Whilst you're waiting for the response do something more productive. Don't be someone who wastes hours on a frustrating problem, we've done it ourselves. Many times we've asked a theme owner for support, and then decided to try and solve the problem ourselves wasting hours and sending our blood pressure through the roof, only for them to reply later with a ridiculously simple solution. Now when we run into a problem, a question is sent off to the appropriate person and we do something else in the meantime.

Next comes the actual content that needs to go on your website. For just about every website you will need a:

- Homepage
- Contact Us page
- Product/Service page(s) - explaining what it is you do

- About Us page
- Privacy Policy page.
- Terms & Conditions page.
- Cookies Policy page (and pop up) - if you are going to use cookies make sure you take the time to read up on current legislation regarding your requirements.

You need to make sure that the pages within your site are easy to find and that your website itself is easy to navigate. This is done through the use of a 'Menu'. A menu will run either across the top or down the side of your website's pages and will navigate visitors to the most important pages within your site. This is called the Main Menu.

The Main Menu is for the most important links you want to push on your website, such as the product or service you're promoting, your contact details etc. There are a number of other pages you'll probably have such as the terms and conditions etc., which you probably won't want to have mixed in with your most important pages but you still need to make them visible to visitors. This can be done by using what is called a Secondary Menu.

Whilst the main menu is the most prominent, the secondary menu, as the name suggests, will not be, it'll have a smaller-sized font and be in a less prominent position, such as the bottom of the page, depending on the theme that you're using.

Plugins are a fantastic feature with WordPress that allow you to do all sorts of great things. From integrating a Twitter feed onto your site through to installing contact forms, image galleries and more.

The vast majority of plugins are also absolutely free. Conduct some searches such as 'best WordPress plugins' to see what is available and what might suit your site. Before installing a plugin we always check its rating and how many times it's been downloaded. We always prefer a plugin with a four out of five rating with thousands of downloads to a five out of five rating with only a handful of downloads. If you get a plugin and end up not liking it, simply deactivate it. Instructional videos are again available on how to use, install and deactivate plugins. We recommend as a starting point you have plugins that cover the following:

- Email sign-up form
- Search Engine Optimisation
- Social media links/social media feeds
- Contact Form
- Google Analytics

Use of Images on your website

Images are really important on a website, poor quality images can make a potentially great website look amateurish. You have a few options, ask someone you know with a really high quality camera to take some good images, use a professional photographer or buy the rights to high quality images to use on your website.

Do not simply save an image off another website or somewhere else online and put it on your website, it'll almost certainly be subject to copyright laws and if spotted you could face a very hefty fine. Don't be ignorant regarding image copyright, this situation can and does happen, and it could leave you with a fine that destroys your business before it even gets started.

ECOMMERCE

If you're planning on running an ecommerce store, meaning an online shop, then WordPress may not be the best solution for you depending on the size of your operation. If you're going to be selling a handful of items then an excellent plugin called WooCommerce should be all that you need.

WooCommerce will turn a designated page of your website into an online shop, allowing you to add products and include a payment system such as PayPal. If you're looking to sell a significant amount of products then a specific ecommerce package will probably serve you better. We have used and thoroughly recommend www.ekm-powershop.com, but there are a number of options available if you're looking for an ecommerce solution, such as shopify.com. If you're technical or want to learn the technicals then you might want to try some free open source options which include:

- OpenCart
- Magento
- CubeCart
- Open eShop
- Abante Cart
- Zen Cart

Whatever platform you decide to use, there are many online videos and tutorials that'll help you set your choice up.

You'll also need the facilities take payments online and we go into this in more detail in the 'Finance' chapter later in the book.

SECURE SOCKETS LAYER (SSL)

SSL is a security feature that encrypts information such as login details and credit card numbers. Data that is sent without encryption is vulnerable to prying eyes. As a business owner you'll be responsible for ensuring that your website is as secure as possible.

Without an SSL certificate your website runs the risk of being identified as unsecure by search engines. This can result in a lower ranking and a warning being shown to visitors that your site is insecure, which will turn them away.

Both you and your customers will know if a website is secure, because the website's address will begin with 'https://'.

Purchasing an SSL certificate is quite straightforward, there are many companies who will take you through the process, and you can usually purchase one when you purchase your domain name. Some website hosting companies offer SSL certification for free when you purchase a website hosting package with them. 'www.123-reg.co.uk' offers a number of packages suitable for a wide range of websites from basic security through to total security for large ecommerce stores. Ensure that support is available from the company you purchase an SSL certificate from, particularly if it's for a more complex website.

When you purchase an SSL certificate the issuing authority will perform checks on you or your business to verify your identity. This process is straightforward and is just to prove that you are who you are saying you are.

Due to the process varying depending on what type of website and level of security you choose there is no *one size fits all* explanation. 'www.123-reg.co.uk' offer a useful tool called 'Which SSL Certificate Do I Need?' which will help you identify what category your website is and what level of SSL it requires.

HOMEPAGE

Your 'homepage' is going to be the first page that most of your website visitors will see. If it looks weak expect your bounce rate (bounce rate is the percentage of visitors clicking away before looking at a second page) to be high.

Too much information on your website can quickly put people off, remember to get your message across and show exactly what you do immediately. The use of a 'homepage slider' using a combination of text and imagery can be a great way of doing this. Many of the themes available on Themeforest.net come with a homepage slider as standard. When completed, compare your homepage to your most successful competitors, if yours isn't as good, as or better than theirs why would anyone choose to come to you based on first impressions?

ABOUT US PAGE

The 'about us' page is of real importance and many website owners don't spend the necessary time on it. On every site we have managed the 'about us' page has consistently been in the top most-viewed pages.

People like to find out more about who you are. Don't just write a few lines about the business, give a description of yourself, why you started the business, who works for you and what they do. Try to make your about us page as interesting as possible, to give a complete stranger a good understanding of your business as well as of yourself and your team (if applicable).

CONTACT US PAGE

If you're in a service business your 'contact us' page needs to be prominent and look professional. It's also important for online retailers, there are statistics showing that around 80% of people visit the contact page before making a payment to an online retail store to ensure there are suitable ways to get in touch if there's a problem.

A weak contact page could be the difference between a potential customer picking up the phone or being put off. Give potential customers as many opportunities as possible to get in touch with you; email address, physical address, contact phone number and social media links should be standard. As mentioned previously, ensure each of the contact methods look professional; a personal email address, a mobile phone number and no physical address will announce to the world that you're operating out of your bedroom, even if you aren't. You may also like to put up images of your office or place of work and members of staff.

PRODUCT AND OR SERVICE PAGES

Product or service pages need to be really well-detailed whilst quickly getting across the main benefits of the product or service in question. You need to quickly get across the benefits of what you're offering to the people who are either lazy online or short on time. Against this you also need to ensure there's a good deal of extra content available for those who like to find out as much as possible before picking up the phone or clicking the 'buy' button.

Adding a good number of images of the product or service can really help increase conversion rates, particularly if you can show something in more detail than your competitors. Look at what your competitors are doing and then do it better. We also recommend including a testimonial or even a few on each product or service page from past customers.

BLOG PAGES

A blog or news page should be available on every website, in our opinion. Read the chapter 'Blogging For business' which goes into detail about what blogs should contain.

IMPORTANT PAGES THAT NEED TO BE INCLUDED

Legal information, privacy policy, terms and conditions and the cookie policy will take a bit more time and careful consideration. There will be variations on these pages depending on your business, for example a sofa retailer will have different terms and conditions to an accountancy practice. Take a look at your competitors' pages for ideas, but don't copy them unless you want to find yourself in hot water. When you have more of an understanding you can create your own content for these pages.

When all of the above has been done you should have a website that looks the part and functions correctly. Before you unleash it onto the world you need to test it to make sure that everything works as it should.

Go to your website and pretend you're a visitor, try clicking on everything, ensure all the links direct visitors to the right pages and that everything works. When you have done this ask some friends and family members to do the same, after spending so much time on your site it can be easy to miss an error. In other words, try and break your website.

When you're happy that your website is error-free it's time to get some feedback before you put it out there to potential customers. Your family and friends will almost certainly tell you that it looks fantastic as they'll be supportive and nice to you; this is pleasant but not what you need. You need criticism; you need to find out what looks weak and what needs changing.

We like to put new sites out on some forums and ask for feedback. A lot of people can be pretty brutal online and like to show off how good they are by pointing out your errors, but take all feedback, good and bad, on board. Don't accept everything people say as true, but if they do highlight some errors that you agree could do with changing then make the changes and start pushing your website online.

SETTING UP COMPANY EMAIL ADDRESSES

Email is an extremely important facility for your business. You communicate with your customers and clients through email and you sell through email. Therefore, having professional emails isn't a luxury it's a necessity. As we mentioned earlier in the book, if you use a public email service which is one that you generally use for personal email then your business will look amateurish. Instead you need to use an email address that is associated with your domain name.

There are a couple of ways to set up a company email address. One way is to pay the company that is hosting your website to provide you with a professional email that matches your domain name. Prices vary depending on what package you want, but a quick Internet search at the time of writing suggests that the average cost of one email address on a basic package is about £5 per month. You'll be able to access your business email via your hosting company's website, which is known as 'Webmail'. This is the same as logging into Gmail, Hotmail or Yahoo mail, where you control your emails on an Internet browser. However, it is far easier and much more professional to use an 'email client' to control your business emails.

An email client is a piece of software that enables you to send and receive emails from your desktop, so you won't need to login to your web hosting company's email website. You might recognise this if you have worked or do work in an office that uses Microsoft Office Outlook or something similar. We'll discuss more how to set this up later in this section, and cover the benefits of using an email client. To get back on topic, paying your web hosting company for an email package has the positive that it'll be easier to set up. However, it'll cost you money and the more email addresses you need, for example for your colleagues, the more costs you'll incur. As you've probably guessed we're all about setting your company up on as little money as possible, so the following option is free.

We discussed earlier in the 'Website Creation' chapter, that if you're setting up your own website we recommend cPanel as your hosting platform due to its simplicity and the tools it provides. Another reason that we recommend cPanel is that you can easily set up free email addresses related to your domain name. Again, due to technology constantly changing we won't go into explicit detail on how to set up an email account on cPanel. However, the process is extremely simple and you can set up an unlimited amount of emails with unlimited storage for no added cost. Again use an Internet search to find a good tutorial on how to set up an email address through cPanel. The platform cPanel will provide you with online access to your email address and account, but as before we recommend using an email client to control your email accounts. The next part of this section will discuss email clients.

Using an email client enables you to access your email from your desktop and eliminates the need to login to your email-hosting website. There are several advantages to this:

• You can access previous emails offline

- An email client can have better features and control of your emails than webmail
- You can have multiple email addresses with different domains all in one place.

To use an email client you can download one or purchase one. Then you link your email client to your email account. If you're using cPanel you can use the auto-configure options to automatically configure your email application with your email account. This sounds complicated, but it's not. You basically download a file and import it into your email client and follow the email client's instructions. Alternately you can manually type the details of your email account in to your email client so that they can communicate. Again there are lots of great up-to-date tutorials on how to do this.

Some free email clients that you can use include:

- Mozilla Thunderbird
- eM Client
- Inky
- Claws Mail

Having a professional email address is only part of the look. You'll also need a professional footer, which sits at the bottom of your email. This is a big branding tool and can enhance your feel of credibility. Any emails sent to clients, especially cold emails, will be assessed by the receiving party. They're more likely to follow your instructions and click any recommend links if your email address, email content and footer look professional.

Your email footer will be tailored to you, but generally it should contain:

- Your name
- Your position
- Your company address
- Your contact numbers
- Your company logo
- Your company website
- Links to other media such as Twitter and LinkedIn
- A privacy policy - Which states how the receiver should handle your email, for example if the email contains information that is privileged, confidential or otherwise protected from disclosure.

How you set up your email footer will depend on your brand, but also what email client or webmail client you use.

PART 2

OPERATIONS

SUPPLY CHAIN

In this chapter we'll discuss the supply chain, which encompasses buying your raw materials from suppliers and then distributing them to customers. This supply chain chapter predominantly refers to goods-based businesses.

As mentioned in other parts of this book, there are generally two ways to increase your bottom line (net profit). One is to increase the cost of your goods. However, the disadvantage of this is that you'll be charging more than your competitors, which means your customers will shop with them instead of you. That is unless your product or service is unique or better in some way, so that you can command a higher price. The other way to increase your bottom line is to lower your operating costs. This means spending less money on all the things it takes to get your product or service to the customer. Organisations can shop round and negotiate prices and they can save a lot of money by optimising their supply chain and making it 'Lean'. Lean is a philosophy and organisational practice to remove "waste" from a business. Regardless of whether you're charging a competitive price or a premium price, every company should be trying to optimise their business to save money. Optimising the supply chain is one of the most obvious ways in which businesses can reduce costs; therefore, throughout this chapter we'll advise where you can save money; however, we won't go into detail about deploying Lean principles.

SUPPLIERS

Anyone you buy products or services from for your business is a supplier. Your web developer is a supplier, your accountant is a supplier, your landlord is a supplier and the companies you purchase your raw materials from are suppliers. However, in this chapter we're going to specifically concentrate on the suppliers who provide you with the goods that you sell.

Local Suppliers

Buying local means buying from the same country you operate in. The closer the supplier is to your company the more local that supplier is. There are several benefits of buying from local suppliers.

The first is that it'll lower your costs, because it reduces transportation costs and takes away the cost of importing. These are the costs of getting the goods from your supplier to your storage facility.

Another benefit to you is the speed of delivery and getting a more predictable fulfilment time. When using overseas suppliers the time taken to fulfil your order can be longer. If your business is operating a just-in-time supply chain then sourcing your goods locally will help you manage this better. We'll discuss just-in-time in more detail later.

Local suppliers can also react faster, so they can quickly supply you with more stock if you suddenly experience a high demand. They'll also be able to create and deliver new goods more quickly, which is essential for industries like fashion. If you're running a fashion business and suddenly a celebrity is spotted wearing a certain item of clothing, consumer demand for that product goes up. Local suppliers will be able to supply you with that product or an adaptation of it while the demand is still high.

Some customers prefer to buy from companies who support local businesses. This is generally for two reasons: one, if you're selling food it'll be fresher if it's local. The other reason is that some people want to support local businesses. Therefore, by buying locally it could make your company more appealing to your consumers. This also has a strong impact on the local economy as it helps to create more jobs and more people in jobs will mean more business for you.

Buying locally is also more environmentally friendly as the reduced transportation reduces fuel consumption and emissions. Again, this is another selling point to your consumers.

Furthermore, buying locally may mean better working conditions. Not all countries have strong human rights and their factories may have dangerous working conditions, child labour, unethical behaviour and low pay. If this is something you or your customers are against then using local suppliers will be a good option. Some well-known companies have had public criticism over their use of suppliers, which is bad publicity. Therefore, you need to ensure your suppliers are fully aligned with your core business values.

Buying from local suppliers also means that it's much easier to visit their premises. By visiting their premises you'll be able to meet your suppliers face-to-face, build rapport and strike better deals and potentially see opportunities that may have been missed if you hadn't met the individual/company. You'll also get to see their equipment and evaluate their operations. From this you'll be able to see if the supplier aligns with your values and expectations. If their operations are in chaos, you might question whether they can fulfil your orders on time. Local suppliers (depending where you're based) can arguably provide you with a higher quality product and you'll be able to review samples and their quality control systems if you visit their premises.

Buying from overseas suppliers may mean you'll come up against language and cultural barriers. With local suppliers, communication will be much easier.

Using local suppliers will also give you greater financial security, which will give you peace of mind. It's much easier to identify if a local supplier is credible and financially stable. If your supplier is abroad you can't just pop down and pay them a visit, without greater expense.

There are some disadvantages that you may find with local suppliers. You might find that limiting yourself to local suppliers means you have a smaller selection of products you can purchase. Some goods just won't be made in your country. You might find that there are a small number of suppliers to choose from. Also the particular products you want may be in limited supply. Local suppliers have higher manufacturing costs than suppliers in India or the Far East Asia, which means local suppliers will be more expensive.

Overseas Suppliers

Depending on your business you might have to or want to use overseas suppliers. This is because they can provide services that you can't find locally and in certain areas like Far East Asia, India and South America, their prices will be more attractive. In some cases, consumers may want products made in a specific country for traditional reasons.

If you're going to use overseas suppliers then you might also want to look at using the services of a buying agent who will source suppliers for you.

Finding Suppliers

There are several websites that link suppliers and manufactures with other businesses. These include:

- www.alibaba.com
- www.aliexpress.com
- www.globalsources.com
- www.tradekey.com
- www.diytrade.com
- www.tradeindia.com

You can also use search engines like Google to find suppliers by typing in what you want, for example 'shoe manufacturer UK', or 'umbrella manufacturer China'. You could also use LinkedIn to search for suppliers.

Supplier Due Diligence

Medium to large-sized corporations have buyers that they send to overseas suppliers to assess their products and their capabilities. If you're starting up then you probably won't have this luxury, but you'll still need to do your due diligence. In case you're wondering why you need to perform due diligence on a supplier, imagine you hand over £2000+ of your start-up money. After six weeks you still don't have your order and the supplier has disappeared. The time taken to get this money back, if you even can get it back, is going to be excruciating and it'll stop you moving your business forward or even starting. Just as bad, what if you do get your product, but the quality is so poor that it's unsellable. Due diligence is an extremely important step in the process of working with any supplier, but especially overseas suppliers that you can't visit yet.

Anthony Trollope, Managing Director of The Wholesale Forums (www.thewholesaleforums.co.uk) provides some simple and powerful due diligence tips, outlined below. These handy tips were posted by Matt on DHL's blog, (2012)

Check business registrations and public documents - if your supplier is based in the UK and they're a limited company, you can check Companies House website for their registration date, registered office, and download their latest accounts. If this information doesn't match with what you already know you'll want to question the supplier.

• www.gov.uk/government/organisations/companies-house

For suppliers based in Europe, you can check the validity of their VAT numbers through the following website:

• http://ec.europa.eu/taxation_customs/vies/

Verify their trade accreditations - many manufactures will be accredited and will have joined credible associations. Look out for things like ISO 9000, which is a quality management standard.

Google names- Google the name of the company and its management team. Your search may show experts within the industry or bad news articles and bad reviews, or things that just don't correlate with your other research.

Trading length - assess how long the supplier has been trading. Their website or any other literature should tell you the supplier's start-up date. The more established the supplier the more confidence you can have. That's not to say new suppliers aren't credible and capable of delivering. A supplier just like you has got to start sometime. In this case you can Google the management teams' background. The new supplier might be backed by credible investors with a management team with strong industry backgrounds.

Check their domain name registration details - using free online tools such as WHOIS you can look at the registration details of a supplier's domain name and review the details provided. The domain name should be registered to the business, so proceed with caution if doesn't match the one published on their website, or in their business registration documents.

- www.whois.net

Call them and ask them questions - you can get a good feel for someone and a company by calling them and asking them some questions. Ask questions around their trading history, how they operate and what their payment, delivery and returns policies are. Also ask them questions about their products and the market. You'll get a gut feeling if you can't get through or someone answers unprofessionally and provides dubious answers to your questions.

Check wholesaler directories and forums - supplier forums such as www.thewholesaleforums.co.uk are great sources of information and advice for dealing with suppliers and obtaining reviews from people with past experiences. You can also check websites like Alibaba.com which ranks suppliers by how trustworthy they are.

Get their trade references and speak to past customers - ask the supplier for any trade references they have and follow these up. Be sure to check out the individuals and or companies that have provided the references to make sure that they're legitimate and have actually done business with your supplier.

Sample requests - if you're putting in a large order or you're having the supplier manufacture a bespoke product you should get a sample. If you're putting in a large order the supplier will probably provide you with a free sample. If you're a small new business they'll likely charge you for the sample. It's worth paying for a sample and finding out the product is terrible rather than spending a large amount and finding your whole order is terrible.

Meet them - if the supplier is local arrange to meet them. If you're a small start-up business dealing with an overseas supplier this probably won't be possible, so make sure you perform the other checks above.

Dealing with Suppliers

So you've picked a supplier or suppliers and you want to put in an order. Firstly, make sure you keep all the research you've done on the other suppliers and their contact details. While you might not want to use their services now you might want to in the future. A good system to store supplier details and your communication history is on your Customer Relationship Management System (CRM). If you don't have a CRM, and we recommend that you do, you can use a spreadsheet.

If you're a start-up business it's highly likely the supplier will want payment upfront for your first order. This is because if you're a start-up you're a high risk client. However, once you build a history and relationship with the supplier they'll give you better payments terms such as 30 days payment, which means you have a 30 day window to pay for your order. If you're wondering why this is important read the chapter on finance, but basically "cash is king" and you need a healthy cash flow. That's because if you have no money in the bank to pay your bills or the banks call in their loans you're going to be in serious trouble.

When you place your order with the supplier, double check with your account manager that they have all your details correct from delivery address to your contact details. Mistakes can happen, and you don't want your order being delivered to some other location, or in case of an emergency they can't contact you because your contact details are incorrect.

When you get your order you'll need to check the contents and quantities are correct. Suppliers, like every business, have many pressures and they'll suffer problems from time to time. If you find a small mistake with your order contact your account manager to fix this. Don't be aggressive, as that's unprofessional and if they stop supplying you, you might not have a business. However, if the order is a complete mess you'll want to reassess if this supplier is the right one for you.

Build a good relationship with your supplier and make them aware in advance of any changes or fluctuations in your orders. You might find that for periods such as Christmas you'll need to increase your order quantities.

While we've stated that you want to pay your suppliers as late as possible, you don't want to miss payment deadlines. If they've given you 30 days payment terms then the latest you should pay is by 30 days. By missing a payment you are damaging the relationship with your supplier. Imagine if your customers didn't pay you on time, and how much strain this would put on your business.

STOCK AND STORAGE MANAGEMENT

If you're selling a product then it's likely you'll store stock, unless you're dropshipping. Dropshipping is a supply chain management technique which involves holding no stock. Instead, the product is sent directly to the customer from the supplier. Please, read the section on dropshipping for further information. The nature and the size of your business will determine how you'll store your stock. You might be storing stock in your home or garage if you're a small online business, the back of your shop if you're retailer, a storage unit or a warehouse if you're a larger business.

There are several stories of entrepreneurs who started an online business where they stored stock in various rooms around the home, only for the business to grow to a point where stock was then kept in large warehouses. Embedding the right processes for storing and managing your stock can be transferred to a larger scale as your business grows, so it's important to manager stock well whether you store stock in a warehouse or in your spare bedroom.

Order delivery check - When you receive your order from your suppliers, make sure you check it immediately. If you're busy running round fulfilling orders and dealing with customer queries it's all too easy to take the order and leave it until later. Upon delivery you'll want to check the quantity and product match what you've ordered. If there are any problems contact your account manager at the supplier to find out what's happened.

Designated areas - Whether you're storing your stock in a warehouse or in a bedroom, you should have organised and designated areas for your stock, which are clearly labelled. That means you know exactly where everything is and you can access it easily. If you don't and you have a large variety of stock you'll spend a great deal of time trying to find the right items. This unnecessary time costs money. For example, you might save one hour a day by having your stock organised and with this extra hour you can now dedicate it to more sales and marketing. Having designated areas with clear labels is also vital to reduce errors. If you're a business that sells similar-looking items, for example clothing of different sizes, you'll greatly irritate your customer and waste money on correcting the error if you send your customer an item of clothing which is the wrong size.

Stock management systems - Make sure you have a stock management system in place. This is to record the flow of stock and can be as simple as a spreadsheet or written down in a stock book.

However, as your business grows and your product range expands, it'll become more difficult to manage it this way. At this point you'll need specialist inventory software. You can get inventory software for free from the Internet and then purchase software with more functionality as you need it.

If you're an online business your web platform may have an inbuilt stock management system, or there may be a plug-in for your Content Management System. Speak to your website developer, if you're using one, and see what options there are. If you're managing your website yourself an Internet search should provide you with options for your particular website. If you're running a busy online store you'll likely need a stock management system that updates in real time and automatically updates your website. That way if you suddenly sell out of a product the system will automatically prevent customers placing any new orders. This will save you time and effort having to go back to the customer to explain that the product they ordered is out of stock and you'll need to refund their money.

Stock takes - The purpose of a stock take is to assess the physical stock numbers to agree with the numbers you've got in your inventory record. Simplistically, if you started off with 20 items and you have sold and fulfilled 5 orders you should have 15 items left. If you find that you have a different number then you have potentially identified a problem either with the system for physically controlling the stock or the system for recording your stock. You might find that stock has been wrongly delivered, misplaced, lost or stolen. These problems cost you money and incorrect orders will damage your reputation. If you're a business with a high turnover of products a stock take every day will likely be necessary, as more movements of stock will increase the chances of errors.

Protecting stock - Your stock has value and you'll need to protect it from water, fire, dust and thieves. Therefore, you'll need to review the area you're keeping your stock. For example, if you're storing your stock in the garage is it safe from water, or will the tap for the hose be a risk? Is your garage securely locked and alarmed? You'll also need an adequate insurance policy to protect your stock. If you're selling any products that are sensitive to temperature such as food or flowers you'll need to ensure the area is at the right temperature.

Stock assessment - Do assess your stock to identify what's selling and what's not.

Just in time (JIT) - Is a "pull" system so you only order and receive your stock in the correct quantity and at the correct time. Why is this important? Storing large quantities of stock has several dis-advantages. It costs more money to store lots of stock because you have to pay for extra storage and also your insurance is more expensive. If you have purchased large quantities of stock that's sitting in storage then your cash is tied up in stock, which affects your cash flow. If you sell perishable goods your stock is likely to go out of date if you stock too much. JIT helps to reduce and stop these problems because you'll store less stock. However, there are some disadvantages to JIT. There will be little room for errors as your stock levels will be low, and if your suppliers don't deliver on time you won't be able to fulfil your customers' orders. JIT doesn't work for all companies so you'll need to assess your company first. If you're a start-up business you won't be able to implement JIT to begin with as you must be able to accurately forecast demand for your products for JIT to be effective.

It's possible that your supplier may also hold stock for you, so ask your account manager if this service is available to you.

PICKING AND PACKING

Before you send your products to the customer they'll need to be picked and packed for delivery. If you organise your storage so that all your products are easily found with the heaviest at the bottom of any shelving, and the most popular product closest to the packing area, you'll make your job and your employees' job much easier, more efficient, and you'll greatly reduce the number of errors such as packing the wrong items.

Your items must be packed for delivery, so you'll need to purchase the right type of packaging for the products you sell. If you sell fragile or delicate goods you might need specialist or extra safety packaging to stop your products being damaged during delivery. If goods are damaged during the delivery you'll not only dissatisfy the customer you'll have to send them a replacement. You'll also have to go the extra mile to delight them enough that they'll shop with you again. Calculate the time, effort and cost of getting it right first time compared to trying to rectify a customer's dissatisfaction. You'll find that it's much easier and more cost effective to get it right first time.

Some companies, as part of their branding strategy, brand their packaging. If you're considering this, you'll need to assess the risk of branding your packaging. If you're selling private goods then your customers might not appreciate you advertising that they shop with you, especially if the delivery is left with a neighbour. If you're selling luxury or expensive goods, the packaging may give this away and increase the probability of the delivery being stolen.

You'll need to store your packaging as well and with as much thought as you store your products. The area you use to package your goods should be well thought out and put in the most efficient place. For example, if your products are kept downstairs and collected by the courier downstairs then packing them upstairs wouldn't be the most efficient place.

You should record who has packed the goods for each order as this'll build up a picture of the operation. You'll be able to see superstar employees and those who may be making mistakes. If particular employees are making constant mistakes, you'll need to find out why this is. Don't jump to conclusions and blame them, it may be the process, such as poorly labelled stock, or they simply may need more training. If your employees are doing this job every day then they'll become the experts, so give them opportunities to make the operations better. Ask them what would make the process simpler and more efficient for them.

Remember to include the correct invoice or receipt and ensure the package is correctly labelled and addressed.

DELIVERY

You've picked and packaged your goods, now what? Now, you'll need to deliver them to your customers. This is a very important function of your business especially if you're running an online business, so don't leave organising your delivery process until you have an order. You need to organise your delivery process and strategy long before you start selling. That means identifying which companies you want to deliver your goods based on costs and service. You can do this by measuring the size and weight of your products when they're packaged and then calling different couriers to establish their prices and the services they offer. The more you use a delivery service the more you'll save money on individual deliveries, so negotiate prices with your courier's account manager. If you're running a start-up you can give a predicted estimate of monthly deliveries.

Customers are sensitive about delivery charges and love when they don't have to pay them. However, this isn't always practical and if you offer a free delivery service it'll reduce your profit margins. That's because you'll be paying for the delivery. This isn't going to be possible if you're a small business, especially as a start-up. However, you may work out that if customers purchase over a certain value they'll qualify for free delivery. What you can do is shop on a competitor's website for similar products and stop just before the purchase. That way you'll be able to see what their delivery charges are.

You'll want to use couriers that collect from your premises, preferably at a specific time. This'll enable you to have your orders ready for that time and you'll also be able to notify customers that if they want delivery today they'll need to order by a certain time.

It's possible that you may need to use different types of couriers for national deliveries and international deliveries if you're shipping to overseas customers. Some examples of couriers include:

- Royal Mail
- myHermes
- Parcelforce
- FedEx
- DHL
- TNT Direct
- Yodel

You may also find that smaller local couriers might offer cost savings and additional services, so shop around. Use an Internet search engine like Google to find couriers in your local area.

You must constantly asses your couriers by listening to your customers. If the deliveries are turning up late, damaged or not at all then your customers are going to be extremely dissatisfied. The problem here is that the courier service is not your business, but the customer doesn't care and they'll see it as part of your service. This means you'll need to constantly review your choice of couriers and ensure that they're meeting your customers' expectations.

If you're selling and posting to overseas customers you'll need to do some extra research around what you're selling. Items that are allowed in some countries are not allowed in others; make sure you do your research so you don't break any laws. Check with your local customs office for further details, if you live in the UK you can visit: www.hmrc.gov.uk.

RETURNS

You will at some point have to handle returns. There are different rules depending on your business type. In the UK, high-street shops don't have to accept returns unless an item is faulty, but there are different laws for online, mail and phone-order businesses, which are covered by the Consumer Contracts Regulations.

For online, mail and telephone orders customers have the right to cancel within 14 days of receiving the goods even if the goods aren't faulty. You must give a refund to customers if they return your product within 14 days of receiving them. Then you must refund the customer within 14 days of receiving the goods back. The customer doesn't have to provide a reason for the return. However, you'll want a facility for them to give a reason why if they want to. This way you can analyse why you're getting returns and solve any recurring reasons. The different laws and regulations are out of scope for this book and the point of this section is how to handle returns rather than the laws, so we'll concentrate on implementing a returns processes.

There are several reasons why people may want to return your goods, for example:

- Wrong order packaged and delivered - your fault
- Unwanted gift
- Didn't like the item after purchase
- Faulty or broken item

- Illegal reasons
- Habitual returns behaviour
- Buying two sizes of clothing to see which one fits with the intention of returning the other

If you're a distance-selling business, such as online or catalogue, returns are costly, so you'll want to minimise them. You lose money on returns due to the delivery charge, the packaging that's wasted, the labelling and printing costs, the time to pick and pack and the cost of the product if it's damaged. You'll never be able to eliminate returns, but you can certainly reduce the numbers. No matter how efficient your picking and packing processes are mistakes happen and the wrong orders can be packed. As stated earlier in this chapter you can reduce this by clearly labelling and organising your stock and reviewing who's picked and packed the orders. For online and catalogue businesses you can reduce the number of returns by providing high quality pictures of the items along with very detailed descriptions. If you're a high-street shop, while you're under no obligation to accept a return that isn't faulty you should still do so. This gives your customers security and they're more likely to shop again with you in the future. If you don't do this they'll not only not shop with you again, they'll also tell all their friends and family.

You'll need to set up a process for checking the items that have been returned. Customers are people too and they may have returned the wrong item or not returned it with all its components. If you're selling luxury products such as expensive watches or clothing you'll need to examine that the real item has been returned and not a fake. You'll want to examine if the item has actually been used. For example, if you're selling clothing you can check the collar for makeup or the pockets for items such as receipts, tissues or anything else.

Keep detailed and up-to-date records of your returns along with your picking and packing records. This information will give you a rich picture of patterns that may occur concerning products, employees, suppliers, couriers, processes and customers. You might find that certain customers are habitual returners who buy goods use them and then return them. You can use this information to stop selling to them. However, make sure you have a full and detailed picture. For example, if a customer has only made two purchases and returned both it doesn't necessarily mean they're a habitual returner. As stated earlier, set up a facility and process to capture why a customer is returning their order. The reasons will provide a guide for your improvements.

With an online business, when you have received the returned item(s) from your customer ensure that you notify them via email, and also notify them when their money has been returned to their account.

Ask your courier(s) about their returns service, which means they'll collect the goods from your customers' address. This is expensive, but if you're a large business that can afford it, it'll give your customers a higher level of customer service and another reason to shop with you. However, you may only want to allow certain items to qualify for free returns. Customers are clever and will purchase a basket full of items they don't want along with the items they do want to meet the free delivery threshold. They'll then return the unwanted items at your expense.

When items are returned because they're unwanted and not faulty then they'll need to be restocked for resale. If you're running an online business we recommend having a separate area for storing returned items. That might just be in a box next to the same new product, but with clear labelling. If you're selling products like clothing they'll need to be cleaned and prepared for resale.

While the UK law says that customers have 14 days to return an item for distance-selling businesses, you may want to extend this in your returns policy, especially around the seasonal periods such as Christmas. Customers may be turned off by such a short returns policy especially for gifts as they tend to buy these early. They'll worry that the person receiving the gift won't have enough time to return the item if it's unwanted.

Make your returns policy easy to understand and easy to find on your website. This gives your customers confidence that they're not going to be left out of pocket if they're not happy. It also gives them the instructions about what to do if they want to return their purchase. It can be highly frustrating for customers if they don't know what to do. Make it easy for them.

For your knowledge and interest, some online companies have based their business model around returns. That is, they concentrate on selling items that customers use regularly and are less likely to return such as beauty products and sports supplements. That way they save significant costs by reducing these problems.

Make sure you have a clear understanding of your supply chain before you start your business. The associated costs of shipping and storing products can in many cases turn products from being profitable to a breakeven or possibly a loss making sale.

DROPSHIPPING

Traditionally the role of a retailer has been to purchase a large amount of stock at a wholesale or trade price and then sell these items to consumers at a retail price. Dropshipping allows a retailer to have goods sent to a customer directly from their supplier, eliminating or reducing the need to hold stock. There are numerous advantages to dropshipping, including not having to tie cash in stock, not having to pay for storage, saving time packing orders and arranging for their dispatch as well as being able to trial new products without making a financial investment. In this chapter we are going to look at how to implement dropshipping effectively as well as some of the common pitfalls to avoid.

Dropshipping in principle is a very simple process:

- Step 1: Advertise products on your website at the recommended retail price (RRP).
- Step 2: Make a sale.
- Step 3: Contact your dropshipper and pay them the trade price.
- Step 4: Dropshipper sends the product out direct to your customer.
- Step 5: You bank the difference.

Unfortunately it isn't as simple as that in reality, if it was everyone would be online making a lot of money from their bedrooms. However, with some of the techniques you'll learn in this chapter you'll be armed with enough knowledge and information to source potential suppliers and negotiate deals that could see you dropshipping profitably.

Here are the first few problems you will need to overcome to be successful in dropshipping:

- Some suppliers will want you to buy their products in bulk and will not want the hassle of packing your items and sending each order out individually to your customers. Convincing them to work with you on a dropship basis can be challenging.
- Companies that dropship will almost certainly already have a large number of people just like you reselling their products meaning competition is fierce.
- As there is no stock, storage, staff or rent costs, online retailers who dropship stock can afford to slash the RRP (recommended retail price) and undercut each other, wiping out profit margins and all but making the process pointless.
- Unreliable dropship suppliers who frequently run out of stock meaning you sell a product to a customer which you can't fulfil. Not fulfilling an order is one of the worst things you can do as an online retailer, bad service, much like bad news, travels fast.

In this chapter we're going to look at how you can overcome these obstacles and make profit from the process of dropshipping.

IDENTIFYING PRODUCTS FOR DROPSHIPPING

First of all dropshipping isn't a suitable strategy for every business. If your core business is based around your passion/interests and your research concludes that dropshipping isn't profitable then don't pursue dropshipping. However, dropshipping can benefit some businesses, or you might decide to set up a dropshipping business that has nothing to do with your passion or interests.

Picking profitable goods to dropship isn't easy and you'll have to consider many things. Remember with dropshipping you're selling goods that already exist, so you must sell goods that have a high demand. You won't be able to create demand with dropshipping like Steve Jobs did by creating and bringing new products to the market. Instead you're following the market.

Google AdWords for Dropshipping

You can use Google AdWords and its keyword planner tool to analyse how many people are searching Google for your good(s). Google provides this information for free and it gives you this data by showing you the total searches each month over a short period of time.

Step-by-step instructions on how to use Google AdWords will become out-of-date by the time you read this book, because it's likely Goole will update and change the platform's layout. However, there are many online tutorials that'll show you how to use Google AdWords, and Google makes it very straightforward to use.

When using Google AdWords to analyse online activity, you can narrow your requirements down by category and by location. If you're selling only to your country or local area then you should concentrate on your local search volume data and ignore any global volume data.

What exactly are you looking for? You're looking for a high level of search volume for your goods in mind. In theory the more people who are searching for your goods the more potential customers you'll be able to sell to.

Google Trends for Dropshipping

For a big picture view you should also use Google Trends. It's different from the Google Adwords keyword planner tool, because you get to see the search volume over a large period of time, over years in fact. Google Trends will provide you with a graph so you can easily identify if your search term is growing or declining.

Google Trends also provides you with geographical information showing you where people are searching for your goods. This enables you to identify where your customer base is heavily concentrated and allows you to form strategies based on this data. For example, if you find that the South East of England is home to most of your customers then you might find it beneficial to work with dropshippers who are local to that area.

Remember to take things into account such as seasons. You might decide that a product is suitable to dropship, but you've not taken into account the high search volume is based on the season. This also could happen the other way around, dismissing a product when it would be good for certain periods of the year.

PRICING STRATEGY FOR DROPSHIPPING

Consumer behaviour changes with price. For example, if you were to purchase a £2000 sofa over the Internet you'd probably want to sit on it first, or even speak to the company who's selling it. This gives you peace of mind and allows you to test the product before purchase. There's nothing wrong in dropshipping items of high value, but you'll need to be prepared to offer extra support to the customer both before and after the purchase.

If you want to make life a bit easier for yourself you might find it best to sell products between £50 and £200. This should give you sufficient profit margins, but reduce the amount of work during the sales and after-sales process.

FINDING DROPSHIPPING SUPPLIERS

There are a number of ways to source suppliers, but finding them is quite difficult. The first obvious one is through an Internet search engine, but suppliers and wholesalers are well-known for having poor marketing. Therefore, it's highly unlikely they'll be on page one of a search engine. They're more likely to be listed on page 67. They can also have terrible websites that look dodgy, so don't let their poor websites scare you away as it's possible they're legitimate suppliers.

Another way is to ask for help on a specialist forum such as: www.wholesaleforum.com. However, the users on the forums may just point you in the direction of online trade directories. Some of these directories charge you a fee to access their database, so if you already know the type of product you want to dropship you're probably best doing a deeper Internet search to find the supplier for free. However, below are some supplier directories you can check out. Please, be aware that we do not endorse any of these directories, and we're only providing you with the links for your research.

- http://www.worldwidebrands.com
- https://www.esources.co.uk
- http://www.wholesaledeals.co.uk
- http://www.salehoo.com
- https://www.doba.com
- http://www.wholesalecentral.com

The above directories list thousands of wholesalers, distributors, manufacturers and dropshippers. Another option is to visit Alibaba, which some people argue as the best site for finding suppliers around the world. For those of you who haven't thought up a product yet, spending some time on Alibaba will open your eyes to numerous potential opportunities. If you know what product you're looking for you can be almost certain that there will be a number of suppliers waiting to sell it to you on Alibaba. Many suppliers on Alibaba are happy to offer their products on a dropship basis.

Offline methods such as using a phone book and trade magazines like 'The Trader' are particularly good for locating suppliers. You'll probably be surprised how many suppliers are within a commutable distance from where you live. You might find it beneficial to attend supplier trade shows where you can visit numerous supplier stands and interact with them.

SPOTTING FAKE DROPSHIP SUPPLIERS

During your search for dropshipping suppliers you're more than likely to stumble across "fake" suppliers. These can be people who act as suppliers, but they're really just someone dropshipping from a real supplier. You'll be able to spot them from the below:

- Monthly fees / membership - Suppliers won't ask you for monthly fees. That's just not how they work. This is different from paying a supplier directory a monthly fee discussed above. Fake suppliers will ask you for monthly fees.
- Public sales - Unless you can confirm you run a legitimate business the supplier should be reluctant to sell to you. That is because suppliers don't sell to the general public. Suppliers will run their due diligence on you before providing you with a wholesale account. If your supplier seems a bit too easy then investigate further.

MAKING CONTACT WITH A SUPPLIER

Once you have a list of supplier phone numbers and email addresses, it's time to make contact. Your goal is to find the suppliers who can offer you the best profit margins and strike a dropshipping relationship. An example email would be:

"Dear Mr Johnston,

I have recently setup a business retailing cooking products. I have found your website and feel that your items will sell very well on my online store.

I would like to discuss with you how to become a trade customer. You can contact me on <telephone number> or sayhello@businesshacks.tips.

Kind Regards,

Jamie Rice"

If a supplier offers a dropshipping service they'll be happy to set you up with an account. However, if the supplier doesn't dropship they might not get back in touch with you. In this case the first task is to strike up a relationship with the potential supplier. Just about every company wants a new customer so the vast majority will reply to you.

The next challenge is credibility; companies won't just give out their trade prices to anyone. Most will ask for proof of business ownership, although some will be satisfied if you have a company email address, whilst others may want references from current trade suppliers. This is going to be the first real hurdle if you haven't run a business before. Your task will be to 'sell' them all of the advantages of doing business with you.

Explain that although you're new to the industry, you're serious about the business. Actions speak louder than words, so if you can, forward them any information such as your website or any company literature. If you're faced with negative responses it's time to really sell yourself. Explain your track record of success in the past whether this was in employment, sports or just about anything; portray yourself as someone who is successful and who will sell a lot of their products.

Should this fail we have found it works to be thankful and understanding of their decision not to do business with you. Say that you have managed to secure a deal with one of their competitors, for example:

"Dear Steven,

I totally appreciate and understand your decision not to accept me as a trade customer due to my lack of trading experience.

Thankfully I have managed to secure a supplier. However, please, don't hesitate to contact me should your stance change in the future.

Kind Regards,

Jamie Rice"

Not taking on a new customer is one thing but then losing that potential customer to a competitor in our experience has often been too much to bear for suppliers who often got back in touch to discuss potential opportunities.

The above communications have been by email, but it's probably easier to contact the supplier by telephone. Speaking on the telephone builds up a relationship much faster as you get to feel out each other's personality. Also from the supplier's perspective people with "get up and go" and confidence use the telephone. Before you phone the supplier make sure you have a list of questions you wish to ask.

While it's important to have all your questions answered and to do your research before working with a supplier, don't take up all of the supplier's time before you've even made a sale. You'll come across as very demanding and hard work, so from the supplier's perspective you'll be seen as a liability rather than a valuable customer.

WORKING WITH A DROPSHIPPING SUPPLIER

Suppliers traditionally sell and distribute in bulk whereas dropshipping involves selling individual items. Packaging and distributing individual items costs more than doing it in bulk, so most dropshippers will charge you a fee for packaging and distribution. You might decide to pass on all, some, or none of the packaging and distribution to your customer.

Your supplier may have a minimum order quantity, meaning you have to purchase a certain quantity of goods before you qualify for dropshipping. Obviously this is to test you out as a retailer and ensure you're serious about the business. It's not likely that you'll want to purchase and store a large amount of goods if you're dropshipping, as this defeats the object of dropshipping. The 'Ecommerce University' by Shopify suggests that in this case you offer to 'pre-pay' the supplier to build a credit with them. For example if you have to purchase £500 worth of goods instead you pre-pay the supplier £500. Now you're probably thinking *'What if I don't sell any of the goods?'* That's why it's important that you do your research and feel absolutely confident that you'll make sales. Once you've sold £500 worth of goods the supplier will be more flexible and not require a pre-paid amount.

ANALYSING TRADE PRICES AND PROFIT MARGINS

The next challenge is dealing with trade prices that are poor. A number of wholesalers may be dishonest and provide you with totally unrealistic RRPs so you need to make sure you do your research. For example:

- Product A - Trade Price £54.99 - RRP £99.99

At first glance a pretty healthy profit margin; the first question you need to ask though is "Are people actually buying this product for £99.99?" This is very simple to check, a quick online search of the product will show you what sort of prices other retailers are actually selling the item for. On many occasions we have done this research and found retailers selling the product online for less than the trade price.

This leaves you with two options, either not to do business with the supplier or work for a better deal. If the product is selling online for less than the trade price we tend to avoid working for a better trade price as the margin would almost certainly be poor even if we negotiated a better deal. In our experience simply showing the supplier the prices other retailers were selling the product for was enough to negotiate a better price. However, you may question that if the supplier is this dishonest what else are they dishonest about? It's always best to work with credible, professional and honest suppliers.

SUPPLIER RELIABILITY

When you have sourced a supplier with a strong, genuine profit margin (this can take a while) the next challenge is to ensure that they're reliable. There are two things that you'll need to ensure: that the products are constantly in stock and that they use a reliable courier that uses signed for/proof of delivery.

The latter is very simple, ask what shipment method they use and if you'll be provided with tracking information for your customers. Finding out stock levels is more difficult but absolutely crucial for online retailers who dropship.

If you bought and sold stock you would manage stock levels and know when you've run out of an item so you would stop advertising it for sale. When you dropship you won't know if your supplier has run out of a product that you're still actively selling. Asking if they keep products in stock isn't enough as they'll almost certainly say that everything is in stock the vast majority of the time, which often proves not to be the case. We got around this by calling or emailing occasionally and saying we'd had an enquiry for 3-4 of their fastest selling items to see if they were in stock. If we were consistently told that items were out of stock we would look to move away and find another supplier as there is nothing worse than disappointing a customer. Dealing with unreliable dropshippers can seriously damage your businesses reputation.

ADVANTAGES AND DISADVANTAGE OF DROPSHIPPING

Some of the advantages of dropshipping include:

- Easy to setup - it doesn't require a great deal of resources (warehousing, packaging etc.)
- Reduced start-up costs - you don't need as much capital to run a dropshipping model
- Geographically unrestricted - you can run dropshipping from any location

Some of the disadvantages of dropshipping include:

- Low profit margins - high levels of competition will reduce your profit margins
- Stock levels - it's harder to manage stock you don't own

- Distribution - if you're stocking goods from different suppliers and a customer places an order which uses those different suppliers it'll trigger different distribution costs. Customers won't be happy if they have to pay several courier charges for one order.
- Supplier mistakes - at some point your supplier may make mistakes and it'll be your job to rectify the problem. Too many of these mistakes and you should change supplier before your customers change to your competitor.

DROPSHIPPING SUMMARY

Dropshipping can be a great way to retail goods you either cannot afford to stock or don't have sufficient space to store. Finding a great product with a good profit margin won't be easy but it can be done. With the knowledge you now have you should be able to: identify a profitable product, source a supplier of this product, negotiate a deal and analyse the product's profitability.

FINANCE

Unless you're opening an accountancy business you don't need to be a finance expert. In fact, unless you're a finance expert you'll need to use an accountant at some point. However, it's still essential that you know how to manage your finances. An accountant can't help you if you've spent all your money and gone out of business through poor financial management. In this chapter we'll teach you good financial management. We'll get straight to the point. We won't go into detail discussing management accounts, financial accounts, or anything technical and we'll minimise any jargon.

THE PHILOSOPHY OF FINANCIAL MANAGEMENT

"It's not how much money you make, but how much money you keep, how hard it works for you, and how many generations you keep it for." - Robert Kiyosaki, Rich Dad Poor Dad

Roughly between 1997 and 2003 there was the famous dot-com boom and bust. In short, due to the rise in the commercial growth of the Internet, venture capitalists threw money at virtually any online start-up. There are a number of reasons why these online companies went bust and many investors lost their money, but one of these reasons was poor financial management. The founders of these online start-ups would spend large amounts of money on travelling via private planes and on plush new offices. Travelling by private planes and plush new offices does nothing to contribute to the business other than waste money.

Now we're not suggesting that you shouldn't spend money, but you should spend it wisely as well as invest it and save it. For example, in the case of the online companies, with better financial management they could have put money aside for difficult trading periods and invested some of it to grow the business.

For simplicity, let's organise your finances into:

- Income
- Expenses
- Assets
- Liabilities

We're going to simplify this even more. The definitions below will slightly differ from professional accounting definitions.

Income - the money your business makes, for example sales.
Expenses - the money that goes out of the business, for example bills.
Assets - what make you money, for example the products you sell, employees in sales who make more money than they cost, any land that you rent out. Assets feed your income.
Liabilities - anything that costs you money, for example your office rent, vehicles etc. Liabilities feed your expenses.

If your liabilities and expenses are more than your assets and income you'll run out of money and go out of business. For your business to be successful you'll need to make more money than you lose. You do this through increasing your income by getting money into your business while also managing your expenditure to keep the money in the business. This financial management philosophy is important not only in business but for your personal finances too. We highly recommend reading *Rich Dad Poor Dad* by Robert Kiyosaki.

Now that we've outlined the essential philosophy of financial management we'll discuss setting up and putting in place the systems to take payments and control your finances.

BUSINESS BANKING ACCOUNTS

A business banking account works very much like your personal account and is nothing to worry or stress about. You simply use this account to store the money that you make through your business and to pay out any expenses, for example to suppliers.

To begin with many people use their personal account to manage transactions, but this can get very messy. This is because you'll need to sort out your business finances from your personal finances. It also has some other complications. For example, if you have a business meeting and purchase a coffee for you and a client you can claim this back on expenses. However, if you're doing all your business through your personal account then it's likely the tax inspector will argue that you may have been having coffee with friends rather than with a client. Therefore, opening a business account makes life easier for you. Also it is professional to charge B2B clients using a business account, because they'll expect to be invoiced with business banking details.

Setting up a business banking account is relatively easy. You simply contact a bank and ask them to set up a business banking account for you. They'll ask you some questions around the nature of your business, how much money you think you'll be making and the name of your business. It's great to see the name of your business on a bank account, debit card and cheque book. It can be a good idea to shop around for the best offers for new accounts. Free banking periods and other preferential offers can be very worthwhile.

Banks are businesses too and they make money from offering this service. Therefore, before you choose which bank to open up your account with you'll need to consider several things:

- What are their transactional costs?
- Do they have a local branch that you can drop in physical money?
- Do they have online banking?
- What are their interest rates?
- Do they have a free banking period, and how long for?
- Do they have an overdraft facility?
- Do they have an overdraft facility for free up to a certain limit?
- What are their overdraft facility charges?
- Do they offer any business support?

Another thing you should do is speak to other entrepreneurs for recommendations on a good bank. However, business managers can vary dramatically from branch to branch with some being very good and others not so good. A recommendation for a certain bank may not be relevant if your business manager is different, so make sure you meet them in person.

A business bank account will enable you to transfer money through physical cash deposits, electronic bank transfers and via payment cards through a chip and pin terminal, which requires the customer to be present. However, a business bank account does not give you the permission to take card payments online, over the phone or by mail order. To take payment via cards using a business bank account you'll need a third?party payment processor like PayPal, which we'll discuss later.

MERCHANT ACCOUNTS

Unlike a business bank account a merchant account gives you the ability to accept credit and debit cards online, over the phone or by mail order. Any money from card transactions will initially go into your merchant account. At this point, you'll not have access to the money, in case the customer decides to return the purchased item and ask for a refund. This money will become available to you once it's settled into your business account.

The application process for a merchant account can be more rigorous than when you open a business bank account, because of the risks the bank takes. Similar to your business banking account you'll want to know the charges, transaction times and you should ask around for recommendations.

You must be aware that if you use a merchant account you are taking on a degree of risk. That is you may have to deal with potential problems like fraud, when people use stolen credit cards, and 'chargebacks', where a customer forcibly reverses the payment to get a refund through their bank.

If you're an online business it may be easier for you to use a payment gateway service instead. This can be slightly more costly than a merchant account, but it does reduce your risks.

PAYMENT GATEWAYS

A payment gateway is an ecommerce application service provider that enables you to take credit card payments online. It's the equivalent of a physical point of sale terminal located in physical stores.

Some examples of payment gateway application services include: Sagepay, Worldpay and PayPal.

You can use either a merchant account or a payment gateway service to take online payments, or you can use both. There are positives and negatives to each. A payment gateway is probably the simpler option to begin with, especially if you want to test the water first to see if your business has legs. You'll also appear as a more trustworthy company if you use a reputable payment gateway service and you'll reduce the risk of having a merchant account.

As stated above there are several payment gateways, but this chapter will discuss the use of PayPal. Setting up a PayPal account is very easy. You simply set up an account with PayPal and link this account with your business account. PayPal will provide you with the facilities to charge your customers for your products and services. If you don't have a business account, which we strongly recommend that you do, you can link your PayPal account to your personal bank account.

PayPal is a great way to start out. Some people argue that the fee rates are too high, so if your business starts to take off and you're doing lots of transactions you may want to consider switching to a merchant account or another payment gateway. However, others argue that you should have multiple payment options to give the customer a choice. People become very cautious when paying for items online, especially from companies they don't know very well. PayPal gives them a degree of safety and familiarity. At the time of writing, PayPal offers buyers using their service a payment protection of up to £500, meaning you can reassure your potential customers that their money is safe when trading with you.

PayPal is largely known for online transactions, but it also offers payment card readers so that you can take payments in person, for example in a physical store. This is something you might want to consider.

BUSINESS TO CONSUMER INCOME

The platform you use to sell your goods and services, be it online, through a shop, or both, will determine how you receive payment. In B2C there is an exchange of goods or services for money. You may receive money in a number of ways:

- Cash - which you may need to deposit in your bank account
- Card payment - which will electronically arrive into your merchant or business account
- Cheque - which you'll need to cash in at your bank
- BACS - which is an electronic system to make payments directly from one bank account to another

BUSINESS TO BUSINESS INCOME

Andrew is embarrassed to say that when he first set up his business he didn't know how to charge B2B clients. He was used to B2C, so he was slightly confused about how to take payment from another business. If you're a little unsure on how to charge clients, don't worry, we'll cover it here. In B2B you'll receive money in the same ways as B2C:

- Cash
- Card payment
- Cheque
- BACS

However, if your services are high value, for example £1000+, it's unlikely that your clients will pay cash. They're more likely to pay via a card payment, cheque or a BACS payment.

So how do you actually charge a client? You raise an invoice and send it to the client who you're communicating with, or their accounts payable department, usually by email, but sometimes by post. We'll discuss invoices next.

INVOICING

An invoice is a document that shows how much your client owes you and how they can pay you.

If you and your client are both registered for VAT then by law you'll need to give them an invoice.

Creating and sending your first invoice is an amazing feeling. An invoice will consist of:

- A clear display of the word 'Invoice'.
- Your company logo.
- Your company name and address.
- The name of the person the invoice is for.
- The name of the client's company.
- The client's address.
- The date the invoice was raised.
- The supply date of the goods or service.
- Invoice number (a unique identification number) - this is just any number that helps you reference the invoice, but never put the number 1 for your first invoice. We like to use the initials of the client's name and the date that the invoice was raised. For example if the client was called 'Sales Training' and the date we raised the invoice was 07/01/2018 our invoice number would be "ST070118". Make sure that every new invoice you create has its own unique number.
- Terms - usually businesses have a payment term of 30 days, which means your client should pay you in 30 days of receipt of the invoice. You may have your payment terms much less

such as 15 days if you're selling certain products or services. Also, don't be surprised if your clients try to negotiate your payment terms.

- A description of the purchase.
- Unit price.
- Quantity.
- Total.
- VAT - leave this at 0 if you don't charge VAT.
- Payment details - (bank account name, number, bank address, sort code, IBAN, BIC).
- A message to say: "Thank you for your business".

It's very hard to visualise without an example, so please, feel free to download our template or search online for examples. You can download our free template by visiting www.businesshacks.tips and inserting your details to make your own invoice. If you don't like out layout the Internet has countless free templates you can download and edit.

When you raise invoices to charge your clients you'll need to store them. Some people like to do this electronically and some people also like to print them off and store them in a folder. We recommend you do both. You'll need these for future reference to see who owes you money and for your accountant.

Once you've raised your invoice and stored a copy for yourself, you then email or post the invoice to your client with a polite message. Please note that you should only post your invoices if your client specifically requests a hard copy.

Some clients, usually large clients, will issue you with a 'purchase order number' that you must put on the invoice for them. A purchase order number enables the client to track their own purchases. If you don't put on the purchase order number they'll send you the invoice back and ask you to put it on. This can delay your payment, so it can be good practice to ask your client what their invoicing process is and if they need to provide you with a purchase order.

CREDIT CONTROL

Credit control is about ensuring your clients pay you the money that they owe you and that you only work with organisations that can pay.

In B2C when customers purchase goods or services, they generally pay for the item on purchase. However, B2B clients normally pay within a specific timeframe, which starts from when the client receives your invoice. This will vary depending on your terms of payment, your client and the products and services you offer. For example, if you're selling high-valued goods your payment terms may be that clients will pay you within 30 days. If you're selling lower-valued goods then your payment terms may be payment upon receipt. If you're dealing with a large client with strict financial procedures they may impose that any suppliers will have to agree to payment terms as large as 60 days.

Knowing when your clients should be paying you is important. There's a famous business saying: "cash is king", which refers to the importance of cash flow for the overall health of a business. In other words, if you don't have cash in the bank and your suppliers, the bank(s) or anyone else you owe money to calls in their debts you'll go bust. Having strong credit control processes ensures sufficient cash flow. You should see cash as the blood supply of your company.

Every month you should check who owes you money, if your terms are 30 days and you see that clients haven't paid you within these terms, you'll need to chase these debts. To chase your debts you call the client that owes you money and ask them for a status update on the invoice you sent them. They'll usually ask you for the invoice number and they'll investigate the delay. Sometimes invoices can get lost, or they may be just late with payments. A gentle polite nudge will usually push them into paying. Always follow up the phone call with a thank you email and copy of the original invoice. This is so that they don't forget about you after you've put the phone down, but also so that you have a record of communication with the client. This record of communication is important when there are problems with payment and a situation becomes a legal issue. Your communication records will be needed for court proceedings. This is unlikely, but it's something you should be aware of.

When chasing your debts it's important to remember that they're still your client. You should not do or say anything that's unprofessional, aggressive or threatening as you'll want to continue the business relationship. It's not uncommon for clients to go over your payment terms, because as we said before invoices get lost and delays do occur.

BUDGET

Your budget is the overall sum of money you allocate for expenses, which you'll then further break down into categories such as marketing, supplies and other. You'll have an overall budget for the year from which you'll assign an amount to each month. The objective is not to go over this budget each month.

Why do you need to budget? You'll need money to set up the business and keep it running. That money could be used on sales, marketing, stock, office, virtual office, phone bill, travel, meetings, the Internet and other expenses. As you can see these expenditures need to be controlled as costs could spiral out of control. To keep the numbers simple, if your business income is £1000 a month, but your expenditure is £1500 then this isn't sustainable and it won't be long before you're out of business. Even if you're making profit, poorly-controlled costs will be eating into this profit; putting a budget in place will reduce your spend and increase your overall profit.

You can download a free budget template at www.businesshacks. tips. This is a simple template which helps you categorise your expenditure, your budget for that category, your actual spend and the difference between your actual spend and your budget.

A budget isn't set in stone and you'll need to analyse your budget at the end of each month by calculating the difference between the budgeted figures and the actual spend. From this you can deter- mine if your budget was in line with your actual numbers or if it wasn't. It's important to examine why the actual numbers varied from the budgeted figures. Through this analysis you'll be able to determine any problems or opportunities. For example, you may have discovered that you're not spending what you predicted on telephone calls. Instead you could adjust your budget to increase your marketing spend.

CONTROLLING COSTS

There are several ways to increase your profit margin. One is to increase your prices. However, this isn't always possible and may result in your customers shopping with your competitors.

Another way of increasing your profit margin is to reduce costs. Many people get this wrong, but the idea is to reduce costs whilst keeping your business running efficiently and effectively. That may seem obvious but it's not uncommon that a business will cut costs so much that their business operates badly. For example, Andrew's local gym cut staff so much that they had no staff on the counter. You would see queues form as people wanted to sign up, but they'd get so frustrated waiting they'd leave and join another gym. This company successfully cut costs, but they also lost business at the same time. This is not what we want to achieve. However, you can reduce costs intelligently. You do this in several ways.

One, always negotiate supplier prices down. If you negotiate at least 10% off all of your suppliers you'll save a significant amount of money. However, don't haggle too hard. Not so much that your supplier doesn't value your business and reduces their quality of service to you. A supplier will always treat its most profitable customers best.

Two, always shop around for the best deals. For example, if you're paying for insurance don't accept your first quote and don't just accept the insurance quote from your existing supplier year after year. Look for alternative suppliers and use comparison websites. Using another example, when booking a hotel for work is it necessary to purchase a five-star hotel room, or can you find an alternative cheaper hotel room? While it's important to reduce costs, don't fall into the trap of purchasing something cheap and useless which in the end will cost you more money. For example, if you need a designer, but you chose to save money by picking one who is ridiculously cheap, if they take weeks to produce the work or they steal it and several months later you discover your design is actually copyrighted, you'll have to find a new designer and with all this work you'll have actually spent more money than if you paid for a quality designer to begin with.

Now you can probably see why so many people get this wrong as it's about striking the balance between reducing the cost, and keeping the quality. It's fine to get things wrong and make mistakes, but learn from them.

TAX
At the end of the financial year you'll be able to claim tax back on certain expenses, therefore, it's imperative that you keep all your

receipts. Organise you receipts by month to make life easier. We're not going to go into depth on tax, but you need to use an accountant. Ask around for any recommendations for a good accountant.

USEFUL LINKS
- Invoicing - www.gov.uk/invoicing-and-taking-payment-from-customers/ overview
- Business Tax - www.gov.uk/browse/business/business-tax

CUSTOMER SERVICE

Customer service is the service you provide your customers before, during and after a sale. Before we begin, it's important to know that returning customers tend to spend more money than new customers. There's been lots of research on consumer behaviour and many studies show that acquiring new customers is significantly more expensive than keeping existing customers, therefore, it pays to have good customer service. The level of customer service required and the systems you need to put in place will vary depending on what your business is. Customer service seems like such a simple function, but it's highly complex and it can make or break a business. This chapter will point you in the right direction by giving you an overview of customer service, so that you can implement the right type of service into your business.

"Customer service shouldn't be just a department. It should be the entire company." - Tony Hsieh

Customer service can take many forms, including:

- Face-to-face customer contact, such as in shops, restaurants, at reception areas, business meetings etc.
- Email correspondence.

- Telephone contact.
- Website.
- Online chat facilities.
- Social media.

Having these options is simply not enough, you must be great at them or you risk irritating your customer to the point they never shop with you again and tell all their friends and family never to shop with you. Have you ever tried to contact a company via telephone only to be faced with a slow bureaucratic automated system that you must go through to reach the right department? Then you're faced with an excruciatingly long wait, so before you've even spoken to anyone you're having a difficult time. Then when you do get someone on the phone you're connected with an overseas call centre and both you and the call handler are having communication troubles.

Have you ever wanted to contact a company and been unable to find their details on their website? Have you ever been in a shop or a restaurant and you've had to wait a long time to be simply acknowledged? If you've ever been faced with customer service issues like the above your first instinct is probably to blame the frontline employees. However, most of the time it's not the fault of the frontline employees but a problem with the customer service process.

HANDLING CUSTOMERS

It's very important that you handle your customers correctly, and to do this you must have the right processes in place. You might not get it perfect at first, but as long as you listen to your customers and are seen to be trying to improve your customer service your customers will support you.

Online - you should make your purchasing processes and access to information as simple as possible for your customers. Having your customers click through unnecessary links and searching the page for the next step is bad customer service. On your website ensure that your contact details are easily findable. You may also want to implement a messaging form to help you manage customer complaints better. If your business gets lots of enquiries on varied topics you can categories these customer enquires using the online messaging form. Simply having the form or providing an email address is not enough, you must also act on the enquiry you receive. If you're a small business, handling enquiries immediately, especially if you get a large amount, might not be possible. Remember customer enquires take you away from other duties such as selling, marketing and fulfilling orders. What you can do is dedicate a certain amount of time during the day to specifically handle enquires. However, while you might not be able to handle a customer enquiry immediately, you'll need to send an immediate response to let the customer know you've received their email and a timeframe you'll get back to them by. Make sure you actually get back to the customer within this timeframe as you'll lose their trust if you don't.

Many customer enquiries will be similar so you can save time by having a Frequently Asked Questions Page (FAQ) on your website. If the FAQ page still doesn't answer their question give them the option to contact you. Again many of the enquiries will be similar so you can create stock/template emails that'll save you time. However, do not send the customer a stock email in its original form, as you'll need to personalise it with the customer's name, order/enquiry number and your name. It's important to personalise the email and put your name or the customer service representative's name, because people want to deal with real people. If they feel they're going down an automated system they'll feel frustrated, especially if they're trying to contact you regarding a problem. Your emails must be written with professionalism, politeness and empathy. Remember to be very sensitive with what you communicate in an email. Any confidential information such as bank details should be conveyed over the telephone.

If your customers need immediate contact then you might want to consider installing an instant chat service. This saves the customer the money and hassle of calling.

Face-to-face and verbal - if you handle your customers face-to-face or over the telephone you must be just as professional, polite and empathetic to their situation. You'll need to judge what type of service you give the customer. For example, the type of customer service given by a waiter at a high-end restaurant where they may call their customers "sir" and "madam" would be totally different to the customer service given in a business meeting with a client.

As with online enquiries it's important to acknowledge the customer's enquiry even if you're unable to deal with it at the present time. For example, if you're helping a customer and another customer is waiting for you, by saying *"I'll be with you soon"* coupled with a smile will temporarily satisfy the customer until you can be with them. Obviously don't keep them waiting all day and if you can direct one of your colleagues to help them even better.

Flexible Customer Service Processes - a friend of ours nearly walked away from a garage recently. He arrived at the garage early so that he could put his car in and then get the train to work. However, the customer service representative said she couldn't take the car until 9am even though the time was 8:50am. Now there might have been a perfectly legitimate insurance reason that she couldn't take the car before 9am, but our friend wasn't told this. He was left baffled. If the customer service representative wasn't taking the car before 9am because of company procedure then what they have is an inflexible process. Let's look at another example, have you ever waited in a long queue to buy something only to get to the front where the customer service representative tells you it's the 'returns isle' and that you must queue back into the 'payment isle'? Well, this is another inflexible process.

A flexible process is a business process that follows a particular route, but if something unexpected happens the people involved in the process can adapt it to the situation and temporarily change the way it works. For example, Andrew was going for a job interview several years ago, but when he arrived at the train station he realised he'd forgotten his wallet, which contained his train ticket and money. He explained this to the lady who worked for Virgin Trains, and she very kindly gave him a new ticket free of charge. She also wished him luck for the interview. We can imagine that the standard procedure is to only let people travel on the train who have a valid a ticket. However, in this unique case the customer service lady went over and above by flexing the process and issuing Andrew a new ticket. The Virgin brand is very well-known for providing its employees the autonomy to make decisions that'll help their customers. You can read more about the Virgin brand and their customer service philosophy in Richard Branson's book *Like a Virgin*.

We want to share with you another example of great customer service. There is a company called Zappos which sells clothing online. Zappos is famous for its customer service and their number one core value is "Deliver WOW Through Service." The CEO of Zappos, Tony Hsieh, often likes to tell a story about customer service at the end of his presentations, and we'll share the story here. Tony was in Santa Monica, California, at a Skechers conference. After a long night of drinking, a small group of them headed up to the hotel room to order some food. Tony's friend from Skechers tried to order a pizza from the room-service menu, but was disappointed to learn that the hotel didn't deliver hot food after 11:00pm. In their intoxicated state, a few of them including Tony persuaded her into calling Zappos to try to order a pizza. Bearing in mind Zappos is an online clothes retailer and has nothing to do with Pizza. She turned on the speakerphone and called Zappos, and explained to the Zappos customer service representative that she was staying in a Santa Monica hotel and really wanted a pizza, that room service was no longer delivering hot food, and that she wanted to know if there was anything Zappos could do to help. The Zappos representative was initially puzzled by the bizarre request for pizza, but the representative put the caller on hold. The Zappos representative then returned two minutes later, listing the five closest places in the Santa Monica area that were still open and delivering pizzas at that time.

"The customer is always right" - you've probably heard of the phrase the customer is always right. This isn't true, the customer isn't always right. It's good customer service to provide the customer with what they want, but sometimes a customer or a potential customer can waste your time and effort. If you have a particularly demanding customer who's draining your resources, but is spending very little or no money at all with you then it may be best to let them go. We had one particular potential B2B customer who constantly asked us for information and connections. At first we were very happy and keen to help this potential customer. However, after a period of time we had to simply stop replying to their emails as this potential customer wasn't going to spend any money with our company. When you reach a point that you feel it's best to not work with a particular customer, you still must handle this in a tactful, professional and polite manner.

UNDERSTANDING CUSTOMER NEEDS

Professor Kano of the University of Tokyo developed a very useful model called the Kano model, which will help you better understand customers. You can see a copy of the Kano model by doing an Internet search for 'Kano model'.

In the Kano model there are three main areas: 'Must Be', 'One Dimensional' and 'Delighters'.

Must Be - these attributes are taken for granted by the customer, but if they're not met the customer will be greatly dissatisfied. For example, if a customer buys a mobile telephone they expect the telephone to be able make and receive calls. If the telephone doesn't make or receive calls the customer will be greatly dissatisfied. However, if the mobile telephone does make and receive calls it won't result in higher customer satisfaction. Therefore, these attributes are a "Must Be". These customer needs are often referred as "the unspoken" needs. Using another example, if you book a hotel room, you expect it to have clean bed sheets and to be neat and tidy. You certainly wouldn't expect to ask for a clean and tidy room.

One Dimensional - these attributes result in customer satisfaction when met and dissatisfaction when not met. These are typically "spoken" and sometimes referred to as "satisfiers". In other words the customer will often state that they want these. For example, more miles per litre for your car will equal more satisfaction, and less waiting time at airports will equal more satisfaction. These customer requirements are often related to features and service delivery such as: cost, ease of use and speed.

Delighters - these attributes will delight the customer and increase customer satisfaction, but will not dissatisfy the customer if they're missing. For example, free Internet access on public transport will delight customers, but they don't expect it, so they wouldn't be dissatisfied if it wasn't present.

An important point to remember is that consumer expectations change over time. That is, if you delight customers, over time these 'Delighters' become 'One Dimensional' and then these become a 'Must-Be'.

Another point to remember is that delighting customers costs more money and these costs are passed on to the customer. Therefore, while there are customers who love to be delighted you may also have customers who want a basic product or service. They'll see no added value in the extras.

CUSTOMER SERVICE TECHNOLOGY – CRM

When you go to the doctor or dentist, you expect them to know you and your medical history. You don't expect to keep telling them what you're allergic to or any previous medical conditions you've had. Your customers and clients feel the same way. They expect you to remember their requirements, their preferences, their contact details, their order history and many other things. It's impossible to remember all these details, especially if your customers run in the hundreds or thousands.

A good way to keep track of your customer or client activity is through the use of customer/client relationship management software (CRM). A CRM is basically a database of information about your customers and their activity.

There are several ways to install a CRM. You can have it installed on your business premises where it would be maintained by you or an IT person, or you can have it web-based also known as in the cloud where the CRM is hosted by a CRM provider. Another way is to use an open source CRM, which you would install on your website domain. This method is free and it's also in the cloud. If you've followed the website creation chapter and you're confident with building websites using the hosting software 'cPanel' you can use the built-in app 'Softaculous' to install an open source CRM. If you've used a web development company to build your website, it's worth asking them if they use 'cPanel' and if they could recommend installing one of the free CRM's from 'Softaculous'.

At the time of writing, some of the free CRMs that are available in 'Softaculous' are:

- Vtiger
- SugarCRM
- Zurmo
- Tine 2.0
- X2CRM

Some other free and open source CRM software solutions include:

- SuiteCRM
- CapsuleCRM
- Insightly
- FreeCRM
- Bitrix24
- ZohoCRM
- Splendid CRM
- OpenCRX

You don't need to use 'cPanel' and 'Softaculous' to install your free open source CRM. If you're familiar with transferring files across the Internet using an FTP client then you can also do it this way.

Not all CRMs are the same and they'll have different features. As you grow you might need to use more space and functions, which may involve you having to upgrade to a paid service. Do your research and test the different platforms to find the most suitable one. A CRM is a good investment if you're marketing a lot of customers.

There is a separate chapter on email marketing and it discusses the use of email marketing software. Ideally you want to use a CRM that also has the facility to do mass-email marketing. This is much better practice than using a separate CRM and separate email marketing platform. This way you can control and track what emails go to what customers and you'll be able to see the communication history.

CUSTOMER SERVICE SUMMARY

Customer service is a large subject and the level of service varies depending on your industry and target market. However, this chapter should give you enough information to get started, so that you can understand their behaviour and implement the right level of customer service for your business.

PART 3

SELLING

SALES

A sale is when a transaction takes place for goods or services in exchange for money. There's a difference between sales and marketing. Marketing is a series of activities that creates awareness of your business and your products, whereas a sale is when a customer makes a purchase. The two functions overlap and work together in harmony. Sometimes marketing activities will lead smoothly into a sale. However, sometimes buyers need to be guided through the buying process before they make the purchase. This is especially true for high-priced goods or major sales in B2B where the purchase can make or break someone's career.

How you sell your products or services is different depending on your business. For example, if you run a B2C high street shop selling clothing, it's highly unlikely that you'll use cold calling as one of your sales methods, but you might make a conscious effort to sell on the shop floor; whereas if you run a B2C business such as a stock brokerage then you'll likely use cold calling to reach high-valued clients. If your business is B2B then it's probable that your company will use cold calling to achieve sales.

Whatever business you run will require some form of sales, whether that's cold calling, door-to-door selling or simply having a conversation with a customer on your shop floor. You'll need to read through this chapter and identify which methods are the most suitable for your business and adapt them for your needs. Regardless of which methods you use, the fundamentals of sales are the same: ask questions, listen and then provide the buyer with exactly what they want.

In this section of the book we've broken up the sales process into manageable, bite-sized categories, structuring it in a way that allows you to easily find what you need for most of the problems you'll face in selling. The content and examples within this chapter are focused around B2B businesses simply because B2B sales, in our opinion, is slightly more complicated than B2C sales. However, the principles and techniques are transferable to B2C.

Selling is a skill and like any skill it can be learnt and improved through practice. It's a common misconception that selling is a natural talent. While there are naturally talented people in all aspects of life, including sales, the saying goes: "Hard work beats talent when talent doesn't work hard."

KNOW YOUR TARGET MARKET

Before you can sell anything you must completely understand your target market and why they would buy what you're selling. This sounds simple, but we've met with so many people who had the wrong strategy and approach to sales. They used a mass-marketing approach and hoped for the best.

Imagine you're selling adrenaline-fuelled skiing holidays. Would pitching to the elderly be the right target market? Probably not. In this case your target market might be 18 to 30-year-olds. Now imagine you're selling adrenaline-fuelled skiing holidays with expensive luxury apartments and night clubs. Your target market becomes even more niche and your demographics might be 22 to 30-year-olds with a high disposable income.

Take the time to review what you're offering and who would buy it. If you're selling a new accountancy software system, would the CEO of a company be the best person to sell to? Maybe not, the Finance Director would probably be the best person to speak to first. This all does depend on the company as they come in different sizes, but we're sure you get the point. Only sell to the people who make the buying decisions on what it is you're selling.

Telephone Sales

This section explains how to sell over the telephone. We'll introduce you to the basics of telephone sales and then show you
how to implement these techniques, step by step.

WHAT NOT TO DO

Let's begin with a list of what *not* to do:

1) Don't be over familiar

You'll naturally want to build a fast rapport with clients so you can
start making money. Clients strongly dislike it when sales professionals are overly familiar without first investing time into building
a relationship. This is more easily understood if you've ever been
cold-called by someone you don't know and they ask questions such
as: "how are you today?" or "how is the weather where you are?"
While these questions may seem innocent, on the telephone they're
irritating to clients when they don't know the caller. You can only
ask these types of personal questions when the client knows you.
Whenever you're speaking to clients for the first few times, always
keep the conversation professional and business-related.

2) Don't sell too soon

Imagine you and your partner have just had your third child and you're looking for a new car: a car that can seat three children, hold several prams and still have room for your shopping bags. The minute you walk into the showroom a car sales professional approaches you and tries to sell you a two-seater sports car. As beautiful as the sports car is, it's completely the opposite of what you want and need. The problem here is that the sales professional tried to sell too soon. Instead, they should have asked insightful questions to build up their knowledge in order to guide you to your ideal vehicle. Don't sell too soon.

3) Don't be pushy

Don't try to close a deal on every phone call. There's a Hollywood myth to cold-calling and selling, wrongly promoting the notion that if you don't close a deal every time, you're not a good sales professional or entrepreneur. This is simply not true. You cannot force your clients to buy your products if there's no need. They'll simply stop taking your calls if you're too pushy. You need to be professional and build relationships with your clients in order for them to trust you.

4) Don't be scared

It can be scary calling clients, especially if you're going up the hierarchy. People are generally nicer and more helpful the higher up you go. This is simply due to the fact that to manage people you need to be a good people person, so these types of people get promoted. However, this is not the case for every client and you'll encounter rudeness on occasion. Don't let this scare you, because in general people are pleasant by nature. If you act professionally, they will treat you professionally. There is less competition at the top. Most people, including your competitors, will be too afraid to call the people high up. From a business perspective you should always aim to be where there's less competition, so don't be afraid to go right to the top. Remember, they're just people. You may have difficulty reaching people at the top via telephone, but you can use the telephone to get their email address. From there you can sell via email.

5) Don't pester your clients

While it's important to win sales and ensure your clients don't forget you, don't pester them by calling too often. You'll present the impression that your business is not doing well if they feel you're calling too frequently. It'll appear as if you're desperate for business. We would recommend you call clients once a month. You may call more if it's necessary, for example if you're actually working with them. You should also call back one week after your first introductory conversation to see if they've read the company literature you've sent them. This will speed up the process of them remembering your name.

It can be all too easy to fall into any of the traps detailed above, so be aware of them, and avoid them!

ASKING QUESTIONS

"A wise man can learn more from a foolish question than a fool can learn from a wise answer." - Bruce Lee'

This is not as straightforward as it appears. We found this difficult initially. Some people are naturally inquisitive and ask questions with ease. We, on the other hand, would over analyse and assume we knew the answers.

"If I had an hour to solve a problem and my life depended on the answer, I would spend the first 55 minutes figuring out the proper questions to ask. For if I knew the proper questions, I could solve the problem in less than 5 minutes." - Albert Einstein

The general rule is: ask a question, and then stop talking. With practice, questioning will become a natural part of your conversation. We would recommend that you spend a great deal of time developing the art of questioning, because it's the foundation of sales.

OPEN QUESTIONS

An open question is a question that cannot be answered with a simple yes or no. They encourage conversation and help to build strong relationships with your clients. They're also the questions that provide you with the most information. An open question begins with one of the following words: Who, What, Why, Where, When and How. Some examples include:

- How do you normally purchase <your product>?
- What suppliers do you use?
- Why do you favour those particular suppliers?
- When is the best time to catch you on the phone?
- When do you expect to be making a new order?
- When does the contract end with your current supplier?

If you're not yet naturally asking questions, create a question sheet, print it out and stick it where you can see it while on the telephone. At the same time, practice on your friends and family. Ask them open questions, such as:

- How was your day at work?
- How did that make you feel?
- Where did that take you?

When you practice something enough times it becomes habitual and you'll no longer need to think about it; it will happen naturally.

CLOSED QUESTIONS

A closed question is one that provokes a "yes" or "no" answer. These questions will not provide you with detailed information, but they're a powerful tool for closing and getting definite answers, for example:

- Are you the person who purchases <your product>?
- Are you happy to call me with your next order?

When entrepreneurs or sales people first start it's quite common for them to ask too many closed questions. If too many closed questions are asked at the start of the telephone call it can cause the conversation to end abruptly. You should base your conversations around open questions and only use closed questions if you specifically need a "yes" or "no" answer, or to close the conversation.

ADVANCED QUESTIONING

A British psychologist called Neil Rackham developed a very powerful selling system called SPIN® selling. Rackham and his team analysed more than 35,000 sales calls made by 10,000 sales professionals in 23 countries over 12 years. The system enables a sales professional to uncover the client's implied needs, develop these into explicit needs and then offer the client a solution to those needs. This is achieved through a sequence of four question types. This is extremely powerful for consultative selling. The four question types are as follows:

1. Situation Questions

Situation questions are fact-finding questions about your client's existing situation. For example:

- How do you normally purchase <your product>?
- How often do you purchase <your product>?

- What suppliers do you use?

While situation questions are an essential part of your information-gathering process, they must be used wisely. Your clients will quickly become bored if you ask too many. The reason for this is that the questions only benefit you. According to Rackham, successful sales professionals ask fewer situation questions, but each one has a focus or purpose.

2. Problem Questions

Problem questions uncover your client's problems, dissatisfactions or difficulties. If your client doesn't have any problems then there are no grounds for your services, so these types of questions help you to identify your client's implied needs. Funnily enough Rackham found that problem questions are powerful for smaller sales, but not as effective in larger sales. Some examples of problem questions include:

- What problems do you usually face when purchasing <your product>?
- How satisfied are you with your current supplier?
- What problems would it cause you if your supplier couldn't deliver?

3. Implication Questions

Inexperienced entrepreneurs and sales people will usually start to sell after they've asked problem questions and identified a problem. However, this will just cause the client to raise objections. Instead, successful sales professionals ask implication questions. Implication questions amplify the problem you've uncovered as it forces the client to review the effects, consequences or implications of their problems. Some examples include:

- If your current supplier couldn't deliver on time, how would that affect you?
- If your current supplier's product didn't meet your quality standards how would that affect your operations?
- What would happen if you didn't act on this?

4. Need-payoff questions

Once you've built up the client's problem so that they perceive it as more serious, you should switch to need-payoff questions, which demonstrate the value of your services. Need-payoff questions shift the focus of the client's attention off the problem and onto the solution. At the same time, the client starts telling you the benefits of your service. We discuss objection handling later in the book, but Rackham suggests that if you use need-payoff questions correctly you'll face less objections. Some examples of need-payoff questions include:

- How important is it that you solve this problem?
- If you only received <your product> just in time would that help to solve your storage problem?
- If you're spending that amount on a service with no guaranteed success, would a service where you only paid for delivered results help you?

Rackham states that SPIN(r) selling is "the way most successful people sell on a good day when the call is going well". You might find that you won't be able to ask all these questions in one call, but instead you may have to ask them in a sequence of calls over a period of time.

THE POWER OF SILENCE

You should be aware of the Pareto Principle, also known as the 80/20 Rule. This principle is named after Vilfredo Pareto, an economist who identified that 20 percent of the population owned 80 percent of the wealth. This principle is applicable to many walks of life, especially business. In business, 80 percent of your business comes from 20 percent of your clients. When selling, you should only talk 20 percent of the time while your client talks 80 percent of the time. You may be on the telephone, but your clients should be doing most of the talking. When they talk, they reveal their buying motives. When you've asked a question, do not feel the need to offer a selection of answers, or to answer the question for the client, for example:

- "I thought you'd be interested in <your product>... Or, not"

Remember the general rule is: ask a question and then stop talking. The above example would be better phrased:

- "What did you think of the brochure I sent you?"

If you ask a question and the client is silent, do not feel the need to fill the silence. While this is an uncomfortable situation it's an extremely powerful one, especially during a negotiation. The silence will feel longer than it actually is and your client will appreciate the time to think. Silence is also a powerful way to get the client to expand further on their questions. This works very well in face-to-face meetings. If you want your client to keep talking after they've answered a question, remain silent and they'll immediately try and fill it with extra information.

LISTENING

Once your client begins talking and opening up to you, ensure you listen intently. This seems a simple task but many sales professionals struggle with listening. They focus so much on trying to think of what to ask next that they forget to listen to what's being said. At the same time, it can be difficult to listen when you're trying to write down what they're saying. While it's essential that you keep the conversation going and record notes, the whole conversation is counterproductive if you're not actually listening. Worst of all, the client will know you're not listening if you ask an irrelevant question straight after they've just spoken about a different topic. Have a list of stock questions on your desk, so that you always have questions to ask and you don't need to worry about what to ask next. To show that you're listening, ask questions relevant to what they've just said. When you're taking notes about your client keep them short, one word per point if possible. Whilst on the telephone it can feel awkward if the person listening is completely silent. Show the client you're still on the other end and that you're listing by making verbal confirmations, such as:

- Mmm
- Uh-huh
- Yes
- Ahhhh
- Okay
- Does that mean...
- I don't understand
- I understand

It's important that you wait until clients have finished making their point and not talk over them with your next question. It's okay to leave a short silence to ensure they've finished speaking before you begin speaking. To help the client build confidence in you and show them that you understand, paraphrase back to them what they've said.

FEATURES ADVANTAGES AND BENEFITS

Features, advantages and benefits, also known as FAB, is a powerful method of tailoring your sell to the client's needs.

A feature describes a characteristic of what you're selling, such as its colour, size and shape.

An advantage is what the feature does.

A benefit is how a feature meets the need expressed by your client, such as: cost saving, ease of use, safety, increased productivity and time saving. A benefit is only a benefit to your client if they've expressed a need. For example, if your client isn't looking for that particular benefit, such as ease of use, then you're actually talking about advantages. Therefore, advantages and benefits are similar, but an advantage becomes a benefit if your client explicitly expresses a particular problem. Remember the difference between the two.

If we were to sell you a pen, and explained that "it's a black inked pen", that doesn't tell you anything useful. Only that the pen is black. However, if we know you scan a lot of your hand-written documents and you suffer from many admin errors, we can use FAB to say the following: "It's a black inked pen, which means you'll be able to scan your documents more clearly resulting in fewer admin errors." Notice how we've discussed a feature, an advantage of that feature and the benefit to the client.

Clients buy benefits not features. While it's important to discuss the features of your product it's essential that you guide your client from features to benefits as we did in the example above. You can do this by using connecting phrases:

- The benefit of this is...
- This means that you'll...
- As a result...

Sometimes entrepreneurs and sales professionals state features, because they wrongly believe it's a benefit, or they think the client can connect the benefit to the feature. Clients can't always connect benefits to features, so be explicit with them. To ensure you've actually got a benefit, put yourself in the client's shoes and ask yourself:

• So what?

If you can't ask "so what?", then you've drilled down enough to reach a benefit.

THE POWER OF THREE

There is something powerful about things in threes. The psychology of it is beyond the scope of this book, but it is believed that the human brain can only take in and analyse, efficiently, three pieces of information.

If you look around you'll see that the power of three is culturally ingrained. You'll hear politicians using it; you'll see it in the marketing of large corporations and you'll see top sales professionals using it. Some examples include:

- The three blind mice
- The three amigos
- An essay has a beginning, middle and an end
- The three wise men
- 1st 2nd 3rd
- Tony Blair's three main priorities in government were: "Education, Education, Education."
- The three R's: reading, writing and arithmetic
- Three Men and a Baby
- Small, medium and large
- Ready, aim, fire
- The Lion, the Witch and the Wardrobe

What this means is that your clients are most likely to remember the information you provide if it comes in threes. Have you ever been on the telephone to a sales professional and they tell you so much information that by the fifth point you can't remember the detail of the earlier points? Have you ever asked someone for directions and after they give you the third road or direction, you just can't remember?

Keep your information in three succinct points. Now we can take this further and combine the power of three with benefits. By selling to your client using three benefits you'll be delivering an extremely influential pitch that they can, and will, remember.

Whether you're selling over the telephone, through an email, face-to-face or through a presentation, use the power of three to organise the structure of your sell. Break it into three parts: an introduction, middle and an end.

LEARN TO ASK

"If you don't ask, you don't get." - Mahatma Gandhi

If you want something in life you have to ask for it. If you want your clients to use your services you'll have to ask them to.

"If you don't ask, the answer is always no." - Nora Roberts

Depending on how assertive you are, asking for things can be quite scary, especially if you're afraid of rejection. As Nora Roberts said, if you don't ask the answer will always be no. That means if you don't ask clients for meetings, or for their business they won't give it to you. Practice asking your clients for things, such as:

- Can I come and meet you?
- Can I have your direct telephone line? I promise not to abuse it.
- Can I have your email address?

Taking this beyond business you'll be amazed at what you get in life if you ask for it. We encourage you to do this outside of work. If you're in a restaurant ask for a free side plate of chips, or ten percent off the bill. Ask someone you find attractive for their telephone number. Ask someone you admire if they will mentor you, or go to dinner and share their knowledge with you. You might read this and think "I can't possibly do that". If you don't ask, the answer will always be "no" and you won't get anything. The odds are stacked in your favour. If you get an "OK" you've achieved your goal, if you get a "no" then you've lost nothing.

CLOSING

Leading on from the last section is the art of closing. We must make a clear difference between closing and closing techniques. Closing is when you get a commitment from your client so that the relationship progresses to the next stage. For example, this could be a meeting with your client. Closing doesn't always mean closing a sale, which it's more commonly known for. Closing techniques are techniques that help you reach a close. As I mentioned earlier closing is usually associated with closing the sale, but this is now very old-school thinking and in today's world you won't be using these traditional closing techniques to close the sale. Instead you'll use them to close stages that progress the client forward, for example a meeting. We'll show you how to book meetings with clients later in the chapter. Closing is notoriously difficult for sales professionals and entrepreneurs most probably because it can feel rude and awkward. It also sets you up for the possibility of being rejected. There are usually two extremes: one, when the sales professional tries to close too soon and close too much, making the client feel pressured; the second extreme is when the sales professional won't close, which makes the client feel irritated. Returning to Neil Rackham's research, he found that when selling low-value goods an increased use of closing made more sales. However, in high value goods an increased use of closing decreased the chances of making a sale. In other words, closing techniques become less effective as decision size increases. There is a famous saying in sales: "always be closing", also known as ABC. This is very outdated and wrong. If you try to close your clients from the start they'll feel pushed into something they don't want, or something they're not ready for yet. The idea is to guide your clients not push them. Instead of "always be closing" think "always be consulting." There is no mysterious secret to closing other than asking your client for some commitment and then staying quiet until your client speaks first.

Traditional Closing Techniques

There are several different types of closing techniques, which work well in the initial stages of winning a client, such as getting a meeting or the client giving you a vacancy to fill. However, these techniques work less well when closing a sale.

Gentle close:

- Do you feel that we could help you solve that problem?
- Do you feel a meeting would benefit you?

This is a gentle close because it's nonthreatening and the client won't feel pushed. It allows your client to either say "yes", or come up with a reservation. If the client comes back with a reservation, you then go back to consulting and questioning.

Alternative close:

- I'm in your area on the 18th and 21st, are you around for a quick meeting?

In this close you're asking them to choose between two alternative options.

Assumptive close:

- This looks good to me. I can get a proposal to you by the end of next week?
- You probably want to get started on this now?
- So you'll call me with your next order?

This type of close assumes that the client wants to progress forward with you.

Conditional close:

- If I can get the price down by 10% would you be happy to move forward?

This close is best when your client has one condition that they can only work to, such as a limited budget.

Invitational close:

- Why don't you try me for one order and if you like the way we work together, you can look at taking things forward?
- Why don't you just try one order to benchmark us against your preferred suppliers?

This close invites the client to test your services with no long-term commitment or risk.

Empathy close:

- I'm confident that I can solve this for you based on everything I know. What else do I need to do in order for us to work together?
- Some of my best clients have "felt" the same way. That was until they tried my services.

This close takes into account the feelings of the client and demonstrates that you understand them.

Puppy dog close:

- Why don't you try my services for a period? We won't charge you, and you'll be able to see if they're the right fit for you.

The puppy dog close comes from pet shops when customers are hesitating over buying a puppy. The shop keeper lets the customer take the puppy home for the night and if they change their mind they can bring the puppy back the next day. The seller knows once the customer takes the puppy home they'll never be able to bring it back, which closes the sale.

You can use these types of closing techniques to move the client forward. Remember, if the client says "no", that just means "not right now". Remain relaxed and confident and the client will believe in you.

When to Close

You must close otherwise it'll irritate your client until they become so impatient they leave the telephone call. For example:

Entrepreneur: What else do you need to know?
Client: Nothing, I think you've covered everything.

Entrepreneur: Great, Are you sure I can't go through anything else with you?
Client: No, honestly, but now I've got to go.
Entrepreneur: (desperate) But we've gone through everything?

In the example above the entrepreneur doesn't know how to draw the conversation to an end, so the client leaves. As you can see the idea is to close, but the key is to close at the right time. If you never close the client will leave irritated, but if you try to close too early the client will feel pressured. Therefore, you need to ensure the client is happy to move forward. Take the following example:

Entrepreneur: (assumptive close) I'm glad you liked the brochure, I'll place an order for you to be delivered to you over the next few weeks?
Client: Wow, hold on, what's your rebate period?
Entrepreneur: (alternative close) I'll send you our terms of business, which contains the rebate period, so can you take a delivery Tuesday or Thursday?
Client: (pressured) Hold on. What are you covering up?

It's obvious in this example that the client becomes irritated when they're not ready to move forward and the entrepreneur tries to close. This makes the entrepreneur look pushy and sinister. An entrepreneur with good sales skills would check to see if the client is happy first before trying to move the client forward. For example:

Entrepreneur: It looks like we've covered everything. Can I check you're happy with everything, or do you have any reservations?
Client: Yes, you haven't mentioned your rebate period.
Entrepreneur: I'll tell you about that now. If you're not satisfied with your product you can have a full refund after one month, but this decreases by 50% after two months.

So when exactly is the right time to close? As the conversation draws to a conclusion and the client has no reservations then you should summarise the client's problems and your benefits, which will then be followed by your close. For example:

Entrepreneur: It looks like we've covered everything. Can I check you're happy with everything, or do you have any reservations?
Client: No, that's everything.
Entrepreneur: (summary) So your current supplier isn't providing you with the products on time. As a result, your team is left idle and your customers are left waiting, costing you time and money. I can certainly help you with this. All our deliveries are guaranteed to arrive on time.
Client: Yes, that sounds good.
Entrepreneur: (closing) Then the next logical step would be to come and visit you. When are you free for a quick meeting?

The next step will depend on your client's situation, it could be a meeting or even to place an order depending on what you're offering. Notice how the conversation has naturally progressed to the close rather than forcing a close. Also notice that the sales person hasn't asked, but instead told the client what the next logical step is. This is extremely important in closing.

In summary, use closing techniques to progress the client forward. The close will come naturally as you ask the right questions, but you must close otherwise no progression will be made. To close, firstly, check to see if the client has any reservations. Secondly, summarise what they've told you and explain the benefits. Lastly, close by telling the client what the next logical step is. In the later stages, when the client wants to buy, you won't need closing techniques.

OPENING A SALES CALL

Whether you're opening the call for the first time or the tenth time, always:

- Introduce yourself using both first name and surname

- State what company you're calling from

- State why you're calling

- Ask for permission to continue. The permission to continue might be to ask questions or ask if they're free to speak.

From a very young age most of us are taught not to speak to strangers and that strangers are bad. Even as we grow into adults we carry these negative associations with us. Therefore, it's important to introduce yourself upfront so you're not seen as a complete stranger. Even on the tenth or twentieth call you should open your calls in such a structured way.

BODY LANGUAGE FOR TELEPHONE SALES

"It's not what you say, but how you say it." - Anon

When you're on the telephone to your friends and family you know if they're lying down or rushing from one location to the next without even having to ask them. You can tell if they're happy, sad, worried, anxious, excited, in a rush or ecstatic. You know this because the sound, pitch and tone of their voice are different depending on their activity and mood.

People become more aware of how you're speaking when you're on the telephone. The reason for this, we can imagine, is that their hearing and imagination becomes heightened by the absence of your physical presence. Therefore, if you slouch in your chair during your telephone calls your body will feel too relaxed. The sound of your voice will change due to the physical structure of your body being in a more crunched up position. If you were to say a powerful phrase, such as: "I'm enthusiastic to work with you. You can be confident that I'd deliver exactly what you want," but you said it from a slouched position. Your client won't feel your enthusiasm or your capability. If this was your first telephone call to a client this would be their first impression of you.

Although you're on the telephone, and your clients can't physically see you, they visualise you by your voice. Therefore, your body language needs to be in a strong and dynamic position. Sit up in your chair with your back straight and your head up. This posture opens up your throat and stomach making you sound clearer, articulate, confident and professional.

If you have a difficult client or an important telephone call, stand up and walk around during the call. You'll feel more powerful and this will transfer into your voice. Most importantly, find a style that suits your personality.

DEALING WITH REJECTION

While in the office have you ever been offered a drink when you're not thirsty, and replied "No, thank you"? Were you rejecting the person or the drink? Have you ever offered a drink to someone in the office and they said "No, thank you?" Did you feel rejected? Probably not because you accept they're not thirsty, just as you're not thirsty sometimes.

There are times when your client isn't buying for whatever reason and they say "no" to you. It's important not to take it personally.

They're not rejecting you or your product for any reason other than the fact that they're not buying at that point in time.

More experienced sales people and entrepreneurs understand this and they realise "no" really means "not right now". At some point in the future, your client will be buying and they will need your services. What determines your success is whether you have the ability to keep calling back. Eventually you'll call at the right time, send an email at the right time, or build such a good relationship that they call you.

In a way it's that simple, but from experience we know how mentally difficult sales can actually be. That's why it's so important to run a business in something you're absolutely passionate about. We've been there when every telephone call is followed by another "no". It can be demoralising and you can start to question whether it is your ability as an entrepreneur. Remember that if you're following the techniques in this book, it's not you, or your ability.

How you see rejection is largely down to your mentality and life experiences. Top entrepreneurs know they're not going to be successful 100 percent of the time. Instead they see it as a challenge. Winning first place in a competition, a football game, or any type of event is only rewarding if you've had to work hard for it. It says you've had to fight and crawl through fire to get there. Top entrepreneurs love to hear "no", because they love the challenge of turning it into a "yes".

There are techniques to help you with any mental barriers you're facing. Try to turn it into a game and see how many clients you can get to say "no" before you get a "yes". If you're new to selling, jump in the deep end and face your fears by making as many calls as you can. The best way to conquer your fear is to face it head on.

Once you've had a few rejections the impact will be less mentally draining, as your mind adapts to your environment.

See rejection as a good thing, because it'll make you a stronger person. Colonel Sanders, the founder of Kentucky Fried Chicken (KFC) was turned down 1000 times before he got a "yes". In sales you may hear "no" more than 1000 times before you get a "yes". We did, so don't let it knock you. Return to this section often to reconfirm you're doing your job well. Realise that you're good at your job and eventually the hard work will pay off. Keep telling yourself this every day.

Now while it's impossible to close a meeting or sell your services on every phone call you will at some point need to evaluate the situation if you're not getting any meetings or sales. It could because you need sales training, it could be the wrong time of year, or it could be because there isn't a need for your products or services. However, don't jump to these conclusions after one day of selling on the phone or even two weeks of selling on the phone. You would need to do this over a period of time.

FINDING CLIENTS

I n order for you to sell your products you'll have to find clients to sell to. This is harder than it sounds, because not everyone is a client and it'll be a specific person within a company. Therefore, you'll need to know that a company exists and the right person within the company. In this section we'll look at ways to find clients.

DRIVE ROUND

After visiting clients, take some time to drive round the area and look at surrounding companies. There could be other companies worth marketing. Look out for commercial vehicles and advertising boards for any companies that may need your services. If you're driving, have a colleague, friend or family member write down the names for you. If you're alone, use an audio recording device such as a Dictaphone and say the names of the companies. Many mobile telephones now have a recording facility. When you get back to the office you can use the Internet to find the contact details of any potential clients within those companies. If you're in a situation where you can't do a drive round, use Google Maps street view to do a virtual drive round.

BUSINESS DIRECTORIES

Check business directories both online and offline for companies that could use your services. When working a particular area, we like to get a list of all companies in that area and go through each one to see if they're worth putting on our marketing list.

LINKEDIN

LinkedIn is a quick and easy way to find new clients. When logged into LinkedIn, go to a search engine, such as Google, and type in: LinkedIn + Area + Job Title - (replace 'area' with the area you are looking to do business development in and 'job title' for the position that your client would hold). Then press 'enter'. This should bring up results of people in your area with that job title.

NEWSPAPERS

Read local newspapers and online news every morning to identify any new businesses that have been set up. Reading local news is also a good way of identifying any change that is happening. The news doesn't have to be a negative change.

WHO ELSE SHOULD YOU BE SPEAKING TO?

Depending on your services you can have multiple clients within a company, and once you have earned the trust of your client it is fine to ask:

- "Who else should I be speaking to within your company?"

You might be speaking to the top person, but the mangers below them may be in charge of their own suppliers. You might be speaking to a manager who has someone above them, or a colleague next to them who uses or needs services like yours. Keep asking questions and keep asking for things.

SALES VISTS AND MEETINGS

A successful recruitment consultant once told us that "It's very difficult to sell over the telephone. Instead sell the meeting, so you can sell in person". That was good advice, but not 100 percent true. In large complex sales, meeting with a client is probably a logical step in the relationship-building process. However, in some sales environments clients may buy without ever having met the entrepreneur. This is especially true if they're buying in distress which means they need the product immediately. Therefore, you can indeed sell successfully over the telephone without ever meeting your client. However, we state again this all depends on what you're selling and your client. Some prefer not to have a meeting while other clients might not work with you unless they've met you.

Always measure your sales-to-meeting ratio. We know a sales professional who analysed his sales-to-meetings ratio and found that every sale he made was from clients he never met. Every client he had met had never given him a sale. He had been on about 20 meetings which, on average, took two hours including travel. That totalled up to 40 hours, which is equivalent to a week of selling over the telephone. Now, this could be because he didn't present himself strongly in meetings, or for some other reason. Regardless, it's an important ratio to be aware of.

187

We're not against meetings, we're against being counter-productive. There are some clients who feel a meeting is essential before they work with you. For the rest of this section we'll concentrate on these clients. A meeting with a client can help you progress the relationship forward. It's an opportunity for you to learn more about the client and for the client to learn more about you. You'll better understand their personality and how they act. At the same time, you'll get a feel for the culture and environment of the company as well as their problems. This should help you provide the right service for them. In this section we'll show you how to book meetings with clients and how to structure a sales meeting with your client.

GETTING MEETINGS

We're going to let you into the biggest secret for getting your clients to meet with you. The secret is to ask. It really is that simple. Just ask if you can visit your client and wait for their response. At the end of your telephone call, if you've established your client's needs, reconfirm their needs and sell the benefits of your services. Then close the call with the following script:

You: (after you've reconfirmed their needs and your benefits) The next logical step would be for us to meet. Do you have a spare 15 minutes that I could come out and see you?

Once you've asked, stop talking and wait for their response.

Client: Okay.
You: I have my diary open, when would be best for you?
Client: Friday at 2pm.
You: That sounds good to me. Do you have an email address and I'll email you a calendar reminder.
Client: Yes, it's...
You: Thank you, I look forward to seeing you then.

Keep it as basic as that and you can't go far wrong. Of course you'll come up against many objections, but instead of dwelling on the rejection acknowledge it and then move past it. For example:

Client: I'm not in the market right now.
You: No problem, hopefully I'll get to meet you at some stage in the future.

If you've already spoken to your client previously and have built up some connection, then try the following approach:

You: Hi <client's name>. It's <your name> from <your company>. How are you?
Client: Hi. I'm good thanks. How can I help you?
You: We've spoken a couple of times on the telephone and I'd like to be more than just a voice. Do you have a spare 15 minutes that I could come out and see you?

If your client says "yes" then get a date in the diary. If they say "no", acknowledge it and then move past it. Ask more questions to build rapport and gather intelligence. For example:

You: No problem, hopefully I'll get to meet you at some stage in the future. While I've got you on the telephone, you said last time that your current suppliers were constantly late, how is this affecting you at the moment?

Or:

You: No problem, hopefully I'll get to meet you at some stage in the future. While I've got you on the telephone, I just want to run our end of month discounts by you.

Alternatively you can try and handle the objection and persuade the client that a meeting would be beneficial to them, which we will go through later in this section.

BLOCK BOOKING

Try to block book your meetings in specific areas. This will save you time, time that you'll want to use for selling. Block booking your meetings is when you visit several clients in one day who are all located in close proximity. That means they can be in the same company or in neighbouring companies. Some clients don't want to meet you when they're not in the market for your services. They feel that it's a waste of their time and your time. However, they'll be more inclined to meet you if they know you're in the area or in the same building; therefore, if you get a sales visit try to get visits with surrounding clients off the back of it. Try the following script.

You: Hi <client's name>. It's <your name> from <company>.
Client: Hi.
You: On <date> I'm visiting <company> which is just down the road from you. I should be finished about <time>. Since I'm in the area would you be free for a quick meeting?

OBJECTION HANDLING FOR GETTING MEETINGS

When you try to book meetings with your clients some will give you objections. In some cases clients give you objections just to see how you handle them. In this section we'll go over some common objections clients give to avoid a meeting, and what you can say to handle the objection.

You: Hi <client's name>. It's <your name> from <your company>. Are you well?
Client: Hi, I'm good thanks. How can I help you?

You: We've spoken a couple of times on the telephone and I'd like to be more than just a voice. Do you have a spare 15 minutes that I could come out and see you?

Client: I don't think that's necessary at the moment. We don't have a need.

You: I was hoping you would say that. It's actually best we meet when you don't have a need. It'll save you time in the long run, for when a need arises I'll be ready and prepared for you.

Another line you can use:

You: I'm interested in your company and while there's nothing happening now, I genuinely want to know you and understand your business for when you do have a need.

Another common objection from clients is:

Client: I'm too busy.

Some possible ways to handle this objection:

You: I'll only take up 10 minutes of your time.

You: I'll just pop in briefly.

You: I know you are that's why a meeting now is best. It'll save you more time in the future when you're just as busy but also needing to solve the problem of...

You: Why don't we book a meeting far ahead when you have more time, let's say in a couple of months? It really will be brief. I have my diary open, do you have a less busy time available?

PREPARING FOR THE MEETING

"By failing to prepare, you are preparing to fail." – Benjamin Franklin

The first thing you should do is check whether you have the correct address of where your meeting is. Some companies have multiple sites, which can be confusing. Always clarify this on the telephone when you book the meeting. However, if you haven't, and you're hesitant to call back, you can call the receptionist and they will clarify this with you.

Next you should find a colleague who can go to the sales meeting with you. A sales meeting is always better with two people for several reasons:

- Your colleague can take notes while you communicate with the client
- The meeting is less intimidating for you if there are two of you
- You can review the meeting afterwards to ensure nothing was missed

We understand that you may not have a colleague, so don't let this put you off.

Plan your route to the client beforehand, so you're not late. If you expect you're going to be late call the client and let them know. While you should do everything in your power to be on time sometimes unexpected events happen. Clients usually don't mind if you're late as long as you have the manners to inform them in advance. If you don't inform them they'll spend that time waiting for you reflecting on how poor your service must be. You'll also become extremely stressed, which will affect your behaviour in the meeting and no one wants to work with a person who's stressed.

Now you know exactly how you're going to get to your client you'll want to know more about your client and their company. You should:

- Speak to your colleagues who are dealing, or have dealt with the company and ask them for any information you should know. Clients dislike having to repeat basic information about the company to different people in the same company.
- Check the company's website so that you fully understand their services and products.
- Type the name of the company into a search engine, such as Google, to see if there is anything in the news. Sometimes your visit can fall around the time of a merger, acquisition, growth or even around the time of job threats.
- Do a search on your client on Google and LinkedIn to iden-tify any information about their professional background or interests. You can use this information to ask them more per-sonal rapport-building questions.

If you find out any interesting information about the company, or you're unsure about anything, bring it up in the meeting. There have been times when we've had to ask exactly what the company does as it wasn't explicit on their website. The client will usually agree it's confusing.

First impressions are extremely important. As soon as the client sees you they'll start to make a visual judgement about whether you have the ability to work with them. The rule is always to dress better than you think you should, or one level above. The reason that dressing smartly is important is that your clients subconsciously perceive a well-dressed person as a higher quality product. They will subconsciously feel that if you can take care of yourself you can also take care of them. Imagine if you were going for surgery and in your consultation the surgeon turned up looking scruffy. You'd probably question whether they cared and whether you were in safe hands.

Dressing smart is only halfway there. Ensure your hair is neatly cut and that you have brushed your teeth. If you haven't had time to brush your teeth and have had to resort to chewing gum, lose the chewing gum before you meet the client. There is nothing more unattractive than chewing gum in front of your client.

There are several things you should take with you to every sales meeting:

- Several business cards
- Several working pens
- A clean A4 writing pad
- Your company's sales literature
- Terms of business
- A sample of your product
- Testimonials
- Case studies or a portfolio

People like to touch and feel things before they buy. It's why clothes shops have changing rooms and why you're encouraged to take cars on a test drive. Once you've tried the product you're more likely to make a purchase. If you're selling a service it can be difficult for your clients to get a feel for it. Therefore, by taking business cards and company literature you make your business more tangible for your client.

SALES MEETING STRUCTURE

The best sales professionals don't sell, instead they consult their clients. The following sales meeting structure will help your meetings feel more consultative rather than like a sales pitch:

1.   *Introduction* - making the client feel at ease
2.   *Questioning and consultation* - learning about the client and their problems
3.   *Reconfirming* - demonstrating you've listened
4.   *Selling / product demonstration* - showing them how you can solve their problems
5.   *Closing the meeting* - asking for their business, another meeting or some progression.

Introduction

The introduction is when you first meet the client and you start to make them feel at ease. You might meet the client in the reception area and then walk with them to their office. It's important to remember that from this point the introduction has already started. In other cases you might be taken to their office by an assistant. In this case your introduction with the client starts when you're introduced to them by the assistant.

However, your client may ask the assistant what they thought of you, so treat the assistant how you would treat your client. Always greet the client with a firm handshake and a smile. Earlier in the book we discussed how clients like you to stick to business. However, it can be awkward to go straight into business if you've met your client in the reception area and you need to travel together to their office. You can make the conversation both personal and business-related at the same time. For example:

You: I noticed on your LinkedIn profile you used to work in America. That must have been fun. How did that come about?

This has an impact on several different levels: firstly, it shows you've prepared for the meeting; secondly, most people love to talk about themselves; thirdly, while it's personal it's still business-related, so the client won't feel threatened.

Another example:

You: Thank you for meeting with me today. You must be so busy with the recent expansion.

Don't fall into the trap of looking around the room for an interesting topic to discuss, such as a photograph or a golf trophy. They'll have met many sales professionals who've wasted their time talking about non business-related subjects. By keeping your introductions business-related, but on a personal level, you can guide them into the next stage of the meeting with ease, which is questioning and consulting.

Questioning and consultation

At this stage you'll ask the client questions about their business, their needs and their problems. Your client should be doing most of the talking while you do most of the listening. Ask them lots of open questions to get them to open up, but ask closed questions to get specific answers. Save the closed questions for the later part of the meeting. Reread the section on questioning and SPIN(r) selling at the beginning of this section of the book to refresh your memory.

If the client has already given you specific information on the telephone, don't ask the same questions again. However, you should reconfirm what they've told you over the telephone by reflecting it back to them and asking them if the information you have is correct. This will demonstrate that you've been listening to them. Remember to maintain eye contact, because we perceive people who cannot hold eye contact as untrustworthy and unconfident. In between writing notes keep looking up at your client. It's better to get your colleague to write the bulk of the notes while you stay fully engaged in the conversation.

Reconfirming

This stage involves reconfirming what the client has said to you. It shows the client you've listened and understood what they've said. It also enables you to correct anything. To guide the client into this stage you might say something like the following:

You: Okay, so you're dissatisfied with your current supplier because 40% of their deliveries are late...

At this point the client will be nodding and agreeing with you, which puts you in an ideal position for actually selling.

Selling

This is the only stage when you actually sell. While you'll have your standard pitch you'll want to tailor part of it to match what the client has told you during the questioning and consultation stage. Ensure you sell the benefits of your recruitment services, for example:

You: Okay, so you're dissatisfied with your current supplier because 40% of their deliveries are late. This is causing bottle necks and you're losing customers as a result of these delays. We guarantee all our deliveries to be on time and we're so efficient at doing this we base our payment by results...

Once you've pitched your services to the client, you'll want to close the meeting. Before you do this make sure there are no barriers or reservations by asking the client if there are any barriers to taking the next logical step.

Closing the meeting

There are two situations the meeting will be taking place under: one, the client is buying; two, the client isn't buying.

Here are some example closes for each situation:

The client isn't buying:

- How would you feel about working with me when a need arises?
- I can see that you're not ready yet. How about we meet again when you've worked things out?

The client is buying:

- The next logical step is to place an order.
- The next logical step would be to send you a proposal.

Remember, closing is simply asking your client for their business or some progression and then keeping quiet until your client speaks first.

SALES MEETING BODY LANGUAGE

Body language is very important in sales. You need to be aware of your body language as well as the client's. The subject is in-depth and there are entire books about body language. While I think being able to read body language is vital to being good at sales, it can be over analysed. To prevent over analysis we'll just touch on the subject here.

Your Body Language

This is body language you should adopt for your sales meetings.

Acknowledging body language - Sales is all about listening. To demonstrate you're listening nod your head and say things such as: yes, okay, I see, really, uh-huh.

Mirroring - If you observe couples and friends you'll notice their body language is often similar to one another. They subconsciously mirror each other's body language and gestures. When people mirror each other's body language they're saying "we're the same". You can create this feeling by mirroring the body language of your client. We recommend you do this a quarter to half-way into the meeting and don't do it too much, as it needs to be subtle. Judge what you should mirror, as we've been in meetings where the client has sat back with their arms behind their head and their feet on the desk. This probably wouldn't have been good to mirror.

Confident body language - Confident body language is when we open up our bodies and expose ourselves. No, not your private parts, although that would take a great deal of confidence to do in a client meeting, let's leave that one off the list. In simplistic terms if a tortoise is confident that no predators are around it will have all its vulnerable body parts exposed. However, if it feels in danger it will hide in its shell. Translating this into humans, you should keep your body language open by keeping your head up, shoulders back, arms uncrossed and legs uncrossed.

The following is body language you should avoid in your sales meeting:

Low confidence - As we stated earlier, when animals feel in danger their confidence levels drop and they retreat into themselves like the tortoise. This is to protect vulnerable body parts, make themselves smaller to be less of a target and to hide from their predators. Humans also display this type of body language when they lack confidence. They turtle their head into their shoulders, hide behind their hands when they talk, cross their arms and cross their legs. Avoid all these types of body language and try to open out more. The very act of opening your body language will make you feel confident, because your emotions follow what your body does.

No eye contact – We mentioned earlier that people who cannot hold eye contact are perceived as untrustworthy. It also shows a lack of confidence. Keep looking your client in the eye. It's fine and natural to break eye contact and you should, because too much eye contact is threatening. So what's the right balance? Keep looking your client in the eye, but break eye contact to write notes and during conversations.

Their Body Language – Throughout the meeting you'll want to assess their body language, so that you can read their mood and adapt your questioning.

Barriers – When we don't like something we try to put a barrier between us and what we don't like. A classic example is hiding behind a pillow when watching a horror film. When people don't like someone or what someone says they'll cross their arms and lean away. During your meeting if you see this display of behaviour you'll need to overcome the objection before moving forward. Try a different tactic to get them to open up. However, be aware of your environment, if the room is cold your client is likely to cross their arms and legs to keep warm rather than because you said something.

Clock watching and fidgeting – If your client keeps fidgeting, looking at their watch or the clock on the wall, they're likely saying I've got somewhere else to be. Never assume, so to ensure it's not a passing glance or an uncomfortable chair ask them how they're doing for time, if they need to go they'll tell you. It's not good to rush your pitch and leave. It can sound desperate, the same as when you rush what you need to say on the telephone. The client won't be listening properly either. Instead, explain how important this meeting is to you and how much you'd value working with them, so ask them if you can rearrange for a later date.

Buying signs – The client is buying into you when they display gravity-defying body language. This will look like steepled hands, raised eyebrows, sitting forward, nodding of the head, smiling and verbally agreeing with you.

Closing body language – When you close a client and ask for their business using any of the closing techniques we discussed earlier, the client is likely to squirm in their seat and shift around. This isn't necessarily a bad thing. Stay relaxed and stay silent. Let them speak first.

NEGOTIATING

Negotiating is always the most fun part of selling. The key is to make everyone feel like they've won. When you and your client both win you help to build a stronger relationship. Always think long term. If you begin negotiating and you win, but the client feels they've lost, then they're unlikely to ever to do business with you again. If you negotiate and you lose while the client wins you'll be feeling as if your skills aren't valued, and you won't make money.

Our first rule for negotiating is: try to avoid negotiating. It's best if the client accepts your terms of business. We've seen sales professionals, especially new ones, say to their client: "Our fee rate is 20% of the cost, but our fees are negotiable." Avoid making statements like this, because you're inviting your client to negotiate.

Our second rule for negotiating is: always start high. You can always lower your fee, but you can never go higher once you have given the client a number. There is also a psychological effect of going in high, because it makes any lower number feel like a win to your client.

Our third rule for negotiating is: never speak first. The first to speak is the first to lose. If you feel that negotiating is the only option, when a client asks you to lower the fee rate, never give them a number first. Remember, once you give them a number you can never go back up. Instead, bounce it back to them and ask them what they had in mind. When you ask the client to give you a number, you'll hear in their voice that you've put them on the back foot. The reason they're on the back foot is because they fear that their offer will be rejected. They'll typically say something like: "I was thinking about X%". You can now take this offer if it's a good offer, or reject it by asking for a higher fee rate. You may even say something such as: "I'm sorry, but I couldn't possibly work at that rate, due to the amount of work involved. I could do X percent."

Our fourth rule for negotiating is: don't care about the deal. This sounds like a weird rule, but hear us out. Have you ever noticed that when you're in a relationship you get more offers from other people? Do you notice when you're in a job you get approached by people for other jobs? Do you notice when you have lots of work on you then get more work much more easily when you do sales?

This happens for two main reasons. The first is the law of being relaxed. When you have lots of work on, your sales calls have a relaxed carefree tone. This is because you don't need the business. When you have a partner, you're more relaxed around other people and you're not trying to impress. This makes you more attractive to other people. The next time you're in a bar or club observe people in the room. You'll be able to tell who's single and who's not.

The second reason is due to the law of scarcity. People want more of the things there are less of. In 2003, British Airways announced they'd no longer be operating the twice daily Concorde flight from London to New York, as it had become uneconomical to run. The very next day sales increased. Nothing had changed about the service of the flight it had simply become a scarce resource, so people wanted it more.

Negotiating has the same psychology. If you're dealing with only one client and you're desperate for a deal, the client will sense this and go in for the kill, because they subconsciously sense your vulnerability. However, if you have lots of business going on and the client offers you a ridiculously lower fee, you're more likely say "Thank you, but no thank you." Your relaxed and confident attitude will no doubt put them off trying to negotiate in the first place, or negotiating too hard.

Therefore, always play with a poker face and never show your cards. Even if this is the only deal you have on the table, act as if you're in demand and your time is scarce.

Our fifth rule for negotiating is: never give anything without something in return. If your client asks you to lower your fee rate, and says they absolutely cannot go any higher, you should ask for exclusivity, or to be their preferred supplier for future work. Try to see that everything has a value during your negotiation. If they take something away, you ask them to replace it with something of equal value. You might say something, such as: "If you can agree to give me exclusivity, I'll agree to drop the rate to 15%."

Our sixth rule for negotiating is: hide your emotions. Professional buyers will try to reduce the fee as low as possible. Don't take this personally it's just a game and not an attack on your services. Nothing bad can come from negotiating, even if the deal doesn't go through there are plenty more out there. Therefore, you have nothing to be nervous or worried about. The best way not to sound nervous is to keep your sentences short and direct, for example:

Client: I can only work with you at 15%.
Nervous Entrepreneur: Erm... let me check with my partner and I'll get back to you, or Erm... I'm not sure, can we not work at 18%?
Confident Entrepreneur: I can only work at 20%.

If you wanted to sound more empathetic: I wish I could, but I cannot go lower than 20%.

Confident Entrepreneur: I can go down to 19%, if you agree to...
Confident Entrepreneur: I couldn't respect myself if I dropped my fees to 15%.

Our seventh rule for negotiating is: walk away if the deal is unprofitable. If the client is squeezing your profit or demanding unrealistic expectations then you should walk away and find a more profitable client.

In summary our seven rules for negotiation are:

- Try to avoid negotiating
- Always start high
- Never speak first
- Don't care about the deal
- Never give anything without something in return
- Hide your emotions
- Walk away if the deal is unprofitable

WRITTEN SALES

If you want to make sales, not only do you have to be good in verbal sales, but also in your writing. Your ability to sell through the written form will dramatically increase your sales. Everything you write is a sell, every email, every e-shot and every blog. In this section we'll show you how to improve your sales writing skills, we'll concentrate on emails, but the principles can be taken and adapted to other sales literature such as brochures.

Firstly, we want to draw a distinction between marketing and selling with closing. You're always marketing and selling, but this doesn't always lead to a close. When you email a client something as simple as:

Hi Steven,

Thank you for your time on the telephone earlier. I've attached a news article that I thought you'd be interested in with regards to our conversation.

Kind regards,

Andrew Leong

You're marketing, selling and consulting, but you're not trying to close a deal. This is a simple way to connect with and build a relationship with your client. It shows them you're interested in them, and that you're more than just a person who's trying to take their money. You don't need to close a deal on every occasion for you to be good at sales.

USE AIDA

AIDA is a well-known acronym used in marketing and advertising to help with copywriting. It describes a common list of events that may occur when your client engages with your sales literature. You should check that your sales literature contains the following elements:

A = **Attention:** attract the attention of the client.
I = **Interest:** raise your client's interest by writing about information that is relevant to them, potentially solves their problems and offers the advantages and benefits of your services.
D = **Desire:** using specific words and language patterns will create desire.
A = **Action:** make it extremely obvious what the client has to do next if they want to progress forward, and make it as simple as possible.

GET TO THE POINT

There is a common misconception that if you provide lots of information with facts and figures the client will be so impressed that they just have to buy. Instead, what happens is the client will see a massive email that they won't bother reading and it'll be deleted. If by some chance they do read it, by the time they get to the bottom of the email they'll have lost the point.

For that reason, you need to get to the point in as few words as possible. Steve Jobs, the late CEO of Apple, was a master at this. When we were younger we used a device called a Walkman to listen to music while on the go. It was bulky and ugly. We had to carry several tapes that stored the music. Each tape could only hold about 12 songs, so it was very inconvenient. Then Steve Jobs created the iPod, a highly sophisticated device for storing and listening to music. It did away with tapes and CDs and it looked good. On selling the iPod, Steve Jobs did it beautifully with the following phrase:

"1,000 songs in your pocket."

No technical jargon, just straight to the point. Keep this in mind when you write your emails and e-shots. Get to the point in as few words as possible. Clients are more likely to read your emails if they're short and they can see the whole message on their screen without having to scroll down.

EMAIL STRUCTURE

Different emails have different structures and as you build rapport with your client your emails may become less formal, but no less professional. In other words, you'll write more conversationally.

However, to begin with it's always best practice to write your emails in a structured way. If we return back to the power of three your emails should be structured as follows:

1.   Strong introduction or opening
2.   Main body
3.   Close / call-to-action

Following this structure while keeping your emails short will make them look professional. This will attract the recipient and persuade them to read.

GOOD ENGLISH

You don't need to have a degree in English to be good at writing sales literature. You can massively improve your English language with just a few simple tips. The famous writer George Orwell states six rules for effective writing:

1. Never use a metaphor, simile, or other figure of speech which you are used to seeing in print.
2. Never use a long word where a short one will do.
3. If it is possible to cut a word out, always cut it out.
4. Never use the passive where you can use the active.
5. Never use a foreign phrase, a scientific word, or a jargon word if you can think of an everyday English equivalent.
6. Break any of these rules sooner than say anything outright barbarous.

WAYS TO IMPROVE YOUR WRITTEN SALES

One of the best ways to improve your writing is to copy others until you find your own style. You'll only want to copy those who are successful, so ask your friends, colleagues, family members or anyone that ever gets sold to for copies of all the e-shots and emails that they have ever received that caused them to engage or buy.

Look at each email and e-shot to see if they have any trends. Look at the use of language, the structure, the length and the use of formatting. Look to see if the e-shots used any numbers and percentages. Then see how many times numbers were used. Were they used lots or were they used sparingly?

You should notice some common features, but also some unique features that you can start adopting in your writing. The next time you buy something save the description or the sell, even if it's just a customer review that convinced you to buy. Then analyse the writing and see if it could be implemented in your sales writing.

EXAMPLE EMAILS

We always learn best when we see an example. In this section we'll write some basic examples that you can use to adapt into you own style. We've specifically chosen these emails, because they got a reply from clients. In this case we've used recruitment as the business for the examples.

Introduction email after your first telephone call:

Hi <name>,

Thank you for your time on the telephone earlier. As discussed, I'm a specialist recruitment consultant working for a company called <company name>.

<company name> has been around for <X> number of years and we offer a tailored and professional recruitment service to our clients.

I have attached a brochure for your information, but you can also find out more by visiting <company website>.

I will call you towards the end of the week to collect your thoughts, but if I can help you beforehand, please, do not hesitate to contact me via telephone on: <number> or via email <email address>

Kind regards

<your name>

When you cannot get the client on the telephone:

Hi <name>,

We've not spoken before my name is <your name> and I work for a company called

<your company>. I've not been able to catch you on the telephone.

I'm a specialist recruitment consultant working for... based in your local area.

I'm keen to work with you and wondered what the best way is to communicate with you?

Kind regards,

<your name>

Email after a Promotional Campaign

We once sent out a promotional brochure with a chocolate bar called a Kit Kat. We then sent this email to the clients we couldn't get on the telephone:

Subject: How was your Kit Kat?

Hi <name>,

We've not spoken before my name is <your name> and I work for a company called

<your company>. I've not been able to catch you on the telephone yet to introduce myself more formally.

I sent you a package recently and I hope you enjoyed the con-

tents. As you know, I'm a specialist recruitment consultant working for... based in your local area.

I would relish the opportunity to work with you. What would be the best way to communicate with you?

Kind regards,

<your name>

SALES WORDS

There are certain words that you can use to make your e-shots and emails more persuasive. Type into an Internet search engine: "sales words" and you'll get several websites offering you a comprehensive list of words that you can refer to. Here are a few sales words that you can use:

- Accomplish
- Achieve
- Award-winning
- Benefit
- Best
- Clear-cut
- Completive
- Complimentary
- Dependable
- Effective
- Experienced
- Ensure
- Excited
- First-class
- Free
- Guarantee
- Improve

- New
- Now
- Proven
- Quality
- Qualified
- Results
- Safe
- Simple
- Top
- Unique
- Winner
- You
- Your

Use these words intelligently and don't fall into the habit of using the same words too much otherwise your messages will lose their effect. There are online thesauruses that you can use to search for alternative words. If you prefer a physical thesaurus, buy one and keep it on your desk.

When writing an email to a client watch out for how many times you use the words "I", "I'm" and "I've" versus "you" and "your". If you use the word "I" too much the email becomes about you. The email should always be about your client. You'll want to make the reader feel special, as if you're talking to them personally. To achieve this use the words "you" and "your" more than "I".

PROOFREADING

You have a busy and demanding job running your own business. You're running round making telephone calls, visiting clients, and building a business. No matter how confident you are as a writer you'll on occasion feel short of time. While established clients do turn a blind eye to the occasional spelling mistake or typo, an email to a new client must be perfect. This is because it's their first impression of you.

When you're exhausted and you feel that you've no time to spare, you'll still have to write e-shots, emails and blogs. This can lead to you rushing your written sales work. Do stop and slow down, because once you click the send button you can't get it back. Always get someone to check your work and if necessary save your work and come back to it with a fresh pair of eyes.

OUTSOURCING YOUR SALES LITERATURE

If you want to you can outsource the creation of your sales literature for very little cost. You can find online freelance writers who will write sales literature from as little as £6 upwards. You'll also find online people who can write your emails, sales literature, blogs and anything else you need.

Why would you pay for someone else to write sales literature for you? If you're not a natural writer it can sometimes take several hours to write a good piece of work. You might just be extremely busy and not have the time to write something with passion. Therefore, for £6+ it would be worth someone else doing it, so you can either spend more time on other tasks you're better at or more time on your social life.

Door-To-Door Selling

D oor-to-door selling is a sales method whereby a sales professional or entrepreneur walks from house to house or business
to business trying to sell a product or service. Before we begin,
we want to be clear that to be successful at door-to-door selling it
doesn't mean you need to make a sale at every door. While a sale is
the aim, clients may not be in a position to buy, but because you've
knocked they're more likely to bear you in mind when they do need
to make a purchase.

Door-to-door selling is a highly effective method of sales, and it's
highly effective because many people won't do it, or give up after
their first experience. It does take guts and perseverance to make
door-to-door selling work. For example, if you're selling building
services such as brick laying you may knock on the door of 50
houses; 20 of them may not answer the door, 25 may politely say
they're not interested, four people might be rude or slam the door
on you, but one gives you work.

That could be thousands of pounds worth of work, and then future
work from referrals.

Billionaire entrepreneur John Paul DeJoria launched his hair care company selling products door-to-door while living in his car. At the time of writing, according to Forbes, DeJoria is worth $2.8 billion.

In this section we're going to give you three door-to-door sales strategies that you can adopt depending on your business and personality. If you're shy you can simply try the more subtle approaches and then progress to the more "outgoing" approach.

Whichever approach you take, you'll need to show confidence and enthusiasm regardless of how you feel or what you have experienced previously. That means on the last door you knock at you need to be just as confident as the first door. You're likely to experience rudeness, but you mustn't let this alter your state or rock your confidence. Their behaviour is their problem, not yours. To portray confidence never apologise or act as if you've disturbed someone, for example by saying: "Sorry to bother you, I just wanted to...". The words "sorry", "bother", and "just" make that sentence lack confidence.

Remember, selling is about asking questions to find the client's requirements. If the client has no requirements at this time, thank them for their time and move on. Always ensure that you address the decision maker. For example, if you're selling home insurance then the decision maker will likely be the home owner. However, if you're selling cosmetics, it could be anyone in the house.

Approach One: Door-To-Door Marketing

We've called this 'door-to-door marketing' because the emphasis is on the marketing rather than the selling. In this approach you would simply knock on the door, introduce yourself, provide the client with some sales literature such as a leaflet or a business card and ask them if it's something they're interested in. If the client is interested you would then ask them questions to find their needs. If they're not interested thank them for their time and move on.

Approach Two: The Call Back Approach

In this method you post a catalogue or brochure of your products or services along with your business card. On each catalogue attach a handwritten note introducing yourself and explaining that in the next couple of days you'll be knocking to collect the catalogue. Now the client expects your visit, and if they want to purchase something in the catalogue they could mark it off on an order sheet.

When you knock and ask for the catalogue you can ask if anything interested them. Remember to ask for the decision maker before asking for the catalogue back.

Approach Three: Traditional Door-To-Door Selling

In this approach, you're knocking on the door, asking for the decision maker and then using questions to identify needs. This is different from the first two approaches which are gentle and to some extent rely on your sales literature. In this approach the client may not realise they have a need until you've asked them thought-provoking questions. Obviously this approach requires a lot more skill, which you can develop by progressing upwards from the first two approaches.

All the questioning techniques that are used for door-to-door sales are the same as telephone sales, which are explained earlier in the chapter: Telephone Sales.

SALES SUMMARY

While this section of the book is quite extensive, it still only touches the surface of sales. However, it'll provide you with enough tools and techniques to win business. Like everything else in life, selling is best learnt through practice.

PART 4

MARKETING

ADVERTISING

I n this chapter we're going to look at some of the different offline advertising opportunities available to businesses and those which may, or may not work for your company.

"Nobody counts the number of ads you run; they just remember the impression you make." – Bill Bernbach

You can have the best product or service in the world but if no one knows it exists you won't have a business for long. Advertising is important; it can potentially make or break a business so you need to understand how to do it right. Advertising strategies that work well for one organisation could bring little or no results for an organisation in a different industry. There is no 'one size fits all' method of advertising so we're going to look at many of the offline advertising methods available and evaluate them so you can decide if they are suitable for your business.

Advertising will only work if you do it consistently and don't rely on a small number of channels. If you embrace a good mixture of advertising and continue to push your business through these methods consistently your business will start to be noticed.

Due to 21st century online advertising being at the forefront of most people's minds many are missing out on more traditional methods which can still be very effective, and in many cases relatively inexpensive. We'll look at some of the methods available starting with the least expensive.

SHOP WINDOW ADVERTISING

Putting an advertisement up in a local shop window is an extremely cost-effective way to advertise your business, it can cost as little as £0.50 a week. Shop window advertising will be more, or less effective depending on the type of business you run; think about what people will look in shop windows for. If you are advertising home repairs, cleaning, car repairs etc. this type of service can yield great results from shop window advertising. However, if your business is a digital marketing company or a financial firm your prospective clients probably won't respond to such an advertisement.

If you decide this form of advertising may be worthwhile for your business don't just place an advert in any shop. Do your research by taking the time to observe which shops have the highest footfall and which shops your customers go to. It can also be worthwhile to think about whether your advertisements should go in wealthier or less wealthy areas, or perhaps a mix of both depending on your product or service.

With amounts such as £0.50 a week many wouldn't think about negotiating but it's very unlikely that you'll see great results from one advertisement in one shop window. To get results you're going to need adverts in a number of shops, and 50p every week in every shop can start to add up. The most effective way to negotiate is to offer a lower weekly amount for a long-term advertisement e.g. 3 months at £0.50 should cost £6, if you offer £4 and settle with £4.50 - £5 after negotiating, the savings can quickly add up. If you place ads in 20+ shop windows, which is what we would say is necessary to see a good level of response, the savings will quickly accumulate over the year. Savings allow you to spend on other complementary forms of advertising.

If you think that this form of advertising could be for right for your business be sure to: research the areas where you will be placing your adverts, negotiate a good deal, start small and evaluate the results before rolling this form of advertising out to a large number of shop windows.

LEAFLETS

Leaflets can be a very effective form of advertising for the right type of business, and this can range from window cleaners to law firms. We often see very poor-quality leaflets which have probably been produced that way to save money. We're all for saving money when it comes to business expenses, but don't mistake cost control for purchasing cheap products and services. No matter what your business is, appearance matters. Your leaflet may be the first time a customer comes in contact with your business, so poor-quality marketing material will portray your business as poor quality.

When designing your leaflets you'll want to use the skills of a graphic designer, see the 'Branding' chapter for creating your brand. Even when you have a great design, a leaflet without a great message is far less likely to produce results.

"Nobody reads ads. People read what interests them, and sometimes it's an ad"- Howard Luck Gossage.

Be different from your competitors. Give people receiving your leaflet a real reason to read it and the desire to find out more about who you are and what you do. Some of the features a good leaflet should have:

- Keep it brief, too much information will put a reader off, get your message across quickly.
- Use a headline that intrigues.
- Have a clear message, whether that is explaining what you do, and or why people should use you.
- Have a strong *call-to-action.* This means tell people exactly what to do and give them a reason for doing so, for example "Visit our website to receive <insert offer or promotion here>"
- Provide contact information; email address, website, contact phone number and physical location if applicable.
- Make sure the fonts used are easy to read, the text is a large enough size and that it's been proofread.

The printing industry is very competitive but there are still many companies charging much more than others for exactly the same product, so do your homework. Don't just go with the first person who quotes you. Ask for the specifications, in particular paper quality. A leaflet printed on cheap-looking paper may leave a poor impression so take the time to visit a printing company and see what type of paper quality you would like.

When sourcing a printing firm we always look for the most competitively priced contender who also has a track record for producing excellent quality material. For this reason we like to use eBay as the pricing is often far cheaper than going into a physical store, and we get to see feedback from past customers. If you would prefer to go to a physical store and meet a printer to strike a deal it can be a good idea to check online prices first to give you leverage when negotiating on price

Be aware that ordering a low number of flyers, such as 1,000 or less can be quite expensive; if you're happy with your design, can't see any changes happening in the near future and have the capital available, go for a larger volume order. It'll bring the cost per flyer down dramatically.

Once you have your leaflets it's time to put them to work. Make sure you speak to your council about the laws relating to leafleting within your area, as you can't go into a town or city centre and start handing them out without receiving authorisation. There are strict laws relating to leaflet distribution and very severe fines can be handed out, so make sure you receive the official green light *in writing* from the council before you hit the streets.

Going door-to-door with leaflets can be a very effective way to get your flyers in front of potential customers. Whether you're going to go door-to-door yourself or hire a company to do it for you, make sure you think about what you're doing. Who is your target audience? Where do they live? You won't have much success promoting a premium product in an area that's less likely to have residents with enough disposable income to purchase it.

The next golden rule with going door-to-door leaflet dropping is the time of day you do it. If you do it during the day most people will get home from work between 5-6pm, pick up all of their mail and put all of the flyers together and move them straight to the bin without anything more than a passing glance. If your flyers go out between 6pm - 9pm the vast majority will still end up in the bin but the key difference is that the majority of people will be picking up your flyer on its own, giving you a significantly higher chance of receiving engagement.

Leave your flyers in your car or have a good amount of them to hand when you're out and about. When you go into a shop (normally independent stores will be more receptive) to buy something ask the manager or store keeper if they would mind you leaving your flyers on show.

Success rates with flyers will be low, no matter how well you do it. Don't expect to be inundated with enquiries just because thousands have been distributed. For an enquiry, the person receiving a flyer would need your product/service at that moment in time and not already have a business that they have used before. But don't be disheartened! Although the people who see your flyers may not become a customer at that moment in time your business may now be on their radar. Staying on their radar is what will make an enquiry more likely if they need your product/service in the future.

DIRECT MAIL

Similar to flyers but with a more tailored approach is direct mail. A well-written letter sent to the right person can result in new business. For new customers this is more suited to B2B, but for existing customers selling new products you'll be able to do direct mail if you have stored your customers' contact details.

The cost of this form of advertising will be based on the volume of mail you send out. It's not just the price of a stamp but also the cost of envelopes, paper, printer ink and the time it takes to create a letter, source addresses, pack envelopes and go to the Post Office.

Many people make the mistake of creating a generic letter starting with something such as "To whom it may concern". If you're going to do direct mail, do it properly. Take time, do research and find out the name of the person you're writing to. It's time consuming but you'll be far more likely to see results. Finding the name of the person you're looking for can be done using LinkedIn (see the social media chapter for more detail) or calling and asking the receptionist who the relevant person to address your letter to would be.

In many ways, rules for the content of the letter itself will be very similar to the rules applied in the Written Sales chapter. Don't write a huge amount of content that is going to put someone off reading it at first glance. Keep your direct mail short, to the point, explain what the benefit is of using your product/service and have a clear call-to-action.

To have more people open your mail take the time to handwrite the envelope instead of using a label printer, and put a stamp on yourself instead of using a franking machine; these two simple tips will make a big difference. A letter that looks personal will stand a much greater chance of being opened compared to one that looks corporate.

If you think direct mail could be a good advertising opportunity for your business, it can be a good idea to trial it with a small number of prospective clients and gauge the results. Keep a record of who you send mail to and get in touch with them to make sure they received it and ask if they have any questions, this is covered in greater detail in the Sales chapter. Direct mail should be a part of a strategy and not used by itself. Make sure your letters are followed up with a telephone call, email, a meeting or something else so that your prospect knows and understands your business.

COMPANY CLOTHING

Wearing clothing with your company branding on is, after the initial costs of printing, free advertising every time you wear it. Businesses can also give away free company clothing to customers as a gift, resulting in more people promoting the business as they go about their day-to-day lives.

Company clothing can be a low-cost method of advertising your business. Promotional clothing can cost less than £10 per item and potentially be seen by thousands of people depending on where and how often it's worn.

Make contact with a few printers to see how much it'll cost to have your logo and/or website address printed or sewn on some polo shirts, jumpers and jackets. Again this method won't result in your phone ringing off the hook with enquiries, but it's about getting the all-important brand recognition, making potential customers on some level aware that your business exists, which over time leads to sales.

If you walk around in company clothing you may be surprised how often you're stopped by members of the public who have a query; make sure you have good quality business cards with you to hand out. We also like to ask for their phone number or email address so we can get in touch if we don't hear from them; a smart phone is ideal for this, if you don't like using this type of technology make sure you keep a pen and contact book with you.

Depending on your business the type of promotional clothing you choose will vary, options include hooded jumpers, T shirts, polo shirts and much more. Think about your line of business and what type of promotional clothing (if any) may be suitable for your business, and decide whether the investment is worth it for the exposure your business will receive.

VEHICLE ADVERTISING

If you own a vehicle, getting some advertising on it can yield great results and gain excellent exposure. How far you go with vehicle advertising will depend on your budget and your willingness to alter your vehicle; at the top end of the market vehicle wrapping and signage can run into hundreds of pounds, whilst removable magnetic adverts can be made for less than £30. Your vehicle will then be acting as an advert for you at no further additional cost and will be seen when you're driving around town, parked in the supermarket and even outside your home.

The energy drink company Red Bull has used vehicle advertising successfully for some time. The company initially decided that instead of using its whole advertising budget on expensive, more traditional forms of advertising it would go for *guerrilla* advertising tactics. Red Bull wanted to get out and be seen, actually putting its drinks in the hands of its most likely consumers by driving around in a promotional vehicle. This type of engaging creativity helped to make Red Bull one of the leading brands in energy drinks and this method is still used today. Your business may not have to be as extreme as this but think about your target consumer and how your business may appeal to them. Is there a form of advertising you could be doing with your vehicle to gain exposure?

TELEPHONE DIRECTORIES

Telephone directories aren't the dominant force of advertising they once were, far from it. Think about your line of business and the customers you have, are they the type of people who might still use a physical telephone directory? If so, even if you're not quite sure, it can be well worth placing an advertisement, particularly if your business model means that receiving one client could more than pay for the cost of the advert.

There are some fantastic deals now available due to the competitive nature of 21st century advertising with its various forms. If you're thinking about it, get on the phone to some of the directories, tell the sales staff you're interested in placing an advertisement. Discuss your needs with them, provide them with your contact details and find out the price. We will always negotiate and say that it was more expensive than we had planned, thank them for their time and say that we'll think about it; then wait for the calls offering lower prices. If and when we're happy with a quote we'll go ahead and advertise, but only then. Never let yourself be badgered into paying to advertise by a pushy sales person; before you even speak to someone decide the maximum amount you would be willing to pay for the advertisement and never go above it.

MAGAZINE AND NEWSPAPER

Magazine and newspaper advertising can be very expensive so proceed with caution. This form of advertising can be necessary for many businesses as they need the exposure that national advertising can facilitate, but if you only have the budget to run one small advertisement it may be worth thinking twice. Advertising is all about gaining awareness initially, having an advert in a newspaper or magazine is great but it needs to be done consistently in order to have a positive effect, and this can become very expensive.

As with everything, research is pivotal, speak to the company to find out the costs of advertising and ask for their print deadline dates. When you have these it's time to look at the publications, ask yourself if they are good quality, whether many people actually purchase them, how many adverts are in there and would your advertisement be lost in a sea of similar adverts?

The reason we mentioned asking for the deadline date is that this can very often be the best time to buy. Magazines and newspapers will have sales staff with targets to meet, you can get some fantastic deals on deadline day. Get in touch and explain how much you would like to spend and ask what you can get for your money. It never does any harm to ask for discounts or for them to stretch your money further, the worst they can say is no. If you're offered a quarter of a page ask if it can be made into a half page ad for the same price and don't be afraid to walk away from the deal if they say no, there are plenty of other places to spend your advertising budget.

Do remember that although a cheap price is great, if it's a cheap price in a magazine/newspaper that has a low readership then it may well be wasted money, so do your research. Think hard before you spend your cash and don't get tempted by salespeople to push up your spend with bigger and bigger adverts.

Local newspaper and magazine advertising will be considerably cheaper than the nationals but the same rules apply, just because the price is right don't jump in. Do your research and if you do decide to go ahead work smart to get the best possible price. When we have advertised in magazines we had one sales account manager who got to know us as a client who would only take a large-sized ad for a very low cost, so she would only ring when she had a big advert available and was willing to let it go for a low price on deadline day. We'd get a couple of calls a year and got some fantastic adverts out for a fraction of the usual cost.

It's important to remember that the magazine needs to be read by your target market. For example, if your company sells fast-food burgers, a national health and fitness magazine isn't going to be the best place to advertise. However, if you sell high-end fashionable clothing for men, then a magazine read by fashion-conscious men with money to spend will be appropriate.

If you do decide to spend the money on an advertisement in a newspaper or magazine, ensure that your campaign is strong. The car hire company Avis used the advertising agency 'Doyle, Dane & Bernbach' to run an extremely successful advertising campaign. It had a strong message which embodied the business and its values. It ran with:

"Avis is only No.2 in rent a cars. So why go with us? We try damned hard. (When you're not the biggest you have to.)"

The advertisement went on to say that because they weren't the biggest they had to work even harder to make sure that the customers they do have receive the very best experience. This message helped to see a turnaround of the business and shows how a strong message in advertising can have dramatic effects.

PRESS RELEASES

A press release is a written document for members of the news media to publish on their media outlet such as a newspaper or magazine. Writing a press release can give your business exposure in newspapers and/or online articles. The challenge for many is to create a press release that's genuinely interesting and worthy of being published.

Think about your business and you personally. Whether you're just starting out and have a story to tell, or if you've been established a while and something interesting has happened, writing a press release can result in free, good-quality publicity that'll portray you as an expert.

It's a good idea to start by thinking where you'd like your press release to be published, you can then tailor the content to best match what the particular outlet might be interested in publishing. You can choose to target:

- Local press and websites.
- Industry-specific magazines and websites.
- National press.

What and how you write will depend on the nature of your business, the topic you're writing about and the type of press you're targeting. Some general tips to get off to a good start with writing a press release include:

- Have a strong opening line or title that interests the reader enough to continue.
- Make sure that it's interesting to others, what's interesting to you and perhaps even your business sector might make dull reading for others.

- Keep it short and to the point, around 3-400 words is usually about right.
- Be able to quickly explain why your press release is important and deserves attention.

Sending a press release by email is the quickest and often the most effective way. Make the email subject line intriguing; journalists will receive many press releases each week, so make sure yours stands out immediately. On the following day it can be a good idea to call the journalist and ask if they received the press release, this is your opportunity to find out if it's going to press and if not, why not. If it isn't deemed worthy to go to print ask for a bit more information to enable you to write a piece next time that'll be more suitable for the outlet.

LOCAL DIRECTORIES

Door-to-door booklets containing local businesses are posted in most areas and can be an effective, low-cost way to advertise your business. However, remember to think about your business and if it fits with this type of publication. If you're a builder, painter and decorator or tradesman then this form of advertising can be really worthwhile as many home owners keep these booklets in a draw then look through them when they need something doing. Think about your business, the area the booklet is distributed in, the people reading them and come to a decision about whether this form of advertising is right for you.

TRADE SHOWS

Whatever the size of your company you should be able to find a trade show or event that you can exhibit at that is suitable for your budget. Exhibiting at trade shows and events is hugely important as it gets your business and yourself recognised by potential clients and others in the industry.

Before you book an event do your research. Spending money and taking a day out of the business to stand in an exhibition hall will be a frustrating experience if there are very few people there. Find out when the last event was organised and how many people attended.

Make sure you get the best possible price. There are usually *early bird* deals available and then last minute offers. If you have a pretty flexible schedule it can be a good idea to wait for last minute offers. If you do decide to get a last minute deal, make sure you negotiate on the price.

Some of the most popular exhibitions sell out well in advance. If you're just starting out in business don't overstretch your budget. Many organisers will try to sell a larger space and make it sound appealing, make sure you have a maximum budget and don't exceed it. It might be worth starting small and getting the feel and hang of smaller trade shows first.

Getting a stand at a trade show or event can result in a number of leads when done right. Here are some of our tips on how to get the most out of an exhibition or trade show event:

- *Don't be shy* - if you spend the day sitting down and not engaging with those passing your way, opportunities will literally be walking away from you. It can be difficult if you're naturally a shy person but you'll soon get into the flow of making conversation. If you think you'll struggle, it can be a good idea to bring someone else who is more outgoing and proactive with starting conversation, preferably someone comfortable with sales
- *Give attendees a reason to stop at your stand* - whether you have some sweets, biscuits, balloons, or a raffle, whatever it might be, give people a reason to come over.
- *Get their details* - whether it's an email address, contact

number or a physical address try to get something so that you can keep in touch. A good way is to get people to drop their business card into a fish bowl to enter a raffle.

- *Have samples* - this will depend on your industry but you should be able to show those visiting your stand what it is you sell or do. If you sell a service you should have case studies and other literature to demonstrate your business. Perhaps have a promotional film playing.
- *Give them something to take away* - whether it's a promotional item with your logo on or a sample of what your business offers make sure you give visitors something to take home, it'll help them remember your business. This can be anything from pens or key rings to information packs.
- *Follow up* - collecting email addresses, numbers and business cards is a fruitless activity if you don't use them. Get in touch a few days after the exhibition to thank them for speaking to you on the day. Try to arrange meeting for a coffee or to visit their offices if it's a person you'd like to get as a client.

WRITE A BOOK

Another method to advertise your business, your personal brand and increase your credibility within your industry is to write a book. The idea of writing a book isn't to make a lot of money from book sales, although that would be nice; it probably won't make you a lot of money, but it will:

- Give you a platform to shout about your ability, opinions and expertise
- Provide you with speaking opportunities
- Help you be seen as a leader
- Help you increase opportunities for sales

Getting your book published by a large well-known publisher is very difficult; if your book is a specialist book in a small niche market and you're an unknown, the chances of you getting your book published are very slim. However, we live in fantastic times where self-publishing is extremely simple and the costs are relatively low. We'll explain how self-publishing works and then we'll explain how you can self-publish.

In the self-publishing world, people have tended to sell their books through their own website using an ecommerce system, through the website Amazon, or by using both methods.

We've not well-versed in "old school" self-publishing, but what we can imagine was the case before self-publishing became a lot easier was that you would have had to purchase lots of physical copies of your book and then try to sell them. The problems here are:

- Storage - you have to store lots of books, enough to reduce the purchasing price
- Cash flow - your cash flow is reduced as your money is tied up in stock
- Distribution - you'd have to package and distribute your books costing you more money and time
- Risk - there's no guarantee you'll sell the books meaning you could lose money

Advances in technology for self-publishing have completely eliminated the above problems. Changes in consumer behaviour have driven these advances in self-publishing. People used to go to physical bookstores to purchase books. However, with the Internet, the Kindle and tablet computers, people can purchase and read electronic books (eBooks) with a few simple clicks. EBooks, like all electronic information, can be duplicated in seconds without cost. Therefore, if you sell one eBook or a hundred thousand eBooks there are no additional production costs, and there's no storage cost. Amazon Kindle Direct Publishing (Amazon KDP) is a platform by Amazon that enables you to upload and sell your eBook through Amazon, and it's extremely easy to do.

What happens if you want a physical book? Again, thanks to advances in technology you can have physical copies of your book without buying or holding any stock. Amazon has another self-publishing platform called CreateSpace and they'll produce and distribute your physical book on customer demand. In other words, they only print-on-demand, so CreateSpace will handle the customers' money on purchase, Amazon will then take a fee for the production and distribution of your book and then send you your profits at the end of the month. CreateSpace and Amazon KDP work in harmony, so you can publish your book on both Amazon KDP and CreateSpace seamlessly.

Selling your book through Amazon rather than through your own ecommerce site has many advantages:

- Print-on-demand - stock can never run out
- Huge customer base - your book will be more likely seen through an Amazon search than a Google search. Consumers tend to search Amazon for books rather than Goole or any other Internet search engine
- Credibility and trustworthy - consumers will be less likely to buy your book on your ecommerce store, whereas on Amazon they'll be completely at ease
- International availability - extends your potential customer base and sales potential
- Low costs - no shipping, returns or inventory costs
- Professional look -as long as you've worked with a great cover designer and formatting experts, Amazon published books look fabulous

There are other options for you to self-publish your eBook. However, due to the sheer pulling power of Amazon and their extremely easy-to-follow self-publishing setup, we highly recommend using Amazon KDP and CreateSpace.

How to write a book is a book in itself. However, it's actually not that complicated, so we'll touch on the subject here. We won't tell you how to be a bestselling writer and author, but we'll give you enough information and a step-by-step process that's easy to follow, so you'll be able to write your own book and get it self-published.

1. Can you write? - if you're able to structure words, sentences and paragraphs together then you can write. You don't need to write like George Orwell, but you'll need to be able to explain yourself in the written form. Remember, your book is about your business, you're not trying to write a compelling novel. If you're not confident in your writing ability, you can always outsource this to a writer known as a 'ghostwriter'. However, you must control the costs and analyse your return on your investment if you're considering using a ghostwriter. It's common for people to doubt themselves and feel that they're not credible enough or skilled enough to write a book. Remember, you're the expert in your topic, so you have every right to write and publish a book. While we're stating you don't need to be a literary expert to write a book, you do need to be extremely passionate about your subject. Writing a book just for the sake of writing a book would be reputation damaging, a waste of time and a waste of money. Your passion, or lack of passion, will show in your book.

2. Planning - you need to know what your book is going to be about, who the target audience is and how the book will be structured. Knowing these things will massively help you direct and shape the book. Always write with your audience in mind. Your whole book is about them and enabling them to

achieve their goals. You can use brainstorming (see chapter Business Idea Generation) to come up with book ideas and chapters. Then use the chapter titles as the guide for your writing. Some questions to ask: what problem does my book solve? Who would buy this book?

3. Research - search Amazon for similar books. Is there a gap in the market? Are there lots of books on your topic? What's the bestseller? You should also buy some of these books to see what they're like and see what's missing from them. There are lots of books on business, but we thought they were too light and that they told readers "what" to do, but they didn't tell readers "how" to do it, hence the birth of *Business Hacks*.

4. Writing - you don't need any specialist software to write your book, a simple word-processing software package will do. The author of *Fifty Shades of Grey*, E L James, wrote it on her Blackberry phone while on the way to work. Also the author of the 'A Song of Ice And Fire' series, George R. R. Martin, writes on a DOS computer.

Writing a whole book is a daunting task, so you need to break the writing process up into easy bite-sized chunks. Using your plan, you could aim to write a chapter a week or every two weeks. We recommend writing in the evenings and not during business hours if your business is a nine-to-five business. Remember your book is to help you win business it's not an alternative revenue stream. Therefore, writing your book during business hours when you should be working on your business is counterproductive.

5. Editing - you'll need to read your book over and over to make it better and fix mistakes. However, your book will need to be proofread and edited by a professional editor. Finding an editor can be difficult and it's very hard to send your manuscript, that you've spent hundreds of hours on, to someone you don't know. You start to get paranoid thoughts about

how they'll run away with your bestselling book. We're going to be extremely kind and give you the contact details of our book editor. Her name is Zoe Markham and her website is: markhamcorrect.com. Drop her an email and tell her about your book.

6. Book title - your book will need a compelling title that not only tells the reader what the book is, but catches their eye. Book titles like *The Naked Trader* by Robbie Burns are great at attracting attention while telling the reader what the book is about. Amazon isn't just an ecommerce store it's also a complex search engine. Your book title will need to contain keywords that'll make it easier for your consumers to find. You'll notice this book has a long, drawn-out title: *Business Hacks: A Guide for Entrepreneurs and Start-ups.* This title was specifically created to hit three key words: 'business' 'entrepreneurs' and 'start-ups', because that's you, our target market. You probably typed a search phrase with one or more of those keywords, which got the book in front of you.

7. Book cover - have you heard of the phrase "Don't judge a book by its cover"? Well, consumers do judge a book by its cover. If your front cover looks amateurish and unattractive consumers will simply ignore your book, which is a shame if your content is great. Our advice is to get your book cover professionally done by a specialist book cover designer. The designers of our book cover are Peter and Caroline at bespokebookcovers.com.

8. Formatting - once you've finished editing your manuscript with your editor you'll need to get it "formatted" into the appropriate file for upload. The manuscript text will also need to be put in the right place on the page for printing. You can do this yourself, but if book formatting isn't your speciality then outsource this. We use Ebook Launch at ebooklaunch.com, so feel free to contact them and tell them you want it formatting for CreateSpace and/or Amazon KDP.

9. Upload - now you've got your book cover and formatted manuscript for CreateSpace and Amazon KDP it's time to upload them. There's an order to do this. Your CreateSpace is your physical book, which will be sent to you to check and approve before you make it accessible to the market. That delay of ordering, receiving and reviewing your physical book is why you want to do CreateSpace before you make your eBook available through Amazon KDP. Uploading your manuscript on CreateSpace and Amazon KDP is very easy. We won't document the steps here, because they'll probably change by the time you read this. However, follow the onscreen instructions and you can't go far wrong. Both CreateSpace and Amazon KDP have communities with very helpful people who can help you through every step of the way.

10. Sales - your book isn't going to sell itself, and being on Amazon isn't enough. This is where most authors go wrong. They forget that books are actually a business that require marketing and sales. Therefore, you'll need to promote your book to make people aware of its existence. Use the skills and tools you'll learn from this book about marketing to market your book. You should put links to your book on your company website and social media pages. You may also put a link to your book on your email signature. This will really help your credibility when communicating with prospective clients via email.

Now that you have the knowledge to become an author all you need to do is start writing.

ADVERTISING SUMMARY

This chapter is by no means exhaustive of all of the available methods of offline advertising but the above should give you a good understanding of the strategies required to ensure that you advertise in the right places and for the right price. Remember not to get disheartened when advertising, if something doesn't work for you, analyse the problems, then either fix them and try again, or look at something new, but don't give up. Advertising your business can be frustrating and expensive, but if you're not constantly looking for new customers, if your existing clients dry up your business could be in trouble.

"Stopping advertising to save money is like stopping your watch to save time." - Henry Ford

NETWORKING

I n this chapter we're going to look at the art of networking. "People buy from people" is a saying that we very much believe in and this is very evident at networking events. If someone likes you they're more likely to do business with you than a stranger. Networking events usually take place first thing in the morning, which can start from anywhere between 6-8am with an 8-10am close. There are networking events after 5pm, but we often find that these can be quieter as many people are tired after a long day at work and decide to go home instead. A smaller number operate during the working day, usually at lunch hours. It's a good idea to attend a selection of events if you can and find which ones work best for you.

"The richest people in the world look for and build networks, everyone else looks for work." - Robert Kiyosaki

Going to networking events takes time out of your day when you could be busy working on other things in your business. We do understand the frustration when people tell us they don't see results from attending networking events. Usually this is because they've only been to an event once or twice and didn't get any business from it, so they never went back. This is a common beginner's error, as networking takes time.

We've attended countless networking events and it's been extremely rare for us to walk into an event, strike up conversation with a total stranger, explain our business and make a sale. It's happened, but it's very rare. The reasons for this are quite simple: one, they don't know who you are yet; and two, everyone who attends a networking event is going to promote their own business. They aren't going as buyers they're also going as sellers. If you understand this you'll become a better networker.

HOW TO FIND NETWORKING EVENTS

It's very easy to find networking events, but finding good networking events can be a lot harder. Using LinkedIn, EventBrite and Internet search engines will show events near you. Some events will be completely free, others will be 'pay as you go' or have a yearly membership fee with an additional payment required each time you attend. Everyone is different and what is a great networking group for one person might not be the one for you, it's all about the people who are there and if you feel that you fit in with the group.

Unfortunately there isn't a quick way to filter between the good and bad events, you need to get out there and attend. You'll almost certainly waste a few early mornings and early evenings but be positive and view it as getting a step closer to finding the right event for you.

APPEARANCE FOR NETWORKING

You should dress well and appear presentable when attending networking events. This includes: clean shaven, tidy hair, trimmed nails, fresh breath and a well-pressed suit. This sounds like common sense, but we're always shocked by at least one person at every networking event that we attend.

When you attend a networking event you represent your business.

We have met a number of individuals representing accountancy firms, financial advisors, solicitors etc. wanting to look after our business, but we feel if they can't look after themselves they simply couldn't look after our business. We understand this is very judgemental, but business by nature is judgemental and everyone goes off first impressions, at least to some extent. Speaking to other business owners we're not alone in thinking this way. If someone is representing their business and they look shabby it makes their business appear shabby. Clothing and appearance are of tremendous importance, so dress in a way that makes you look and feel successful. We're not suggesting you turn up in a £1000 Hugo Boss suit, we're simply implying you should dress smartly.

The next point will depend on how comfortable you are doing this, but we like to wear one thing that stands out. We do this for two reasons: firstly it is a conversation starter; and secondly it makes you both stand out from the crowd and be memorable. You might choose a bold tie (never wear any type of comedy/cartoon-related tie), noticeable cufflinks or very colourful socks. Just don't wear them all at the same time.

How you act is even more important than how you dress. If you sit quietly in a corner looking lonely you won't have much success. For the introverts amongst us going up to complete strangers isn't easy so you'll need to practice. Make sure you have strong body language when both standing and sitting, no slouching, hold your chin high and portray confidence even if you don't feel it.

When you meet someone, a good firm handshake is of great importance and something you should practice if you're not used to it. After shaking hands the conversation will begin, so ensure your body language is correct, speak clearly and audibly and try to enjoy the experience.

PLANNING BEFORE THE EVENT

If possible get a copy of the delegate list before the event. A delegate list is a list of everyone who's attending the networking event. Expect some people on the list not to turn up, especially if it's a free networking event. Once you have the list identify companies and people that you'd like to speak to; when you've done this go over to the event organiser and say that you would like an introduction. Don't be afraid to build a relationship up with the event organiser prior to the event as it can make asking for an introduction even easier.

The delegate list also has another purpose. For a number of reasons you may not get a chance to speak to the people you want to. After the event you can send those individuals an email explaining that you were hoping to talk to them, upon a reply you can either try to setup a meeting with them or arrange to meet at the next event. Some events won't hand out the delegate list, but they have it on the wall, so simply take a picture of it with your camera phone.

NETWORK TACTICS

Upon Arrival

Arrive on time or earlier if possible to maximise your networking time. Introduce yourself to the event organiser and ask them if they could introduce you to those you've targeted on your list as mentioned above. The event organisers are almost always more than happy to help.

Who to Talk To

Try to avoid 'serial networkers' as you'll find that a large number of these people spend all of their time networking and doing very little business. These individuals will be hard to identify when you start attending events, but when you start seeing them at every event they'll become apparent.

Avoid individuals from multi-level marketing organisations, business development and sales staff, only because you might find that they're mostly interested in selling their products or services as opposed to building a relationship. You may have different experiences when you network, but we have found we have considerably greater success with people who run their own business, or directors, as ultimately they're the decision makers.

Try to avoid the 'comfort zone' of spending the entire networking time attached to someone in the same position as you who is new to networking and possibly just as nervous. Time is money, you aren't going to this event to make small talk with someone you'll never do business with, and you need maximum exposure from your time out of the office.

Who Should You Try To Talk To?

It's easy to go and speak to someone standing alone, but you only get your business across to one person. Instead, speak to a group and you get yourself across to 5-6 people in almost the same amount of time.

When you arrive, scan the room, look at the groups of people talking and see where there's an opening (a space which you can easily walk up to and join the group without having to ask anyone to move to let you in), walk over, wait until there's a pause in the conversation and politely ask if you're okay to join in, then introduce yourself. At least some of the group will be experienced networkers who'll usually put you at ease and the conversation will flow.

What to Say

Once you've shook hands and introduced yourself, first ask: "*What do you do?*" People like to talk about themselves and their business. If you ask them to talk about themselves and are genuinely interested in what they have to say they'll pretty much warm to you. The second reason for this is to evaluate how much time you're going to spend with this person. If they're in a line of business which has no relevance to yours or, worse, a competitor, wrap things up politely and move on to someone else. Just about everyone you meet at a networking event can potentially be important, but some are more directly useful than others. When speaking to someone who you may think is of no relevance, bear in mind they may be well-connected, so never be rude. When wrapping a conversation up do so politely, for example "I need to make a quick call", or "I just need to go and speak to a certain person before they leave".

Tailor your business description around what you've just been told about their business. Don't regurgitate the same scripted speech in every situation. An important point leading from this is not to explain every little thing or every service of your business. It's tempting to talk a lot, particularly if it's something you're passionate about, but show restraint, not everyone is going to be as interested in your business as you are. The goal is to have the person you're speaking with walk away with a clear understanding of your business and how you could be of benefit to them, or someone they know.

Some networking events will give you time to deliver a pitch, which can range from 30 seconds to three minutes. Preparation is key, so you'll need practice pitches that summarise your business that last different periods of time. Make sure you get across the name of your company, what you offer and how this can be of benefit. When you start attending networking events you'll be able to develop your pitches and build your confidence.

Business Cards for Networking
If you haven't got business cards with you we recommend not going to the networking event. The reason for this is that you'll be asked for them repeatedly and if you don't have one it'll raise eyebrows

and questions: "Have you forgotten them?", "Have you only just setup your business?", "Have you never been to a networking event before?" In short, not arriving with business cards will make you look unprepared and amateurish.

Your business card represents you and your business, so you need to have an attractive, well-designed card that portrays your brand. Make sure your business card has a strong design, unless you're very good at designing we strongly recommend hiring someone to design your business card, and ensure it's printed on good quality paper. Your business card needs your full name, contact number, website and email address in a clearly visible way. A lot of people like to put a small photograph of themselves on their business card which is a clever move. Networkers will meet lots of people, so they'll end up with dozens of business cards and find it very difficult to remember who the person behind the card was. If you're active on social media then links to your company's social media links can be effective.

A double-sided business card can be very beneficial if you use the back of the card for a promotional offer. People who probably wouldn't get in touch may call or email you in the days following an event to take up the offer, and you'll be able to convert a percentage of these into paying customers. Think about something that you could offer as an appetiser for a potential customer which will allow you to show them your professionalism and demonstrate how you can make their life easier.

Playing the Long Game

Networking is unlikely to provide you with immediate results. It takes time to build up trust. If you meet an accountant today would you immediately give them your business? Probably not, but if you met that accountant and over time got to know and trust them it's far more likely you'd use their services if you required them.

Even if you find that you're networking with people who don't need your services it can still be very worthwhile. If you attend a weekly, fortnightly or monthly networking event with say 12 people, if you only try to sell to those 12 people you are significantly minimising your chances of success. Everyone has their own network of friends, family, colleagues and other networking groups, so your task is to get each person within your chosen networking group to be acting as your representative. This isn't something that'll happen overnight, so again you need to build trust within your networking group. You can offer referral fees as an added incentive for people to pass you work, so that they benefit financially, and it makes them more likely to continue promoting your business.

When you trust the people in your networking group it's good practice to send them referrals. If you know someone who needs flyers and there's a printer in your group put them in touch with each other. You may benefit from a referral fee, but more importantly you'll be cementing relationships and you'll likely get a referral back in return.

Be sure to only send referrals when you're confident that the person in question completes work to a high standard. It can be damaging for you and your business if you make a connection with someone who provides poor quality work or doesn't pay their invoice.

In closing, the above points should help you get off to the best possible start with networking. You'll learn a great deal more from actually getting out there and meeting people, but this chapter should give you the knowledge to make a start.

VOUCHERS

A discount voucher or coupon gives the entitled holder a discounted rate for a particular product or service. For the rest of this chapter we'll define voucher to mean both a discount voucher and a coupon. Vouchers can be provided both offline and online, and your marketing strategy will determine the best method to use, or if you should use both. In this chapter we'll separate offline and online vouchers and explain how each work, the positives and negatives, as well as thinking about whether they could be suitable for your business.

OFFLINE VOUCHERS

Offline vouchers tend to be pieces of paper that customers hand over to the cashier when they make a purchase. They can be accepted as is or scanned with a barcode scanner. Alternatively they may contain a code that is entered online if the customer is making an online purchase with the physical voucher. If you're giving your customers the ability to use the voucher online then you'll need to consider any front and back-end development work needed to your ecommerce website, which will allow the customer to enter the code.

Some companies offer vouchers as a reward scheme to keep customers shopping with them. This type of strategy is a customer retention strategy, which gives customers an incentive to continue shopping with you. If customers shopped with another company they'd not gain any points from you for future discounts. This is also known as a loyalty scheme. Tesco have been doing this for a number of years through the use of their club card. Tesco sends vouchers to its customers based on the amount of points they've collected. You also get this points and voucher reward system with some credit cards.

A different strategy with vouchers is to acquire new customers through the use of discounts. There are several ways to do this, for example handing out vouchers in your local area or town centre to create brand awareness. To reach a wider, more targeted audience you could partner up with online companies and have your vouchers placed in their parcels for customers. In this case, and for it to work well, it would have to be a company that sells products to your target market, but who are not in direct competition. For example, your company may sell healthy prepared meals, and you could partner with a supplement company to have your vouchers packaged in with the customers' orders. In this case while the supplement company sells to your target market you're not in direct competition with each other. The supplement company may charge you a fee for this, or require a percentage of any sales made through the vouchers.

There are several other ways to get vouchers in front of customers such as:

- Working with industry-related magazines who can put your vouchers in copies of their magazine.
- Door-to-door posting of vouchers to customers.
- Sending vouchers via email so that they can be printed off and taken to the cashier when making a purchase.

Can you think of any other ways to get your vouchers in front of your target market?

ONLINE VOUCHERS

An online voucher can be an internal voucher that is sent out to your customers via an internal email shot, or it can be an external voucher which is managed by a third party voucher website such as 'Groupon' or 'myvouchercodes'. As smart phones have grown in popularity, customers also have access to voucher apps through their phones. Therefore, for simplicity, when we discuss voucher websites we mean both websites and mobile phone apps.

Online voucher websites provide customers with vouchers towards a variety of discounted products and services. Companies apply to the voucher website to have their products or services discounted, which are then displayed on the voucher company's website. The voucher company also send out daily emails to its email list with current discounts that are available. This way people don't miss out on any deals because they won't always check the voucher website for what's new. The popular voucher websites have extremely large emailing lists. What this means for you is that you can have your product or service reach a much wider audience through the use of the voucher company's website traffic and their email list. In other words, the voucher websites have a lot of pulling power that you can leverage.

While the voucher company will do their part to make sales you can also do other things to increase awareness of your current promotion, such as advertising your vouchers on your social media platforms or sending an email shot to your email list.

How Online Vouchers Work

When a business is thinking about promoting a product or service on a voucher website the first task is to identify what they'll be selling and if it's suitable for the website. There can often be intense competition to have a product or service listed on the best voucher websites, meaning they can be selective in what they decide to promote.

Get in touch with the websites you would like to use as a platform. Some examples are below:

- Groupon - groupon.co.uk.
- My Voucher Codes - myvouchercodes.co.uk.
- Top Cash Back - topcashback.co.uk.
- Voucher Seeker - voucherseeker.co.uk.
- Quidco - quidco.com.
- Living Social - livingsocial.com.

You'll be asked about your product or service such as what the usual selling price is and the amount you would like it to be sold for. Be aware that the discounted price usually has to be pretty significant in order to be selected for entry.

The amount that the website provider takes can vary depending on the item cost and sector. It's common for the provider to take between 30 to 65 percent of the sale price. If you have a product that usually sells for £10, the new discounted price might appear on the voucher website for around £6. The provider would then deduct between 30 to 65 percent from the £6 sale price, let's say 30 percent for this product, but purely as an example:

£10 minus £4 discount = £6, minus 30 percent (£1.80) = £4.20. Therefore, for each sale of the item that is usually sold for £10, you would receive £4.20.

The suitability of a voucher website will vary from business to business. For some readers it could offer a large volume of new clients and the opportunity to sell slow-moving stock. For others, you can still receive a large number of customers, but will have to work hard to meet the demand for minimal profit margins and potentially not see the majority of these new customers again. For some of you voucher websites would not be suitable at all.

If you've concluded that voucher websites are a good option for your business, be sure to:

1. Analyse the product/service that you wish to promote.
2. Calculate the profit margin after special offer and commission - is it viable?
3. Think about what you want to achieve from using the platform, for example move old stock, increase awareness and so on.
4. Check that you have the systems in place to deal with a large volume of orders.
5. Plan how your business will work to retain the new customers.

POSITIVES AND NEGATIVES OF VOUCHERS
Positives

Quickly promotes new businesses - building a strong customer base in the initial months of operating a new business can prove challenging. Using a voucher website platform allows you to tap into a huge potential audience. Many business owners choose to use such platforms on the basis of making a very small profit, perhaps just breaking even on the foundation that they can build a customer base to sell to again in the future.

Only pay when a sale is made - this can be a very attractive feature to businesses that are looking to promote their products. Typically advertising is an upfront expense with a variable conversion rate. Using a voucher website means that there is no expense unless a sale is made.

Additional sales - taking a restaurant as an example, it could run an offer on a well-discounted evening meal and make profit from additional sales such as alcohol and additional courses.

Shifting old stock - slow-moving stock can be a real pain for retailers, tying up cash and taking up space. Voucher websites can potentially sell these items quickly and increase cash flow.

Negatives

Small profit margins - slashing the Recommended Retail Price (RRP) can be challenging for a business, being charged an additional 30 to 65 percent of the discounted rate can make the process unappealing for business owners.

Not being prepared - it could result in a large volume of sales, so for the unprepared this can be a problem. Before advertising on such sites, ensure that you have systems in place in case you receive a significant volume of orders. Being prepared can include having sufficient stock levels, staffing and capacity. For example, a small Bed & Breakfast business with three rooms would struggle if their promotion resulted in a few hundred reservations being purchased in a single day.

Potentially damaging to your brand - targeting customers that are focused on price doesn't create a loyal customer base. If a competitor offers a better deal than you in the future, those who are price-driven will be more likely to switch. Offering your product or service for a significantly lower price seen by a huge audience can potentially damage your brand with many not wanting to pay full price after seeing what it has sold for in the past. In some ways it can make your brand appear cheap. However, if what you're offering is strong customers are likely to forward your vouchers to friends and colleagues, further increasing your brand awareness and sales.

Deals Don't Get Repeat Business - According to Brown (2011) the voucher website Groupon has a low conversion rate for repeat customers. You may not see the customer again unless they have another coupon. Brown (2011) showed that only around 19 percent of new customers who redeemed a voucher became a repeat customer, although this can vary depending on the product categories.

EMAIL MARKETING

Unlike one-to-one emails, email marketing involves sending one message to many people. Personal emailing services like Hotmail, Gmail or Yahoo limit the amount of emails you can send to people at one time, so you need a specialist email marketing service provider, which we'll discuss later. Email marketing is permission-based only, which means your readers must 'opt in' to your emails and you need to inform them on every email why they're receiving your email. Email marketing can develop how a business communicates with its past, current and potential clients in a cost-effective, environmentally friendly way. Email marketing can be broken into three simple stages:

1. Building a list of subscribers who want to hear what your business has to say.
2. Regularly sharing your knowledge, thoughts and promotions by email.
3. Creating opportunities for your subscribers to become paying customers.

Email marketing is an incredibly powerful tool. In this chapter we're going to look at how to utilise it effectively whilst avoiding some of the common mistakes.

EMAIL MARKETING SOFTWARE

There are a number of companies who offer software that'll allow you to store your list of subscribers and send them emails. In this chapter we're going to look at 'MailChimp' as it offers stunning email designs, is very straightforward, requires no knowledge of HTML and you can start using it for free.

MailChimp offers a free account until you have two thousand email subscribers. Create a MailChimp account by visiting mailchimp.com, enter your details and you'll have an account in a matter of minutes. There are a number of instructional videos on the MailChimp site that cover how to get started and these are well worth a watch.

When your MailChimp account is created you'll need to create a 'list'. A 'list' is merely a list of your subscribers, give it a name e.g. 'My first email marketing list' and then start adding email accounts of those who have subscribed to receive your emails, if you have any. If you don't have any email addresses to add yet, don't worry, we'll be covering that later.

We're going to look at three different types of email campaign; 'Regular Ol' Campaign', 'Plain Text Campaigns' and 'A/B Split Campaigns'.

- Regular Ol' Campaign: This allows users to design and customise emails with images, social media links, a number of fonts and much more. Unlike sending an email from a regular account you'll be creating what can be a visually stunning email which will require no knowledge of HTML. All you need to do is 'drag and drop' the content you want in the email, it's straightforward and there are lots of support videos and tips on the site should you run into difficulty.
- Plain Text Campaign: As the name suggests this option will only allow users the option of using plain text. If you are

looking to send a text-only email to your list then this is the one to choose.

- A/B Split Campaigns: This is a great tool for testing how effective things like your subject line and time of sending really are. Using this option you can create two campaigns, which is ideal if you can't decide on what subject line or content to use. MailChimp will send out the two different versions to a small part of your subscriber list, the most successful (the one which receives the most opens and clicks) is then sent out to the remainder of the list.

Adding content to your email will differ slightly depending on which of the above campaigns you decide to use. None of the three campaigns require any technical knowledge and all have a number of great instructional videos available on the MailChimp website and YouTube which will show you step-by-step how to create the campaign.

After sending your campaign MailChimp will show you how it has performed with a 'Report'. The main areas you need to look at are:

- Open Rate - the number of people who opened your email out of the list.
- Click Through Rate - the number of people who clicked a link that was in your email, this link could be to your website or social media channel etc.
- Unsubscribe Rate - how many people clicked to unsubscribe from future emails.
- Bounces - how many emails 'bounced back' and were not received by the recipient.

The MailChimp report will show you how effective your campaign was. If you have a very low 'Open Rate' or a high 'Unsubscribe Rate' then you'll know that your campaign had underperformed. In the rest of this chapter we're going to cover how to make sure your campaigns perform well.

EMAIL TARGET AUDIENCE

Who am I targeting with this email campaign? It's a simple question, but something that a lot of people don't think about, so they miss out on reader engagement and conversions as a result. When you know who you're targeting it's considerably easier knowing what to say to them and how you're going to say it; for example, an email campaign for a luxury product aimed at the middle-aged would be completely different to a campaign for a low cost impulse purchase item aimed at young adults. Think about your audience, your product and how you'd like to get it across to your subscribers.

If you've just started and don't have email subscribers don't worry, we will be covering a number of strategies to legally and ethically build a list of past and potential customers. If you're in the fortunate position of already having a genuine list of people who have subscribed to your email newsletter then you need to think about who they are:

- Why did they sign up?
- When did they sign up? - If they signed up during making a purchase or soon afterwards then they're already a customer and the way you engage with past customers can often be different to how you deal with potential customers. You might organise this by having different "lists" for example "customers" and "prospects".

Whether you have or haven't got email subscribers, the goal is to get more. Even when you perform email marketing very well, the conversion rates are low, so the more genuine subscribers you have the more likely you are to win some business.

ACQUIRING EMAIL SUBSCRIBERS

After identifying your target audience you need to plan on how to drive this type of person to your website and encourage them to sign up for your email newsletter. This'll be different for just about every industry, but they key questions you need to ask are the same:

- Who am I targeting?
- How will I find them and bring them to my website?
- What are they interested in?
- What can I offer weekly/monthly that they'll find interesting enough to sign up for?

You know your business and you'll hopefully also know what your customers like. If you're a retailer then the obvious incentive would be to give some sort of discount or give subscribers access to certain products before they go on general sale. If you're a service-based business then free worthwhile tips or advice can be an excellent way to entice visitors to subscribe to your emailing list.

Your website will need a facility for customers to subscribe. To add a 'subscribe' option on your website is relatively straightforward, particularly if you're using a platform such as MailChimp. As there are slight variations on how to install a subscribe button depending on which email service you're going to use, the best way to learn how to install the button is to watch one of the instructional videos available on the MailChimp website and YouTube.

If you've followed the website creation chapter you might consider installing a WordPress plugin that enables users to subscribe.

EMAIL MARKETING CONTENT – SUBJECT LINES

"64% of people say they open an email because of the subject line"
- Chadwick Martin Bailey.

The subject line will often be the difference between someone clicking to find out more or moving the email into the trash before even opening it. An engaging subject line is of crucial importance if you want your email marketing campaign to succeed. The idea of a subject line is to create enough interest to make the recipient click to find out more. It's not a good idea to create a subject line that has nothing to do with the email's actual content as the recipient will feel cheated.

Analysing your campaign's 'Open Rate' with MailChimp can help you decide if your subject line was effective. If your open rate was very low then the subject line won't have been enticing enough to make the recipients click.

EMAIL MARKETING CONTENT – THE EMAIL
You should be looking to put somewhere between one to three pieces of information in an email campaign, more than this and it can be too much for a reader to quickly scan, meaning it can find its way quickly to the trash box.

Depending on your industry, some of the below ideas for email content won't be applicable, but as with the subject line examples, they should give you food for thought:

- Upcoming events, products or services.
- Tell them what's been happening within your industry (if it's interesting).

- Popular posts you have had on Facebook, Twitter, LinkedIn etc.
- A joke or something amusing.
- A quiz or 'brain teaser'.
- An interview with a member of staff.
- Top 10 ways to...

Put time and effort into what you send out, if you do it well you're far more likely to be rewarded as opposed to just quickly writing up the first thing that comes into your head.

If you can make your readers feel as though they're part of an exclusive club it can yield great results. Have your members find out the latest information before anyone else, get deals, discounts and incentives that aren't available to the general public. Getting someone to sign up to your newsletter is great, keeping them is better.

We're sure you receive a fair few emails every day from companies. Start to take a look at them in more detail and think about how they're getting their message across - does it work? If not, why not? What emails do you immediately delete? What makes you do this? When was the last time you bought something or enquired further from an email? What made you do this? Start to analyse the emails that you receive from companies, learn from their mistakes and best practices.

If your email is 'text heavy' the majority will click delete before reading the opening sentence. Even if you try to keep things to the point, if your content isn't interesting then readers are going to click away and move on to the next. Keep it short, interesting, to the point and have a clear call-to-action.

EMAIL MARKETING FREQUENCY

Depending on the nature of your business and the type of email campaigns you'll be sending, along with the amount of time you can commit to email marketing, will dictate how frequently you should be sending emails for maximum effect. Many companies can justifiably send an email campaign every day and subscribers are happy to receive it because of the news, discounts or other benefits associated with being a subscriber.

You do need to think about how often you're going to be emailing and why this is. Don't start emailing every week if you don't have something interesting to include every week, if your emails become dull your subscriber list will suffer. Sit down and think realistically about how much time you have, how long it'll take you to arrange for news or a special offer to be created and how willing your subscriber list are likely to be to receive emails at this consistency. As a minimum we would recommend a monthly email, just make sure that the content is good.

We know a few people who plan to send emails once a month and on that day of the month they sit down and will produce any email that comes into their head at that point. You need to work smarter than this. Interesting things will be happening in your business and industry; throughout the week or month. Keep a note of ideas that would be good to go in your next campaign, if you find an interesting news article, a funny video or something else that you think would be of benefit to your readers store it and have it ready to go in one of your next email campaigns. This way you aren't searching the Internet at the last minute trying to find something engaging to write about, and we've found it makes for far more engaging emails.

EMAIL MARKETING TARGETS

We have covered your target audience, what you should say to them and how often you need to say it. Next comes one of the most important parts of email marketing: targets. Without targets and goals you'll miss out on making your email marketing campaigns better.

Email targets can range from the percentage of people on your list who open your email, clicking through to your website or a call-to-action right through to increasing enquiries, sales or overall website traffic. As soon as your email campaign has been sent you should keep track of how many people open your emails and how they act on it from your MailChimp account.

From the first email you send you need to analyse its success and make necessary changes. If the percentage of receivers opening the email was very low was the subject line not engaging, enticing or interesting enough? If the click through to your website was poor, what was the call-to-action? Was there a strong enough incentive to make a reader want to click through to your site? It isn't an exact science and what is true for one business many not apply to another so you need to trial your email marketing campaigns, analyse the statistics and use trial and error to ensure that you're engaging with your readers and converting as many as possible to customers or clients.

CALL-TO-ACTION

A call-to-action is the action that you want the reader to take, whether that's to click through to your website or something different.

If you send an email campaign you need a clear call-to-action, without this your conversions will plummet. Don't fall in to the trap of having lots of text with lots of links to your website with the hope that more the links you have the more probability the reader will click. This is too much information for readers and gives them too many options. A clear call-to-action on a specific product or service massively increases conversions.

Giving the recipient a very clear call-to-action along with an incentive and a time restriction will massively increase conversions. For example "Click here to purchase... at...% discount, offer ends at 7pm!" A time restriction gives a sense of urgency and can make the click through and conversion rate much higher.

Whatever your business, know exactly what you're promoting in the email and give recipients a real reason to buy.

EMAIL MARKETING LAWS

Email marketing is strictly regulated and the laws can change frequently so make sure you're up to speed with the latest changes.

Sending an email to an individual that is tailored to that person is perfectly legal. Adding a person to an email list which they've not subscribed to is illegal. You'll have heard of the term 'SPAM' before, quite simply it's an unsolicited email sent to people. The Can-Spam Act came into effect on January 1st 2004 and states that you can be fined for every offence. Every offence doesn't mean how many email campaigns you send, it refers to how many people are on your list. So if you send an unsolicited email to ten people you're potentially liable for a fine multiplied by ten.

There are some very simple common sense ways to ensure you don't send SPAM mail, and some less clear, more complicated laws and guidelines that have come into effect which you need to be aware of.

Looking at common sense first; there are many companies and individuals selling email lists, this can be an extremely bad idea. How can you justify sending an email to a complete stranger who hasn't heard of you, doesn't know your business and hasn't signed up to your email campaigns? Not to mention the fact that these people are far, far less likely to open or engage with anything you send them compared to a genuine subscriber.

We've collated the main things to avoid from the 'Bureau of Consumer Protection' http://www.business.ftc.gov.

- Don't pretend that the email you are sending is a reply e.g. making the subject line 'Re: Your Recent Order'.
- The subject line must accurately represent what the email contains.
- If your email is an advertisement then you need to state that it is.
- Your email must include your valid physical postal address.
- Very importantly, tell recipients how to opt out of receiving future emails. Don't try and trick people by hiding it or putting the 'opt out' somewhere difficult to see. If people don't want to receive your messages anymore then stop them, you don't want your business to become an annoyance. Opting out of your emails doesn't mean they're not going to be a customer anymore, but if you inundate them with emails they don't want then they're far less likely to become a customer. Honour opt-out requests promptly and don't charge for it.
- Even if you outsource your email marketing, if the law is broken then both yourself and the company who sent the email on your behalf can be held accountable.

Different countries have different laws relating to SPAM so make sure you know where your emails are going to and the laws relating to those countries.

AVOIDING SPAM FILTERS

Spending a great deal of time creating an engaging and attractive email for it to be captured by your customers' junk folder is a complete waste of time.

To avoid spam filters and junk folders you'll need to understand how they work. Spam filters use a list of criteria to determine whether

the email received is spam or not. Spam filters are constantly growing in criteria and intelligence every day, because every time a user
sends an email to a spam folder it learns what spam emails look
like. According to MailChimp, below are some common mistakes
to avoid:

- Using too many exclamation marks!!!!!!!!!!
- Using typical spam phrases like "Once in a lifetime opportu-
  nity", "Work at home", "You're a winner!"
- USING CAPITAL WORDS - especially in the subject line.
- Using red or green-coloured fonts.
- Bad HTML, which happens when converting a Microsoft Word
  file to HTML.
- Creating an email that is one big image with little or no text.
  Spam filters can't read images so they'll just junk your email
  to be safe.
- Having the word "Test" in the subject line.
- Sending emails to inactive lists, which are lists that have not
  engaged in the campaigns through opens and clicks. These
  lists have low engagement ratings and an Internet service
  provider (ISP) will bulk your campaigns to the junk folder.
  Eventually they'll block the domain and IP addresses which
  are used to deliver the campaigns.

You can use an Internet search engine to type in: "spam words" or
"spam phrases" to find more detailed lists of spam trigger words
to avoid. MailChimp has a useful tool for checking and telling you
your spam score and what you need to fix called 'Inbox Inspector'.
At the time of writing if you're using the free version you'll need to
pay a small amount for every inbox inspection, but Inbox Inspector
is free for 25 inspections per week for paid accounts.

TESTING YOUR E-SHOT

Before you send your email you'll need to test it. That means send a test email to yourself, your friends and co-workers to ensure it looks right and that there are no grammar or spelling errors or typos.

EMAIL DATABASE CLEANSING

Database cleansing means removing email addresses from your list that you believe no longer wish to receive communications from you, are not receptive to what you're sending or have an email address that is either no longer in use or incorrect.

Sending emails out to a database containing recipients that are not receptive can potentially damage your brand and it'll waste your time and money.

Whether you use MailChimp or a different provider, they'll have an obligation to monitor SPAM. Sending campaigns that have a high number of SPAM complaints, (meaning recipients mark the email as SPAM), bounce or undeliverable rates will mean running the risk of having your account suspended. Cleansing your email database reduces the likelihood of this happening.

Email marketing providers such as MailChimp will offer a report analysing the success of a campaign. Within this report it can show email addresses that bounced back and unsubscribed. If you are using MailChimp, people who unsubscribe will automatically be removed from your database. If you're using a different platform ensure that people who unsubscribe are removed before another campaign is sent.

Emails bouncing back can happen if there is a typo or some other issue with the address, such as using '.co.uk' when it should be '.com'. Emails that bounce back are usually not automatically removed from a database. If an email address bounces back you may need to review the email address and correct it or remove it.

As your database of email subscribers grows, the potential for issues with your database will also increase. Issues can be reduced by only sending content to those who have opted in to receive your emails, meaning you're sending campaigns to people who're happy to receive them. There are some good online tools which can help you cleanse your email lists including:

- www.datavalidation.com
- www.briteverify.com

If you're new to email marketing and only have a small list of subscribers you should be able to cleanse your own database manually. Sending campaigns to quality subscribers will not only reduce the risk of potential bans from service providers, save you time and money, but also increase the likelihood of responses and engagement.

By now you should have good idea of how to send an effective email campaign to your subscribers. Every business is different and how your subscribers react will differ depending on the nature of your business, so there is no 'one size fits all' rule for email marketing campaigns. Start planning what you will send in your first campaign and how you'll make it engaging. After it has been sent, analyse the results and adapt for the second campaign, then continue to analyse and adapt until you have a strong understanding of what your subscribers respond to best.

PART 5

ONLINE MARKETING

Social Media Marketing

Social media websites and apps are created for users to join and make connections with others who they know or are interested in. Social media has in many ways changed the face of marketing and is showing no signs of slowing in momentum. You need to be active on social media or you'll miss opportunities. In this chapter we're going to look at some of the many social media channels available and how you can utilise them for your business for maximum effect.

We want you to personalise this chapter and the advice given to make it unique to your business. There is no magic formula to social media success, if we wrote precisely what to do it would only apply to certain types of businesses. An example we often use is: how would the social media strategy of a funeral directors and a night club be the same? In short, they wouldn't, for obvious reasons. This is why you'll need to personalise this section around your business, implement what you learn and then analyse the results.

It's worth noting that social media platforms and the market are evolving rapidly with new products and apps coming out regularly. Therefore, we'll only write about the most popular social media platforms at the time of writing.

FACEBOOK

Facebook is a free social networking website that allows its users to create profiles, upload photos, upload videos, send messages and keep in touch with contacts. Facebook has 1.28 billion monthly active users as of March 31, 2014 (newsroom.fb.com, n.d).

Firstly, you're going to need a company page. If you already have a company page please still read this section as there may be areas that you haven't implemented to allow maximum exposure.

Creating a company page is a very simple step-by-step process so we won't spend too long on it. If you don't know what to do visit YouTube and search for "how to start a Facebook page" and there will be lots of free step-by-step guides to watch.

Here are some of the common pitfalls to avoid with your Facebook Business Page:

- Creating a Facebook web address that's complicated and doesn't reflect your business name.
- Choosing the incorrect category and subcategories for your business page. If you have a page make sure you check to see that you've chosen the correct one.
- Not including a physical address, email address, website address or contact number. If you don't have a business address it might be better to leave the physical address blank, and we don't recommend putting your home address.
- A weak short description with no 'call-to-action'.
- Nothing to entice a potential visitor to like the page.
- No 'Company Overview', 'Long Description' or 'Mission'. These all need completing in detail, we don't advise just copying and pasting information straight from your website, make it unique for your Facebook page.

Facebook Design

First impressions count, there are an incredible amount of Facebook pages, so you'll need to be different in order to stand out from the crowd. There are many companies and individuals who can design you a fantastic Facebook page for your business. We couldn't recommend this highly enough. Our advice is to have your Facebook company page designed so it looks similar to your website. It can cost as little as £15, for what could be a customer's first impression of your business, so it's money well spent. This also applies to other social media channels such as Twitter and YouTube, personalise and brand your social media channels as much as possible.

If you don't want to make an investment at this stage then at the absolute minimum you need to make sure that your business page has quality images for both the cover and profile photo. These images need to be clear and in the correct size format to ensure they're a good fit. You can find the correct dimensions by doing a quick search online (we won't include them here as the sizes do occasionally change). Carefully select your images, as this is your opportunity to grab the attention and/or interest of a potential follower.

If you have a company logo which doesn't explain your business then it can be better to select an image that does represent your business. If you run a martial arts club you might have a photograph of an impressive type of kick, if you run a clothing brand you might use a t-shirt design that looks good. Use your images to stand out from your competitors, be different and create interest.

You do need to be careful with the images you use for your business profile and cover images. Facebook doesn't allow you to include promotions or links to your website; but this isn't a problem. Think about it, someone might visit your Facebook page for a few seconds and your initial objective is to get them to 'like' your page so that you can build a relationship with them over time. Your images need to create a spark of interest to give this potential fan a desire to 'like' your page and to make them want to find out more. Your website URL in the cover photo won't create that spark of interest.

The types of images you use are going to be different depending on the product or service you offer. Don't just choose any image, carefully think about what images grab your attention, what images would make your customers look twice or curious enough to look into the page further to find out more. When you have an idea of what you think will work, put this type of image into place; after a few weeks or months think about changing it to see if different images can have a bigger impact on your page's exposure.

It's worked for many of our clients, that is, to use a cover photo as a reason to click the 'like' button, sometimes even pointing an arrow at the 'like' button they want them to click! Consumers are incredibly lazy when they're online, so literally pointing out the 'like' button tells them exactly what you want them to do and where you want them to click.

Additional Features for Your Facebook Page

There are a number of companies offering some great apps and templates which you can integrate into your Facebook page. These apps can work in two ways, firstly making your page look more professional and successful; secondly it can make converting fans into customers that little bit easier. Some of the apps we recommend include:

- Integrating a shop with items available on your page for fans to buy without leaving Facebook (apart from the act of making payment).
- Easy to see and fill out contact forms.
- Coupon Codes apps for your followers to use.

Just about every company offers a free trial period which is normally thirty days, take advantage of these opportunities and see if their software improves your businesses social media presence. Just don't forget to cancel the recurring payment if their service isn't working for you. We recommend using a spreadsheet to record what apps you're using and when their free period ends. This way you can cancel them on time and not lose any money.

Facebook and Social Media Updates

Now that we have given some thought as to how your Facebook business page should look we'll cover the type of updates you should be making. This section will be applicable to all of the other social media channels and not just Facebook.

How annoying is it when your personal timeline is filled up with boring, useless or irrelevant updates from individuals and businesses? It's pretty boring, even frustrating and like most people you'll probably skip past them and after a while either block, unfriend or unsubscribe from those concerned.

The majority of people go on social media when they're bored. It's your job to alleviate that boredom. Whether it be through humour, quizzes, competitions or facts (more on this later).

How many times a day should you post updates? It is a tough question, and one that'll be different from sector to sector. If you sell something fun (such as toys or gadgets) then you can justifiably do quite a few posts a day, as long as you're not outright selling. If on the other hand you only offer one or two products/services that are a bit drier than gadgets, for example if you run an opticians, funeral directors or accountants then constant updates are not likely to yield great responses from those consistently seeing them.

You need to update when most of your followers are likely to be

276

online, it sounds obvious but we're often surprised at how randomly some businesses update their status with seemingly little thought to who's going to be online at that time of day. We'll initially assume the vast majority of your fans are residents of your country and in your time zone (if you have a large number of fans in different time zones, which you can find out in your page's admin area, then you'll need to create updates at times that are applicable to their time zones). You need to think:

1. Who are my target 'fans'?
2. How old are they?
3. What type of job do they have?
4. What times of the day/night are they likely to be online and what mood are they going to be in at those times?

The responses you give here should create a good level of insight into the most effective time of the day or night to post updates. Remember that this is not an exact science, if you don't see results go back to this task and reassess.

Now you hopefully have an idea who your target fans are, next you need to get thinking about how to create updates that are going to interest them at certain parts of the day and/or night when they may be using social media.

Let's imagine you're targeting a mid-20s office worker; break down his/her day:

6-7am - Wakes up, maybe checks Facebook on their phone before getting up - your social media channel could give a motivational update which may cheer them up or make them feel more motivated.

8-9am - Breakfast and commute to work - potentially bored on public transport, post an update with a relevant puzzle, brain teaser or quiz to keep them entertained.

9am-10.45am - They're probably hard at work now and not checking social media.

11am - Morning lull, probably a bit tired/bored of working and need some stimulation, this could be a great time to post a joke or funny image if appropriate depending on your industry. If updating with a joke isn't for your business, a link to an interesting article can work well.

12noon-1.30pm - Lunch time, possibly at their desk, or if not they can still access social media with their phone - this can be an opportunity to push a product or service that they might purchase from you.

2-4pm - Hard at work.

4-5pm - Afternoon lull/watching the clock for 5pm - post a link to an interesting article or news item. This doesn't have to be your website.

5-6pm - The commute home, targeting those on public transport again. Keep them entertained and potentially create excitement for a post you'll be doing later on e.g. "We're making a huge announcement tomorrow about a new product", "We're announcing a special offer at 8:05pm, only the first three customers will be able to take advantage of it". If you're making a huge announcement and creating excitement the news must be equally exciting or greater. Otherwise your audience will feel oversold.

7-10pm - Your target audience will either be at home or out doing a hobby or maybe at a meal. Monday-Thursday (and Sunday) they're more likely to be at home than on a night out so on these days you can again target a product/service to push that's relevant to them. Friday and Saturday fewer people will be online during these times so either alter the timing of your updates accordingly or try to interact with those who might be staying in on a Friday/Saturday night.

This is just an example, but look at the volume of updates that don't push a product or service. We advise business pages to be a source of interest, value-adding information and amusement first and selling second. If all you do is push products throughout the day your page's fan base will almost certainly not grow.

Ways to Interact with Your Fans:
Fun - Very few people are going on social media to be serious. It's time to unwind, see what their friends are doing and generally be entertained or distracted.

As long as your industry allows it, your businesses social media channels should be fun, some of the time (not recommended for funeral directors!). Your fans should enjoy seeing your updates and interact with you whether that's through 'liking' your update or posting a comment.

Posting funny or humorous items is not suitable for every business and generally you see this in B2C and less so in the B2B world. This is simply because in the B2B world you need to come across as professional and reliable.

If you find coming up with funny updates difficult, then start sharing updates or images that you find amusing on your business page for your fans to see. When you start to get a good idea of what your fans like, which you can monitor by seeing how many likes, comments and or shares an update gets, you can start testing the water, making your own updates and/or images using a similar kind of humour.

Quizzes and Puzzles - Quizzes can also be a great way to interact with your fans. Create questions then post the answers on your website meaning your followers will have a real reason to click through to your website. The page with the answers on should not merely provide the answers, it should give the visitor the opportunity to look at your best-selling products, read something interesting, find out more about you; in short work hard to make sure that they don't read the answers and then click off.

Expert Advice - You're in business and you know your sector inside out so don't be shy about it. Provide useful updates that answer common questions that you get in your business sector (obviously some sectors won't allow this, for example financial advice). Portray yourself as a fountain of knowledge but try not to be arrogant with it. Giving snippets of information can be a great way to create interest in you or your business, and make readers come to you to find out more.

Informative Links - Posting links to information that your fans will enjoy is a great way of connecting with your fans. Of course you're not the creator of the article, but you'll be seen as the company that provides them with the access to the most relevant news. This'll give people who are interested in your sector a reason to follow you. These people will also get to see your other updates as well.

The effort required for this is minimal. You'll know what's happening within your business sector so when you find an interesting article share it to your followers.

Review Products and Services - This one is aimed more at retailers, or if you're in certain services then it can still work, you just need to think of the right angle. Let's think about a gym owner or a personal trainer as an example. Reviewing workouts can yield excellent results for example "I did X type of bicep workout and I saw Z results. The workout begins with..." This is not pushing a product or service, but instead this is giving your followers a reason to be followers. It's something interesting which they can read and maybe try themselves. This idea also goes back to being seen as an expert.

Imagine this personal trainer posts a review maybe once a fortnight or once a month and gets a really good following from people reading their reviews and trying their workouts. They could potentially get new clients from people wanting to train with them in person due to this exposure. Think about your business sector, what sort of reviews could you offer that your fans and potential fans, would find interesting and want to keep up to date with?

Reviewing products can again bring excellent results if done properly. First thing to note is, you weren't born yesterday so neither were your fans, if you give everything you sell a glowing five star review and anything you don't sell a poor one then it won't take long for everyone to see that your reviews are not independent or trustworthy.

If you have a fantastic product that you're currently stocking, go into detail about what makes it so good, how would it benefit potential users? Look at its weak points also, is it too expensive for example? If it is expensive then feel free to say so but then justify why it's expensive. This way you are showing both the positive and the negative sides of your products, highlighting the positives, explaining the negatives and overcoming reasons why people might not buy the product in question.

Special Offers, Discounts & Sneak Peeks for Fans - Make your fans feel special, maybe even as if they're forming the future of the business. A number of companies use social media extremely well in asking their fans for their opinion, for example in fashion what style of clothing or design they prefer. This can be a great idea as it performs in two ways. Firstly, it's customer research giving you insight into what they like or dislike and why. Secondly, your fans can feel that they're helping you shape the business with what you bring out and when.

The next way to create a sense of loyalty with your fans is to offer them special discounts, promotions or deals which can only be claimed by your social media fans. Offering a discount code for use at the checkout which deducts a certain amount or percentage off the value of the goods can work very well.

Announcing a 10% discount for your followers will not result in a mad flurry of sales. However, if fans are aware that they have access to this code it may tip the balance in your favour when they do come to need a product or service that you offer.

Free Offers - What could you offer your fans for free? Think about it for a while; obviously you don't want to be losing money but do you have an informative product or a service that you could offer to your fans for free, for example an eBook. If so, it's another reason for an individual to follow your business.

Take some time to think about the different type of updates that are available to your business and how you could use these to create a real following for your page.

Creating Exposure without Posting an Update
Updating your status at the right time and with the right comment can be great for exposure but adding comments to the Facebook pages of other companies can also yield fantastic results. When

using Facebook as your business you can 'follow' other business pages; when they make updates you can add comments or 'like' what they've written. Before we look into this further, don't try to 'hijack' their update by pushing your own product, as you'll look desperate and weaken your brand page.

Start off by following a range of other business pages; competitors, similar businesses, large corporations and most importantly pages your target audience are likely to follow. Now when you login and manage your page your timeline will have updates from the pages that you follow as a business.

The way to add comments successfully to other business owners is very similar to the advice already given when creating your own updates: be insightful, give your opinion, provide useful links for further information or even just 'like' the update. In short, you're trying to make people like you and find your opinion valuable.

This won't produce immediate results, but it can start to make people aware of your business. If you start making useful comments, whether they're funny, interesting or otherwise on pages that have tens of thousands of followers, maybe even millions then the potential rewards can make the effort very worthwhile.

Facebook Paid Advertising

Paying for adverts on Facebook is when you pay to have your company advertised on people's Facebook news feed, which is a pay per click strategy (PPC). At the time of writing there are two ways to pay for advertising, which we'll discuss below:

A "boost" is paying Facebook an amount to have an update shown to more people. The benefits are:

- From about £5 you can have approximately 1000-5000

people view your update; great if you're saying something important or announcing a special offer.

- You can choose very closely which sort of demographic will see your update, so you can target your ideal customers.
- It can increase the number of likes your Facebook page gets due to the large number of people seeing your posts.

In addition to boosts, you can also place a direct advertisement on Facebook:

- Again you can target your advertising very closely so your ideal potential customers view it.
- Advertising on Facebook can be a good way to advertise your page as well as your website and potentially increase the number of 'likes' you have.
- As with all PPC you are only charged if someone actually clicks on your advert, it can be cheaper than other forms of advertising and is very accountable.

The negatives:

- In our opinion there's only one negative for paid advertising on Facebook and that is viewers are not in a buying frame of mind. If someone wants to purchase a product then the more traditional route will be to go to a search engine, visit some websites and then potentially make the transaction. Ask yourself, when was the last time you clicked on an advert on a social media channel and ended up buying something?

If you do decide to pay for advertisement on Facebook do your research. Look at current advertisers when you login, what stands out, what doesn't? What intrigues you and makes you want to click to find out more? Adverts are going to differ widely depending on the industry you're in, but the usual key features remain:

- If you have a wide range of products don't try to offer every-

thing, try promoting a single product or service with each advert
- Create interest
- Have a call-to-action
- Stand out from the rest
- Give some form of incentive if possible, such as a discount code

TWITTER

Twitter is both separate and different to Facebook. You cannot post the same updates on both platforms and expect success.

You can follow the tips from the above section with how to update, but the way in which you update needs to be different in order to gain maximum exposure. There are two things that you need to understand:

Hashtags

The hashtag looks like this: #. It's simply a way for people to identify conversations on a certain subject, which will then allow them to read and interact with people from around the world. Also, as you'll learn, they're used by businesses to interact with their target customers.

If you don't fully understand the hashtag go to Twitter and in the search section enter '#football' and you'll find updates from people around the world who've put updates including the hashtag 'football'. Understand that they're all talking about football, some are having a running conversation, sharing opinions or having a difference of opinion...but they're all talking about football in one way or another. Next be more specific, try a hashtag for a local sports team e.g. #ArsenalFC. Then try searching for a hashtag that relates to your business industry, for example #marketing.

Have you checked on Twitter to see which hashtags are currently trending and if any could be relevant to your interests/experience/ sector? If you update your Twitter account without using a hashtag you're missing out on potential views. For example, here are two updates we could use to increase awareness of this book:

- "Our new book is available to buy, learn how to start your own business."
- "Our new #book is available to buy, learn how to start your own #business. #startup"

The first update would only be seen by our followers. The second update would be seen by our followers as well as those looking at the hashtags: #book #business and #startup. We usually recommend no more than three hashtags within a Tweet.

You should be starting to see the potential for your business. We'll take a gym based in Manchester as an example for how the hashtag can be used effectively. Updates could look like this:

- "Come down to our #gym in #Manchester for a free trial. #fitness"

Using the above hashtags means your update will show up when people search any hashtag including: #Manchester #Fitness and #gym. It's a good idea to play with the hashtags to see what words are most effective and provide you with the best exposure. Exposure can be measured in 'favourites', 'retweets' and new followers soon after the update.

The next powerful way to use the hashtag for business is to search hashtags. Using the gym in Manchester again as an example, it's in a certain geographic area so it is common sense to target geographic areas that are within a commutable distance. Example hashtags to search include:

- #Manchester
- #Salford
- #Levenhulme
- #Didsbury
- #GreaterManchester
- And other reasonably close areas

Have a search for a geographic hashtag in your area e.g. #London, read through some of the recent updates and interact with a few people. This can be done by clicking 'reply' on a Tweet that you find interesting. To highlight how powerful this can be, we have just searched #Manchester and found this update:

"Anyone know of a good gym in Salford? **#Salford #Manchester #Gym**"

Clicking reply, introducing yourself and your business with a direct link to your website and maybe a free day pass to get them through the door would be a great start for the gym owner based in Manchester.

Staying with the gym example, here are some hashtags potential customers might use:

- #Gym
- #Fitness
- #Training
- #Treadmill
- #Bodybuilding
- #Running
- #Strength

- #Protein
- #Supplements
- #Sport

Searching for these hashtags will bring up people who are likely to be interested in the service provided by the gym, so it's a good idea to start interacting with these people as it'll increase the exposure of the gym. A single gym is a geographically restricted business so many people your search will find will not be within a commutable distance.

The final stage for searching hashtags is one of the most effective for making sure you get results from people closely matching your target audience. Using the search function to search for two hashtags at the same time; the gym owner might use:

- #Manchester #Gym

Or

- #Manchester #Diet

The list of potential combination hashtags will be pretty long and will bring up individuals and companies that closely match your industry who you can interact with.

The @ Symbol

Using the @ symbol is a way of creating a Tweet that 'tags' an individual or an organisation of your choosing. 'Tagging' someone basically gives them a notification that you have created an update which includes them. An example might be:

- "Hi, @JamieRice we've just built our new website, check it out: www.example.com"

Jamie would receive a notification that this person had tagged him.

The most important thing to point out is that the '@' symbol cannot be used excessively. If you tag people for the sake of it or do it excessively it becomes a lot like spam emails. You'll annoy people and you'll find yourself facing a suspended or even banned Twitter account if you continue. An example of how **not** to do it would be:

- "Visit www.example.com @JamieRice @The_Rich_Rec @ FredSmith @DavidWilliams @JoeTaylor"

Each of these people would receive a notification, but if they've never heard of you before or don't understand why they've been tagged, they'd be within their rights to report the update to Twitter and of course it isn't going to endear your business to them.

A more intelligent way of doing things would be to identify a key influencer within your sector and create a Tweet like this:

Hi @JamieRice I enjoyed your Tweet yesterday on...I've created a new website & would love your thoughts. This way you aren't sending tags out 'en-masse', you're explaining why you're getting in touch.

We would describe key influencers as people who are very active on Twitter (5+ Tweets per day), have a large number of followers (in excess of 5,000) and receive a large number of 'retweets' and 'favourites'.

You can find these people by searching hashtags as mentioned previously. If you run a marketing business, searching #marketing would bring up all of the people Tweeting about this subject. Your task would then be to go onto the profiles of who you think might be key influencers and find out how popular they are by viewing the number of followers they have.

It can be a good idea to make a list of people and businesses that you feel are key influencers that you would like to interact with. It's not a good idea to send out messages to them all at once. Instead keep them in mind, when you have a blog update or a link that you think one of them might be interested in, then send a message over such as:

- "@KeyInf120 - I have just written a blog on...would really like your thoughts on it, here's the link:..."

If you have sent something that the key influencer finds worthwhile they may well 'retweet' you, which will provide you with exposure to their followers which can be a massive boost in both increasing your credibility and your volume of followers.

Retweets

Retweets are a great way to increase your exposure. If you have 100 followers and you post a Tweet, perhaps 5-10 of your followers might see it; the goal is to get 'retweets' from others. A 'retweet' is when another Twitter user shares your Tweet with their followers. If another Twitter user has thousands of followers and retweets your Tweet it's realistic that a few hundred of those followers may see your Tweet. Also, if someone you follow has Tweeted something interesting then retweet what they've put.

Follow Your Competitors' Followers

As you'll have realised by now on Twitter the people who follow your account are called followers. Different social networking websites have different user behaviours and one of the behaviours of users on Twitter is generally to follow an account back if that account follows you. Therefore, you can access the followers of your competitors and make a conscious effort to follow their followers. Their followers will be prompted by your action to follow them and they'll likely visit your Twitter page and follow you back.

Following your competitors' followers is significant because these followers are more than likely to have an interest in what you offer.

YOUTUBE

YouTube can be an incredibly powerful tool when used effectively. It's one of the few social media channels which allows your upload to be viewed 24/7, around the world for days, weeks, months, even years after it's published. Post an update on Facebook or Twitter and you can get some great exposure, but that exposure will range from a few minutes, to hours or if you're lucky days. Create a YouTube video and your message will be out there for the foreseeable future.

One of the main challenges we hear from people when we tell them they should be on YouTube is that they don't want to be in front of the camera. This is a fair comment, very few people are confident public speakers and struggle with talking to a camera, but the best thing you can do is give it a try and make a start. You'll be surprised how quickly your ability can progress. Like every new skill in life at first your videos will be amateur-looking, you'll be nervous and you'll mess up a lot. However, with practice you'll get better and better. If you simply cannot face the thought of looking at a camera why not ask someone else to do it for you. This way you can still have your company message on YouTube. You might have a really confident friend or family member who would relish the opportunity. Failing this, get in touch with a local drama school, as this has yielded great results for many of our clients with amateur actors charging very little, and in some cases doing it absolutely free to get exposure.

A morning of filming can result in dozens of short video clips lasting from just 30 second to a minute in length. This stock of videos can be published over a period of time giving you ammunition for your YouTube channel for months.

However, it doesn't matter how many clips you film if they're not adding value to people. Every business is different but for a general example we'll take a second-hand car dealer and a cosmetics business to discuss the types of videos that could be created. You'll need to think about how the below information could be applied to your business.

Tips and Advice Videos - a second-hand car dealer could create videos with tips and advice to help people, such as:

- Questions to ask a salesman before you buy a second-hand car
- Problems to look for when buying a second-hand car
- Things to ask about buying a second-hand car
- Second-hand car buying tips
- What to look for when buying a second-hand car.

A cosmetics business could create videos, such as:

- Common makeup mistakes
- Beginner's guide to makeup
- Beginner's guide to eye makeup
- 10 tips for perfectly applied makeup
- Hollywood makeup tips

If you create videos with good content that people will genuinely find useful then there is every chance your channel will become a real success and significantly promote your business. We've chosen these video titles as they:

- Target the clients;
- Give the viewers genuinely useful information that they can put into practice;

- Help to build a relationship and trust by helping those who don't know what to do;
- Make the business appear as an authoritative figure within the industry.

Informational Videos - similar to the tips videos but created with a different angle. They don't answer specific questions but give information, for example the used-car dealer might be looking at a second-hand BMW 3 Series. Whilst the tips and advice video would give things to ask a car dealer the informational video would look at the car itself. The informational video would perhaps look at the vehicle's paintwork, give some of the history of the vehicle or perhaps BMW, explain why it is a good or bad car to purchase, examine the interior etc.

For a cosmetics business you could have videos providing information on different makeup tools and accessories and which ones are best for certain looks. Think about your business, you'll have a wealth of information in your head and at your fingertips relating to your sector, products or services. What informational videos could you create?

How to Videos - are a form of informational video, but the information they provide is how to do something. For example, 'How to check a second-hand car before purchase' would be a great video to help your customers.

For the cosmetics business you could do a video on 'How to get the latest celebrity look', or 'How to take your makeup off'.

Showcasing Products - videos showcasing your products can work really well for two reasons. Firstly, it shows potential customers what your products are, their good points and some information about them. Secondly, and very importantly, it can be used for SEO purposes to drive traffic to your site. If you film a clip for YouTube that showcases one of your products, by giving it a detailed description with keywords and a strong title your video can be picked up by potential customers using search engines looking to find your product. YouTube is a very powerful tool, you may not be able to get your website onto the first page of major search engines, but you may be able to get your YouTube video onto page one. At the end of the video make sure you give a link to your product page so it's very easy for viewers to go and buy it.

Customer Testimonials - These can be fantastic to embed on your website and push through other social media channels. People can be very cautious when doing business with a company they've never heard of before. Written testimonials can be very easily falsified, but a video testimonial can make a real difference. The second-hand car salesman could do a very short clip with someone who has purchased a car, of course not every customer will want to do this but it would be worth asking.

The cosmetics business could do exactly the same and have videos of people reviewing their makeup lines or individual products.

You may also want to consider using the leverage of other people's YouTube channels. For example, if someone has a popular YouTube channel with millions of subscribers that focusses on beauty videos, you can ask them if they'd feature your brand or product in one of their videos. There'll be a charge for this, but it'll have your product reach potentially millions of viewers.

Interviews - are good videos you can upload to your channel. For example, in the case of the used-car dealer, interviews with mechanics giving maintenance tips would be very value adding to viewers.

With the cosmetics business, video interviews with models or TV personalities and what they do for makeup would be of great interest to that target market. Remember, video interviews don't have to be in person, they can be over the Internet using a web camera. You can download free video communications software such as Skype and use free screen recording software to capture the interview. Some free screen recording software includes:

- Ezvid - www.ezvid.com
- BlueBerry FlashBack Express Recorder - bbsoftware.co.uk
- Screenr - screenr.com
- Rylstim - sketchman-studio.com
- CamStudio - http://sourceforge.net/projects/camstudio/

One Is Greater Than Zero

Entrepreneur, investor, author, public speaker, and Internet personality Gary Vaynerchuk has a powerful philosophy towards YouTube videos and that is: "one is greater than zero". Many people get caught up in the idea that a video you post on YouTube needs thousands or millions of views to be effective. However, Vaynerchuk believes that quality is better than quantity. For example, imagine you're a business consultant and you post a video on YouTube of you doing consultancy. That video is only seen by 10 people, but one of those 10 people is a Director of a company looking for your services. That Director contacts you and asks if you would visit them to discuss a project. That is far more beneficial than a video that gains thousands of views, but no sales prospects. Therefore, undervaluing just one view is a huge mistake.

Titles and Descriptions

The way people search for videos on YouTube is by typing something in the search bar that matches or closely matches what they're looking for. This means your videos must have intelligent and SEO friendly titles and descriptions if they're to be found.

Video Titles - the title of your video is the most important factor that you need to consider for helping viewers find your video. You'll need to think about what your customers will type in the YouTube search bar or a search engine like Google to find a video like yours. Therefore, your videos should include relevant keywords to ensure high rankings, but also be convincing enough to encourage people to watch. For these reasons, keep to plain text and don't use any symbols. Go on YouTube and look at the titles of videos within your industry and popular videos in general to see examples.

Video Descriptions – a video description is exactly what it says and is used to describe your video and provide any further information. A snippet of your video description also appears under your video in search results, so it needs to be informative and appealing if it's going to convince people to click the link. You'll also want to put a link to your main website in the description so people can visit your website to find out more or make a purchase.

YouTube Comments and Likes

Viewers can like or dislike your videos and make comments. The idea is to get people to like your videos. Don't worry about having 100 percent likes, as this isn't possible. Some people will just click dislike even if they like the video. You can disable comments, but we recommend that you keep them enabled. That way you can engage and interact with people's comments. You might suffer some online abuse, but don't get angry and react with an angry comment back. Just ignore it, but if it's a customer service related issue then try and solve it. In fact you want people to comment as it helps with your video ratings. A simple and effective method to get people to like your video or comment is to tell them to in your video.

If you're ever struggling for video content or ideas leverage the ideas of your viewers. Create a video asking your viewers what they would like to see or if they have any questions they'd like answered. They can do this by leaving a comment for you.

INSTAGRAM

At the time of writing, Instagram is one of the newer social media channels and it's quickly gained momentum becoming a powerful platform.

How is Instagram different from other social media platforms? Instagram is a mobile phone photo-sharing app. It uses the same hashtag and @ interaction facility. However, the main focus of Instagram is pictures you take with your mobile phone, which you can modify to make them look more appealing. Whether you're looking to take some photographs of your products, a sneak preview of a design process or something completely different, it allows your followers to see what you're doing and offer their input. It's extremely important that you take good pictures, because poor-looking pictures will do little for your brand image. Now your pictures don't need to be professional quality, but they do need to look like you've put effort in.

The way you capture followers and interest is to post a picture and tag it with #hashtags that are relevant to the picture or your industry. That way people can find the picture. Like other social media platforms people can like your images, so the more likes you receive the more exposure your image and brand is getting.

Instagram also offers businesses the opportunity to quickly conduct some powerful market research. In a few minutes business owners can search for their product or service and find what people are talking about and sharing. This insight can be invaluable, particularly if you're thinking about trialling a new product and would like some independent thoughts about it. Conducting searches is done by using the hashtag as with Twitter.

Instagram also allows businesses to gain leverage from other people's followers. This is achieved by getting people on Instagram who have a large relevant following to endorse your goods or services. Usually popular Instagram accounts display their business email address as they expect to be contacted for promotional work.

As with Twitter if you follow people, they'll be prompted by your follow and view your profile. If your profile is interesting they'll follow you back. Therefore, you can use the same strategy of following your competitors' followers to increase your exposure.

Have a think about how you could enhance your product or services exposure through the use of Instagram.

LINKEDIN FOR SOCIAL MEDIA

Many people think about LinkedIn as the place to go if they're looking for a new job. It's great for this but it's much more; if you're in business and not on LinkedIn then you're missing out. LinkedIn is in some ways very similar to Facebook but for business professionals and the way you use it should reflect this business nature. In other words if you don't want your clients or customers to read something or see something, don't put it on LinkedIn, or anywhere for that matter. In fact, don't put anything you wouldn't want your clients or customers to see on your personal Facebook either, and obviously not on your business Facebook page.

There are two profiles on LinkedIn that you'll need to be aware of. The first profile is your personal profile, which shows a picture of you, your work experience, your education and a short description of yourself. The second profile is your company profile which shows what your company does, where it's located and displays contact information.

Personal profile - Your profile picture needs to look professional.

Make sure in your picture that you don't have a drink in your hand and you're not enjoying a night on the town. This type of image is perfectly acceptable on a personal Facebook page, but your LinkedIn page needs to show you at your professional best. It may be an idea to have a professional photograph taken or have the background of the image manipulated. If you're a professional it's a good idea to use a picture of yourself in a suit. However, if you're a gym instructor or personal trainer this type of clothing wouldn't represent you or your business. Therefore, do think about what you wear and how you look, first impressions count. Don't put a picture of your company logo as your profile picture as that's what your company profile is for.

On your personal Facebook account you might post updates about what you're doing at the weekend, if something funny has just happened or a joke. On LinkedIn, updates are quite different, we would advise you to keep all updates focused on your business, your industry or sector - keep your personal/social updates to your personal Facebook page. As you get used to LinkedIn you'll get a better understanding of the type of updates members use; the majority will post updates such as motivational quotes, tips, links to news articles etc.

Give your profile page a detailed description, the more that's on there the easier people will be able to find you. Where you went to school, college, university, where you have worked, charity work you have completed, your skills etc.

Next you need to start making some connections. It's against LinkedIn rules to add people that you don't know. However, if you're trying to reach out to a particular client it's always worth sending them a LinkedIn connection request. In the words of Arnold Schwarzenegger: "Break some rules".

LinkedIn displays how many connections you have, but stops showing them after 500+ connections. Therefore, you want to get at least 501 connections. The reason that you want 500+ connections is that you appear well connected, it's a psychological thing. However, at the same time you also want quality connections, so take some time to think about the type of person you're looking to connect with. LinkedIn restricts the number of profiles you can view to first and second connections. This means you need a higher number of connections to get more out of LinkedIn. To get around this you can leverage your visibility by connecting with people who have a significant amount of connections, which will widen your network. A good way to do this is to connect with recruitment consultants in your industry. Many recruiters have a large amount of LinkedIn connections, so by connecting with them you'll have access to the profiles of their connections.

Creating your LinkedIn company page is a must. You need a well-detailed company description explaining exactly what you do, where you're based and a link to your website. Like Facebook and Twitter you can share insightful value adding updates for people to see.

LinkedIn is very different to other social media channels but is extremely worthwhile if used correctly. Think about your business and what type of people could be great connections that could put you in touch with your potential customers, or if you're going to target potential customers direct.

If your company is a B2B company then you, your sales and your marketing employees should be using LinkedIn on a daily basis to discover clients and decision makers. To read more about how to effectively utilise LinkedIn for B2B sales, read the 'Sales' section of this book.

GOOGLE+

Google+ is one of the lesser used social networks, the vast majority of people you meet will have a Facebook account but far fewer will have their own Google+ profile. We generally find the response to be from individuals and some businesses that they have heard of it, know it's worthwhile, but don't actually understand what it is or how to use it.

There's no better way to highlight the importance of a good Google+ business page than by saying that having one can offer your business increased exposure on Google searches. From an SEO point of view many believe that using Google+ for your business can yield great results for your website. Even if you put a small amount of time into your business page it can produce improved local search visibility. Particularly if you also add your physical address to your page and register your business with 'Google Places'.

If you use the Google search engine you'll have probably seen the new website ranking which shows businesses within your local area. Many believe the ranking on this list can be down to how active a business is on its Google+ page. Many believe that businesses which are more active on Google+ and have more +1s (followers) are ranked more highly.

If you create a new page on your website, whether it's a blog or a new product, by posting the link on your business Google+ account with a description or some more information can actually up your rank in search engine results as each update is provided with its own unique URL.

Google algorithms can and do change so the above information about Google+ may change slightly. Whilst change is inevitable if you have an active Google+ account for your business and put time in keeping it updated and post links to your website you'll receive the benefits.

SNAPCHAT

Snapchat isn't strictly a social media app, instead it's a messaging service similar to text messaging. However, it's completely changed the way people communicate. In traditional text messaging the focus is around the text. Snapchat, instead, focuses on a picture, which you can edit using a paint feature as well as add a short text description. The uniqueness of Snapchat is that the picture disappears after a number of seconds. However, it is worth noting that any information sent to a mobile phone cannot be truly deleted.

At the time of writing Snapchat has a feature that enables you to post images and videos for 24 hours called 'My Story'. Famous people and other popular people are using Snapchat and the story facility to engage with their fans. This means you as a business can use Snapchat to engage with your customers. However, this will largely depend on your business type as it'll not be suitable for every type of business.

If you're using popular people on Instagram to promote your goods and services you could also have them promote your goods and services via Snapchat. Usually people who have a large following on Instagram have a large following on Snapchat. People will be more responsive to your product and services if they're advertised by people they follow.

DEALING WITH NEGATIVE FEEDBACK

Sometimes you may receive negative feedback or comments from people on your social media platforms, as social media is a quick way for your customers to communicate with you. Negative feedback is not always a bad thing, so don't panic if you receive any. This is an opportunity for you to improve your business and correct and delight your customers. For example, if a customer is complaining about poor service, listen to your customer and act immediately to correct this. In fact great positivity, public relations and market-ing can come from correcting a customer's displeasure. Don't forget that negative feedback on your social media channel can be seen by others so make sure you deal with comments swiftly and in a way that shows you as proactively trying to make your customer happy.

Sometimes you may just receive angry abuse for the sake of it. This is known as "Trolling". This is by people who in many cases might not have even bought anything from you and just want to attack you. Sometimes it can be angry competitors. Your best course of action in this case is doing absolutely nothing. Their bitterness or anger is self-destructive and deflected by their own behaviour. It can be diffi-cult not to stand-up for yourself especially if you're really passionate about your business, but it's pointless and a waste of time. It's their goal to waste your time, so don't let them. It's your goal to grow your business, concentrate on that. If you receive malicious messages on your businesses social media channels there are tools that will allow you to block or report the individual(s) concerned.

SOCIAL MEDIA SUMMARY

In summary, social media could potentially keep you very busy. If you're quite new to social media there'll be a great deal to take in. Don't allow yourself to be overwhelmed. If you have never used social media before, don't become active on all of the channels straight away. Start with one social media channel until you're con-fident with it and happy before progressing on to another.

If you're used to social media then make sure you're disciplined. Logging in with the best of intentions for your business can quite easily become wasted hours browsing. Have a goal before you login so you don't get sidetracked and when you have completed your tasks log out and carry on working on a different task. Social media is a powerful tool for marketing your business, but entrepreneurs can fall into the trap of hiding behind social media. Social media should form only part of your marketing strategy. You still need to get out there in person to network and knock on doors.

SEARCH ENGINE OPTIMISATION

S earch engine optimisation (SEO) could be a book in itself, and there are many big, confusing books out there on the subject and a few good ones as well. We'll explain to you what SEO actually is in a straightforward way, what you need to be doing to ensure your website is optimised and the benefits of doing so. After reading this chapter and when you get started on optimising your website you'll realise it's nowhere near as daunting or complicated as you may think it is now.

SEO is important for every business and here are just a few reasons why:

- 93% of online experiences begin with a search engine - SearchEngineJournal.com
- 60% of all organic clicks go to the organic top 3 search results - HubSpot
- 44% of online shoppers begin by using a search engine - HubSpot

These statistics show us that a huge proportion of those looking for something online don't have a specific business in mind and are using a search engine to help them find what they're looking for. Further to this, the statistics show that a significant amount of traffic will go to the top three organic (not paid for) websites listed by the search engine. If you can spend the time to get your website to reach a high position on search engine results you'll reap the rewards.

Before we start, remember these two points:

1. SEO isn't rocket science.
2. The job of a search engine is simply to match an individual's search with quality content that answers their question or finds what they're looking for.

WEBSITE CONTENT

If you want your website to perform well on search engines then you need to have good quality, unique content on your site. Competition to be on page #1 of search engine results is incredibly fierce and is becoming increasingly more competitive as the number of websites online continues to grow. By creating unique, useful content your website can be seen by search engines as a resource which helps people find answers to questions and provides them with the information they need resulting in a high ranking.

Unique content is very important. Search engines will penalise you if your website contains identical content to another site, so make sure you haven't got anything copied directly from another online source. Duplicate content can often happen with online retailers who take the product description directly from their wholesaler's website. This is very understandable and justifiable but it can have terrible effects on a website's search engine ranking.

Take the time to create your own unique content on every page of your website. A general rule is that every page on a website should be 300 words in length as the absolute minimum. Anything less than this and it will perform poorly on search engines and it'll be less likely to have a number of quality keywords. We'll discuss keywords shortly. We personally recommend pages to have a minimum of 450 words of unique content on every page; the more quality content you have on your website, the more likely it is that search engines will find it.

Search engines love fresh new content, so if you aren't creating new content or updating your website in some way it'll start falling down the search engine rankings whilst websites that are updated regularly will take your place. This is where a blog can come in extremely useful, in our opinion it's the easiest, most effective way to keep your site updated with fresh, relevant content. See the next chapter called Blogging for Business.

KEYWORDS

Within your website you should have keywords. If you've never heard of keywords before or aren't quite sure what it means, don't worry, it's very simple. Your keywords should reflect your business and what you do, for example a solicitor would have keywords such as:

- Solicitor
- Law
- Legal
- Advice

Your chosen keywords would then be used throughout your website. It is very important to use keywords organically. This means using them for a reason, so you can't write nonsense sentences such as:

'If you're looking for a solicitor, we're a firm of solicitors, so if you're looking for a solicitor get in touch and a solicitor will be happy to talk to you'

A few years ago website owners could get away with this and in many cases cramming a site full of keywords would get it listed very highly on search engine results. However, times have changed. The major search engines identify poor quality content and your site will be penalised when identified. Being penalised by a search engine can have a catastrophic effect on the amount of visitors you receive. Our advice is not to try and trick the major search engines, use SEO ethically and you'll see results over time.

Identifying Your Keywords

To identify your keywords, think about your business and the products or services you offer. Think about what people will be typing into the search engine if they're looking for your particular product or service.

How many keywords you choose for your site as a whole will depend on how big your website is (or is going to be). If you're a tradesman with a small website with about 3-4 pages then you may look at around five keywords for your website as a whole. If you run a large online retail store with 50+ pages you may look to have twenty or more keywords within your site. If you're not sure what to do then we recommend you start small, pick five keywords and start from there. When you see results you can begin adding additional keywords.

When you have chosen your keywords they then need to be placed on every page of your website. Depending on the keywords you've chosen it may not be possible to get them all on a particular page which is okay, but make sure you have at least one of your keywords listed on each page. This is very easy to do as your keywords should be a reflection of what your business does, so they may already be on most of website pages without you even realising it.

Taking keywords to a more advanced level, every page of your site should have its own unique keyword. As an example we'll use the solicitor's keywords as given above; on a page titled 'Personal Injury' within their website the owner would of course want the keywords of the site listed on there (solicitor, advice etc.) but the main combination of keywords for this particular page should be 'personal injury' or a variation of that. Within the webpage's written content the keyword 'personal injury' should be used consistently but not excessively. Think about all of the products you offer and decide what should be the main keyword for each of those pages.

Long Tail Keywords

We really like long tail keywords and have found them very effective for SEO. They're more specific so you'll get less traffic from them but you can come up considerably higher on search results than you would with a standard keyword. You can use a combination of keywords and long tail keywords within your site. The examples below will show the difference between keywords and long tail keywords. Sticking with the solicitor as the example:

- *Website keyword:* solicitor
- *Specific page keywords:* personal injury
- *Long tail keywords:* Looking for a personal injury solicitor for a compensation claim

Website keywords and page specific keywords are highly competitive. You may struggle to place highly on search engine results for these; this is where the use of the long tail keyword comes in useful. Most search engine users would type in '*personal injury*' or '*personal injury solicitor*' if that's what they're looking for. However, a smaller percentage may enter '*Looking for a personal injury solicitor for a compensation claim*' or another variation of this: '*I'm looking for a personal injury solicitor to make a compensation claim*'. Although there'll be fewer people searching for the long tail keyword it'll still happen and your website would place much higher for these results when using it as opposed to a standard keyword.

Think about how your page-specific keywords could be altered to become a long tail keyword. We like to use a long tail keyword on every page of a website if possible.

Geographic Keywords:

How you use geographic keywords will depend on your business, but they can be extremely powerful when used correctly. If you run a business that serves customers in a local area for example hairdressers, a gym, retail store, a restaurant, using that specific location as a keyword can be very effective. The traffic will come from using the name of the town or city as the keyword, for example London, but as with keywords and long tail keywords the geographic angle can also be made more precise for better results, for example 'Mayfair, London'.

As with long tail keyword terms there'll be fewer searches for this, but your website is far more likely to rank highly for this. Examples:

- *Keyword:* Salon
- *Geographic Keyword:* London Salon
- *Precise Geographic Keyword:* Salon in Mayfair, London

Many site owners try to cram as many geographic locations on the bottom of website pages. We don't advise this, as firstly, it doesn't look professional and secondly the search engines will clamp down on it and penalise you at some point.

Don't worry if your business offers a nationwide or international service, you can still use geographic tailoring to give you an advantage for some terms. If you were based in Oxford it can be used throughout the site for example *'We offer a nationwide/international service from our offices in Oxford'*, or made more specific such as *'Adwell, Oxford'*. This can be successful as a lot of people like to buy from local businesses.

GETTING YOUR WEBSITE PAGES SEO READY

After covering keywords we're now going to look at the main areas that should be optimised on every page of a website and how it can be done.

Website Title

This is an important feature that you need to get right. The title of your website basically tells the search engine what your website is about. You only have between 60 - 70 characters to do it in, so it needs to be short, to the point and contain your main keywords that you want to be found for.

Keyword cramming on titles isn't an effective strategy. Search engines can now identify whether a title makes sense or if it is just crammed with keywords. A title such as:

'Salon | London | Mayfair | Stylist | Hair'

Wouldn't be as effective as:

'London Salon offering Hair Styling in Mayfair'

Web Page Titles

If you're using WordPress we can't recommend highly enough installing the 'plugin' called 'SEO' *by* Yoast. A YouTube search will show you a video how to do this in less than two minutes. Using this 'plugin' will allow you to optimise your website's pages in a simple, straightforward way. There are other SEO plugins and soft-ware available for non-WordPress sites, but there are just too many to cover. Using a search engine will help you find the SEO software for your particular website if you're not using WordPress. Make sure you take the time to read independent reviews so that you know the software is good before you install it.

Every page on your website needs optimising, so the first thing you need to do is give each page a title. The logic is the same as the site title above. Again you only have 70 characters available to use, so you need to make sure that as much search-engine-friendly content as possible gets in there.

On every page look at the content that's in there, think about the keywords that are assigned to the page and aim to include as much as possible in the page title. An example for the solicitor's personal injury web page title might be something like:

'Personal Injury Solicitors in Manchester offering Legal Advice'.

When using WordPress this is very easy to do when you have installed 'SEO' by Yoast. Sign into your admin area, find the page you wish to update and then scroll to the bottom were you'll see the plugin: 'SEO' by Yoast. It'll say 'SEO Title', in this field enter the title for this particular page.

Header Tags

Header tags are simply a way of giving your webpages a structure with a main heading and subheadings, just as this book uses headings and subheadings. Just to note, header tags are HTML code, so the reader won't see the actual tags.

The main Header Tag is called <h1> and then subheadings are labelled <h2>, <h3>, <h4>, <h5>, <h6>. The main header of the page would be highlighted and turned into a <h1> tag and further sections of content would be made into <h2>, <h3>, <h4>, <h5> or <h6>. You don't need to use all of the six header tags, so it'll depend on how much content you have. Simply for readability we recommend not going past <h3> for the reason that subheadings nested under subheadings looks messy and becomes hard to read.

The breakdown of header tags might look something like this:

- <h1>Most important heading here</h1>
- <h3>Less important heading here</h3>

Using header tags can make pages simpler to navigate for both users and search engines. To learn more about header tags visit: http://www.w3schools.com/tags/tag_header.asp

Meta Description

A meta description is a small description of what that particular webpage is about. A meta description should be given to every webpage. When you use a search engine to find websites the two to three lines of content underneath the website link is the meta description.

When writing the meta description it's a balancing act between priming it for search engine optimisation and making the page enticing for viewers to want to click on the site to find out more. If you stuff the meta description full of keywords or create content that doesn't make sense or read well then it'll look strange and possibly like nonsense to the people who read it.

Creating good meta descriptions can be a challenge so don't rush them. Think about each particular page, what it is you're offering and or writing about, give a snippet of information to entice the reader to click whilst also trying to include a relevant keyword, long tail keyword and or geographic keyword.

Again if you are using 'SEO' By Yoast on WordPress it's very straight-forward to enter a meta description, as with the page titles scroll to the bottom of the page in the admin area until you reach the 'SEO' By Yoast section and enter the content where it says 'meta description'.

Image Alt Tags

Images with alternative text specified, or Alt Tags, simply means giving an image on your website a name to make it easier for the search engine to identify what the image is. People visiting a website won't see what is included in the Alt Tag unless they hover their mouse over the image.

When uploading an image onto your website you'll see an option to add 'Alternative Text' or 'Alt Text'. Adding Alt Tags will make your website perform better on search engines, particularly if you have a large number of images on your website.

An image on your website may quickly get across a particular product or service to a person looking at it, but without Alt Text search engines won't be able to identify what the image is or what it represents.

Go through your website and make sure that each image has its own Alt Tag description. Alt Tags should not be crammed with keywords, instead they should explain the image within a few words, if you can include a keyword then do so but don't make it your goal.

Sitemap

Search engines want website owners to create sites that have great content which can be easily accessed. A sitemap is a structure or hierarchy of your website's webpages, which makes it easier for people and search engines to find information on your website, and to quickly evaluate the website's content. Without a sitemap installed on your website, search engines may miss key information that's held on your website which can result in a far lower search engine ranking.

For WordPress users there are a number of very simple plugin tools which allow you to create your own sitemap in just a few clicks. You can try 'XML Sitemap & Google News feeds' which is a WordPress plugin. It's very straightforward and requires no technical knowledge, just follow the steps after installation. You can download it here: https://wordpress.org/plugins/xml-sitemap-feed

If you're using a content management system other than WordPress there are dozens of step-by-step instructional videos available on YouTube which will show you how to create a sitemap on your website.

BACKLINKS

Backlinks are important and they're simply when another website has a link to your website. Search engines view backlinks as giving a website credibility. If dozens to hundreds of good quality websites are happy to put your website as a link on their site then it's seen as you must be doing something right.

Before we go any further a word of warning. Creating poor quality backlinks can have the opposite effect and get your website ranking significantly downgraded. Make sure you visit websites before you have a link to your website placed on them. Paying for backlinks can also prove catastrophic as a number of companies are creating backlinks to very poor sites, you will see offers such as "300 backlinks for £xxx". Don't do this and instead build your backlinks organically.

Gaining backlinks is time consuming, there's no two ways about it. You need to find websites that are in the same sector as you or linked in some other way, contact the site owner and ask for a link. They'll normally want something in return whether it's a mutual link back to their site, a payment or some content for their website such as guest post blogging.

When you start building your backlinks speak to people you already know who have websites, whether it's for their own business or some other reason. You'll be surprised how many people you have a connection with who will have some sort of online presence. If you know someone it's very easy to ask for a backlink so this is a good way to get started.

Gaining backlinks from strangers can be a challenge. It's made considerably harder if your website isn't very good. Make sure your site has some interesting content and/or is useful in some way so that high quality websites won't be averse to linking to you. Decide what it is you're willing to offer website owners, whether it is a mutual link exchange, a guest post blog for their website, payment or something else. Then start making contact with websites. It really is a numbers game, many won't even reply to you but don't lose heart, keep putting your site out there, even if you only gain one new backlink a week over time it will grow and become substantial.

There are some simple ways to have quality and reputable websites link back to your website. You can create pages in Google+, YouTube, LinkedIn and Wikipedia which will have links back to your website.

Another good way to get backlinks is to search all your competitors' websites and see what websites link to them. Record these websites and contact them for a link exchange.

INTERNAL LINKS

Search engines like to see internal links within a website, which also help to keep your visitors on your website. In your blog if you mention a particular product or service make it a clickable link that takes the reader to that page of your website. If you're writing a blog make a conscious effort to mention other blogs on your website with links to them. Search engines will be pleased with this and you can direct visitors to exactly where you want them to go, whether that's a sign up page, or to a particular product or a contact page.

EXTERNAL LINKS

Putting links on your site to other high quality sites is known as external linking. It's used less, but something that many believe can have positive effect. This can be done when you're creating new content, such as a blog, provide your reader with a link to a website to find out more or the source of whatever it is you're writing about.

As with backlinking, make sure you only link to websites that are high quality.

PERMALINKS

A permalink is a URL that takes the user to a specific webpage created on a CMS such as WordPress. These are also the links a user sees in the Internet search browser and which they may type in the Internet search browser. When creating pages in WordPress the page will generate a URL like this: 'www.examplewebsite.com/pageid=101'. However, looking at that URL we have no idea where it's taking us, so neither will search engines.

This default permalink ID is very weak for SEO and can make your website appear unprofessional. Ensure you update your permalink settings so that it gets the 'post name' meaning the page name, for example if the page name was 'Contact us' it would look like this:

'www.examplewebsite.com/contactus'. To change the permalinks in WordPress login to the admin area, click 'Settings', then 'Permalinks' then change from 'Default' to 'Post Name'.

This is a very simple job that takes less than a minute to do.

SEO SUMMARY

In summary, SEO needs constant work, but it can pay dividends. You'll need to understand that you'll not achieve success overnight.

If you keep your website consistently updated with fresh content and build links with other websites you're on your way to having a strong SEO system in place. There is a great deal more to be learnt about SEO, but if you're a beginner this is a great start to give you a good grounding in the subject. You'll be able to start working on getting your website onto page #1.

BLOGGING FOR BUSINESS

A blog is a regularly updated website or webpage. It can take many forms depending on the interests and purpose of the author, for example some people blog about fashion; some people blog about food, the list is endless. Blogs, if appealing enough, can attract thousands if not millions of readers. One of the World's most famous bloggers is Tim Ferris, the Author of *The 4-hour workweek*. Ferris has used the power of his blog to sell his books to his loyal readers. In this chapter we are going to look at how you can integrate blogging into your business to build a following and grow your business.

Blogging has other important marketing qualities. Not only can it help you been seen as a leading expert and create loyal readers, Internet search engines like Google love new website content which helps you get up the search engine rankings. The main goal of blogging is to acquire more customers and according to Hubspot, 79% of companies that have a blog reported a positive return on investment for inbound marketing in 2013. Since blogging is free it's a powerful marketing method that your business can utilise. However, simply having a blog won't achieve these goals, your blog must be informative and appealing, and we'll show you how.

Don't worry if blogging doesn't make much sense yet, or if it feels overwhelming. It will all become clear as you read through this chapter.

BLOGGING FOR SEARCH ENGINE RANKINGS

As a business owner you'll almost certainly have a website, but ask yourself, when was the last time you updated it? If your answer is along the lines of: "I can't remember", then there's a possibility that your website is disappearing into the abyss of the vast Internet where 2,500,000,000,000,000,000+ (2.5+ quintillion bytes) of data are produced every day. In other words, if your website isn't creating good, fresh new content it'll be pushed to the back of the line.

Search engines love unique content. If your competitors consistently create great new website content and you don't, they'll almost certainly be ranked higher than you, receive more traffic and gain new customers that could have been yours.

Most entrepreneurs who are new to blogging often struggle with what they're going to write about, many feel that they don't have anything to say. As an entrepreneur you'll be a fountain of knowledge within your sector; you'll know things that other people don't. You just need to think about what knowledge you have and don't assume that everyone already knows what you know, as they probably don't.

Creating Quality Content

Now we're going to look at how to create blogs that supercharge your website's SEO (Search Engine Optimisation) and be found by people using a search engine. Following these steps will help your website get visits from potential customers who wouldn't have come across it without a blog.

SEO is done to get your website higher on search engines so that more people visit. In order for this to happen you need to ensure that your website's keywords are in your blog, for example if you run a clothing business and one of your main keywords is 'jeans' then you want that keyword within the blog. This has to be done sensibly, search engines are created by extremely smart people, if you write nonsense and cram content full of your keywords you'll be found out and your site will almost certainly be demoted as a result.

An example of a good blog for this type of business might be 'How to pick the right jeans for you'. With this type of blog the content might be between 300-1500 words in length. 300 words is usually the minimum if you want your blog to be found by a search engine. Taking the time to write a blog with 1500 words or more has been shown to achieve 68.1% more Tweets and 22.6% more Facebook likes than a post under 1500 words (QuickSprout cited in Hubspot, n.d). Within a blog you could get the keyword jeans into the content between 3-15 times depending on its length.

It's important to note that blogging doesn't provide immediate results. It can take between two weeks to three months for your blog to be indexed and your website to be updated by search engines. Don't be disheartened if you don't see results immediately, writing a good quality blog that contains your website's keywords is laying the foundations for your website's long term success.

LINK BUILDING

Blogs are a great opportunity to place internal links within your website, which search engines love. If the business mentioned above had written a blog on jeans he or she might mention a specific type of jeans that they sell. When mentioning this particular item a clickable link can be added which readers can press to take them to view the product.

Doing this is a success on two fronts; firstly you achieve internal links, which search engines look for when ranking sites and secondly you are directing people who are clearly interested in your products, as they're reading about them, directly to the page where they can purchase the product they're reading about.

Choosing the Right Content

Our favourite way of doing research is to go to a search engine and start typing in your product or service letter by letter. The search engine will then provide you with suggested options based on the most frequent searches. It's also good to add words like 'who', 'how' and 'why' before you enter the letters of your service as it gives more results and shows you what people are searching for. When you see what people are searching for you can create great content that'll provide people conducting these searches with the information that they're looking for.

The business owner retailing jeans may start by typing 'Jeans how to...' we have just tried this and the suggestion was 'how to choose jeans', the business owner would know that this particular search is popular. By creating a good quality blog which provides the user with information they're looking for the jeans retailer could expect his or her blog to perform well over time and potentially be ranked very highly by major search engines.

This is particularly powerful, as a jeans retailer would have to spend a huge amount to be placed on the first few pages of a search engine for terms such as 'Men's jeans'. This is simply due to the size and comparative budget of its competitors. However, creating a blog that helps people who want to find out more about jeans could realistically end up on page one of search engine results without the unnecessary costs.

Remember that the job of a search engine is to bring a person seeking information to the best website with the most relevant information. As a business blogger your job is to ensure that you answer as many questions as possible through your blogs. Through blogging you should be aiming to bring visitors to your website, keep them engaged and bring them back.

Copying Blogs for SEO

You might be thinking a quick alternative to writing your own blogs is to copy and paste good ones from other sites and maybe change the wording around a little. Unique website content is one of the most important reasons for blogging. The main search engines have some of the most incredible algorithms and detectors, so if you copy and paste information from another online source onto your website they'll find out, and fast. The penalty for this type of action is demotion of your website, the complete opposite of what you wanted to achieve when you got started with blogging. If you're thinking about just copying and pasting content from another source then you're genuinely better off not blogging at all. The penalty is fair, when you put time to one side and create new content for your website, we're sure anyone would be frustrated if they saw that content on competitors' sites.

BLOGGING FOR LEADERSHIP

Blogging has another very important role, which is showing readers that you're an expert within your industry. Blogging, when done well, allows you the opportunity to become an authority within your sector. If, for example, you run a business selling fitness equipment then a weekly blog informing readers about the latest exercises, scientific research and sports supplements would over time start to get higher levels of Internet traffic.

Think about your business sector and what you could write weekly/fortnightly/monthly that would show you as the 'go to person' for the latest news and information. Obviously writing all of this from scratch would be incredibly time consuming, so a good idea can be to go around other sites, gain snippets of information about what has been happening in your industry and then creating a 'round up' of the news on your site. However, always remember to reference other people's work in your blogs.

Being seen as an industry expert obviously won't happen overnight, for quite a while your blogs might only get a handful of views which is what stops most people from continuing. If you persevere and write good content then you'll be rewarded. However, like everything in life, it takes hard work and dedication.

GUEST POST BLOGGING

Guest post blogging is something that most people haven't heard of but it can be an incredibly powerful took for increasing the awareness of your business, and bring huge gains for SEO results. The first step is to find a highly reputable or upcoming website that is ideally within your industry. Then make contact with them saying that you would like to write fresh content for their site and get a link back to your website within it.

Duplicate content is again not allowed, the website owners will want fresh content so you cannot just send over a blog that is already on your website. Should you get away with it and have this published on their website (you probably wouldn't get this far) the search engine's algorithms will identify it and penalise you, so make sure that if you're going to do guest post blogging that you do it properly. If you're new to blogging then it's worth spending the first few months building up a stock of blogs on your own website before you look at guest post blogging. That way you'll find your writing style and have an idea of what works and what doesn't.

A lot of people don't see the potential benefits of guest post blogging and don't like the idea of writing unique content to be used on a website that isn't their own, but it really can pay dividends if you partner with the right website. It increases the exposure of you and your business to people that may have never known that you existed and it shows the major search engines that your website is a reputable site. Getting a link back to your website from a high quality website informs the search engines that this reputable website approves of your website enough to 'enough to reference you within its own.

A fantastic tool to find high quality reputable websites that are looking for unique content is HARO which stands for 'Help A Reporter Out! Register with HARO and you will receive a number of emails every week with websites looking for content. Read through the list of articles site owners are looking for, they range from seeking opinions, technical advice, ideas and more. This can be one of the quickest ways to have your business and website link placed on some extremely high quality websites. To register visit: http://www.helpareporter.com/

VIDEO BLOGGING

With platforms like YouTube you have the ability to create video blogs in conjunction with written blogs.

A video blog can be fantastic for businesses as potential customers actually get to see you as an individual, which studies have shown can have a massive impact on converting visitors into customers. The use of a video blog can also make your website more engaging, build trust and keep visitors on your website for longer.

We've worked with a number of clients on video blogging and have found that it can have remarkable results in its own right for SEO. At the time of writing YouTube is the second largest search engine in the world. The result of this is that a video can be found higher on search engines than a website.

A company we worked with recently had worked extremely hard to beat their competitors and gain prominence on page one in results for an extremely competitive sports supplement product. They struggled to get higher than the top of page two. As a different angle they took a handheld camcorder (a smartphone is just as good these days) and filmed a two-minute video in which they held the supplement, spoke about its benefits and read out loud the ingredients. It certainly won't be winning any video awards, but what it did achieve was a position on page one of major search engines and within the top one-third of the page. This was done by giving the video a title that included the name of the product and a very well-detailed description of the video that included relevant keywords. At the end of the video they placed a discount code and a clickable link saying 'Get Yours Now' which took viewers who clicked it to the relevant page to purchase the product. The result was a huge surge in website traffic and a significant increase in sales.

To maximise the full benefits of blogging we suggest that you write blogs, but also work in video blogging too. If you run an email campaign, an advert in a magazine or something similar, it can of course work but only for as long as the campaign runs. When you create a video promoting your business and publish it on a platform such as YouTube or Vimeo it can be viewed 24 hours a day, seven days a week, 365 days a year by people around the globe at no cost to you.

ADVERTISING YOUR BLOG

Your blog has been carefully thought out, well written/videoed and published, now it's time to get it to your readers. In this section we're going to look at ways to give your blog more exposure.

The most obvious platform to push your blog is through social media: Facebook, Twitter, Google+ and LinkedIn being the best for this. This can be done as soon as your blog is published. Our advice is to create a 'teaser' update that makes people want to click the link to find out more and read your blog. For example if you posted "Just published our latest blog about jeans, read it here (link)" you probably wouldn't get many people clicking as it doesn't sound intriguing, exciting or even interesting. If you created updates such as:

- Find out what you never knew about jeans......<link>
- Our latest blog update has been released in the last 3 minutes be the first to read it...<link>

An excellent way to increase the exposure of your blog is by running a competition. Social media channels are an effective tool for this, doing a 'share' or 'retweet' competition on Facebook and Twitter can result in great exposure. Create an update and tell your followers that if the update gets, for example, 10, 20, 50 shares or retweets combined then one person who has given it a share or retweet will receive a prize. The prize can be just about anything, something silly, funny, a discount code or a genuine prize.

You'll almost certainly have an email list of potential and past customers, and if you haven't, read the email marketing chapter. When a good blog has been published, send them an email letting them know about it. You can also ask them to 'like', 'favourite', 'share' or 'retweet' it to their followers if they enjoy it/find it useful. You'll usually get a better response and more interaction from past customers and those who have signed up to your email newsletter compared to those on social media who may have never interacted with your business before.

Often forgotten about but very effective is to tell people about your blog: friends, family, colleagues, people at networking events and anyone else that might be interested. Ask them to read it, tell their friends about it and share it online.

CONVERTING READERS TO CUSTOMERS

As a business owner writing fresh content, don't lose track of why you're blogging, ultimately it's to get more customers. Make sure that when visitors are reading your blog you're doing as much as possible to create and ensure a continuing relationship. Too many business owners just have a page of content on their blog, so visitors will mostly read the information and then click away, this is really missing out on some big opportunities. Have an email signup form on the blog page and give a really good call-to-action to make them sign up. If your blog is about a product or service that the reader can purchase from you, ensure you have a clear call-to-action enticing them to make the purchase.

A lot of businesses don't do this and it's a fundamental error of blogging; someone has come to your website as they're interested in what you're writing about so why wouldn't you give them the opportunity to sign up to find out more? Of course only a small percentage of viewers will sign up regardless of how good your call-to-action is (although a bad or no call-to-action will result in a significant fall in signups) but overtime you'll build up a list of potential customers who you can tell about promotions, special offers, new products or even your latest blog. This is the next stage in building a relationship with a potential customer, the blog introduced them to your business and you'll now keep in touch with the long term goal being to turn them into a customer.

You can convert readers into customers through the use of enticing images. Graphically designed banner ads can work very well on blog pages as they stand out when put next to paragraphs of text. Create advertising images intelligently and don't just show them the product with a clickable link to buy it. You need to create excitement. The excitement can be created with some sort of special offer or discount with a deadline such as "offer ends midnight" or "the next 3 customers". As with email signups the immediate conversion rate from blog reader to customer will be very low. However, you're giving the minority of people who're thinking about buying an easy option to complete the checkout process who may not purchase if the link wasn't there.

WRITING A BLOG

By now you should have a good understanding of how blogging can be beneficial to your business. As with anything, successful blogging won't come overnight and it may take some time for your blog writing to develop, but starting is the key.

When was the last time you had your spelling, punctuation, grammar and ideas put under scrutiny? Probably not since your schooldays. However, as a blogger you'll need to be prepared for criticism if your content contains errors or differences of opinion. Ensure that your content is proofread before it's put online, failure to do so can result in negative comments and lost business. Errors can put potential clients off your business quickly. If the first impression of your business is that it makes sloppy mistakes and doesn't have checks in place, it can damage your reputation.

For those who are really short on time or for whatever reason don't want to write a blog, you'll be pleased to know that this task can be outsourced. There are copywriters around the world willing to create content on your chosen topic for a small cost. Sites such as PeoplePerHour.com will allow you to make contact with copywriters and agree a price for good quality, unique content which you can use on your website. However, always check the work hasn't been plagiarised before you release any money.

Depending on your business there'll be dozens of types of blogs that you will be able to create, but here are some ideas:

- How to guides.

- A list, e.g. 15 reasons to...
- A review of a product or service.
- A news story or your thoughts on a news story.
- An interview.
- An FAQ (frequently asked questions).
- A 'cheat sheet/life hack' guide with tips and ideas.

CREATING ENGAGING TITLES

The title of your blog will be the difference between someone being curious and interested enough to click to find out more, or not giving it a second glance. As mentioned in the SEO chapter, keywords are of great importance and you should aim to have at least one of your keywords within the title, as well as making it sound interesting.

Your blog title can either be short and sweet or it can be stretched out to gain the advantage of a long tail keyword, this is covered in the SEO chapter.

Here are some blog titles that should give you some inspiration:

- 5 Reasons you should...
- What happens when you get... Completely wrong!
- The biggest mistakes on... to avoid.
- How to enjoy...
- 5 tips to help you become...
- 3 amazing facts you didn't know about...

In summary, blogging can be fantastic for business but won't provide results overnight. If you follow the steps above, research your sector and write engaging content or create interesting video blogs then your web traffic will grow over time. Blogging can be a chore but if some of the biggest companies in the world have blogs on their websites then you should as well.

PAY PER CLICK ADVERTISING

Pay Per Click (PPC) advertising is when a business places an advert on a platform such as Google or Facebook. The advertiser is only charged when someone clicks on their advert, which is a major benefit for you. In this chapter we're going to look at how to create a PPC advertisement, choose which provider is right for your business and ways to ensure you get the most out of your budget.

ABOUT PPC

PPC is unlike any other form of advertising. If you take out an advert in a newspaper, magazine, radio or on television the same advert is shown to everyone, so the advert will be shown to people who may or may not have any interest in your product or service.

With PPC advertising you get to decide who sees your advertisement, whether that be a certain age group, those living in a certain area or a whole host of other factors. In other words you can pinpoint your target market. What makes PPC even better for you is that you aren't charged any money if someone only looks at your advert. You're only charged when someone clicks through to your website, so unlike other form of advertising it is highly accountable.

Before we get started we want to make it clear that if you have a poor-quality website or business then no matter how much you spend on PPC advertising the results will almost certainly be poor. Each click is a person, if that person is not confident in your online presence then they'll go elsewhere. Don't start on PPC advertising until you have really scrutinised your website, made sure it's all in working order and looks fit for purpose.

When your website looks great, still remember that many people won't make that purchase or pick up the phone straight away. Many will look at your website, read the information, have a think and perhaps visit the site again before deciding to make a purchase. They may get in touch for more information, particularly if your product or service isn't usually seen as an impulse purchase. A person's buying behaviour change as the value increases.

CHOOSING A PPC PROVIDER

To get started you need to choose one or more companies that offer PPC advertising, such as Google, Bing, Yahoo, Facebook, YouTube, LinkedIn; the list goes on. Don't go with the first company that you come across or assume will be the best, sit down and think about your target customers, what platform might they use the most and respond to? For example, a company targeting teenagers might decide on YouTube advertising whilst another company targeting the over 40s may look at Google.

PPC makes big money for these platforms so there are plenty of great offers around to entice new advertisers. Don't just sign up straight away. Search online for discount codes or even contact the advertising departments directly and say you're thinking about using them and see what freebies they're willing to give you. It's not uncommon to receive anywhere from £25 - £150 worth of free advertising, although receiving the discount will usually require you to spend a certain amount before the free advertising is credited to your account.

Spend time thinking about which platforms you want to spend your budget with, gauge the success rates when running a campaign and make alterations. PPC isn't an exact science, so every business will be slightly different.

GETTING THE MOST FROM YOUR BUDGET

PPC allows you to operate with an incredible degree of flexibility, meaning you can spend anywhere from a few pounds to tens of thousands of pounds a month. Whatever your budget you can advertise with PPC. Your budget can even be maximised and minimised depending on the day of the week or time of the day if you wish. If you run a business that gets the majority of its business from Tuesday to Thursday 10am - 3pm you can maximise your budget for this period, as is the case if you wanted more customers from 5-8pm weekdays. You decide when your advertisements are shown to ensure your budget is not used unnecessarily.

The flexibility with PPC doesn't stop there, if you're running a PPC advertisement and it's not performing well or something is wrong with it, you can simply make the necessary changes. If you put out a poor-quality magazine or television advert, by the time it goes live it's too late to make changes which isn't the case with PPC.

SETTING UP A PPC CAMPAIGN

Let's take a look at actually starting a campaign. We're going to use Google Adwords as the example for setting up a campaign; each platform is slightly different but the overall points raised below will be the same for all.

Go to www.google.co.uk/adwords. Creating an account is quick and straightforward, the only information needed at this time is your personal and business details as well as your billing information so that they can take payment when due.

After your information has been entered it's time to create your first advert. You can search for YouTube videos to watch an advertising campaign being created from start to finish. This will help if you're more of a visual learner.

One of the first questions you'll be asked is whether you would like your advert to be seen just on Google search results or whether you would like it to be seen on Google Search Partner sites, which are just other websites. This is a personal choice, depending on your business and how much exposure you want it can be worth using both Google and the Search partners for a short period of time and then just Google to compare success rates to help you decide which is better for you.

By Location

A fantastic opportunity to maximise your PPC advertisement's success is to choose what geographic locations you would like your advert to be seen in. Unless you have a huge budget we would not recommend making your campaign worldwide or even UK wide. Think about the key towns and cities that you would like to target, you can even narrow it down to postcodes if there are very specific areas you would like to hone in on. Again, mistakes can prove costly with a wasted budget so take a while to think about the areas you want to target and why.

If your business offers products nationwide, geographic tailoring can still be extremely beneficial. If your business sells a product used by industries geographically targeting industrial areas by postcode could see a better return on investment than allowing the advert to be run nationwide. A company selling farming machinery probably wouldn't get many customers from big cities so they could look to geographically tailor their campaign to more rural locations were they would be more likely to make a sale.

Deciding on a budget

When choosing your daily budget remember to multiply this by how many days are in each month so you know what the maximum amount you can spend is per month. That way you know there won't be a surprise at the end of the month with a big bill.

Your daily budget is the most you'll spend, if no one clicks on your advert then there will be no charge. The unused daily budget isn't 'rolled over' so if your daily budget is £10 and you get no clicks on Monday your daily budget on Tuesday would still be £10.

When starting on Google Adwords only invest what you can afford. Don't plough a significant amount of money on the assumption that you'll get a lot of sales in return, it isn't always the case.

Budget Vs Profit

It's important to calculate your daily advertising budget against your profit targets. If your business sells items with a profit margin of £500 then it may be acceptable for you to have a daily budget of £100 as the traffic derived from this amount of clicks could result in a sale resulting in a profit of £400. However, if your business sells items with a far lower profit margin, perhaps in the region of £5 per customer you'll need to think about how much you're willing to spend to achieve a sale and how many sales you'll need each day to make your PPC advertising budget worthwhile. In short, calculate how much you're willing to spend in advertising to achieve one sale and have this as your target, just keep in mind that it'll probably need adjusting later.

Your PPC targets will of course have highs and lows. There may well be days when your PPC adverts do fantastically well and others that are really poor. Make sure you're scrutinising your spend to ensure that you're not making the mistake of, for example, on average spending £30 in PPC advertising to make a sale with a £20 profit.

Cost Per Click

Deciding on how much you're willing to spend every time someone clicks your advert is extremely important. On Google, advertisers with the highest 'cost per click' budget will be placed in the most prominent position, for example a business willing to spend £1.50 per click would be placed higher than a competitor only willing to spend £1.20 per click.

If a business had a budget of £5 per day and a maximum cost per click of £1 they would only receive around 5 clicks through to their website per day. However, if they lowered their maximum cost per click, they could potentially get more traffic from their daily budget. If the business decided to have a maximum cost per click of £0.50 they could potentially get around 10 visitors to their website per day based on their daily budget of £5. Unfortunately for advertisers, the less you spend the less likely you are to be seen so a maximum cost per click of £0.50 may result in no clicks in a day.

Every industry is different and the maximum cost per click you need to ensure you get a steady flow of traffic will vary. We suggest starting with a reasonably high maximum cost per click and then progressively taking it lower day-by-day and seeing at what level you need to keep your maximum cost per click to see results. Many businesses don't do this and have found that they could be spending 20-30% or less per click for the same or very similar results.

CREATING YOUR ADVERT

After deciding on your maximum cost per click and daily budget you'll move onto the advertisement itself. Firstly you'll need to provide the landing page, which is simply the page that people who click your advertisement are taken to. Make sure that your landing page is relevant to your advertisement, if you're selling a certain product don't have your PPC advert take the visitor to your website's homepage, take them directly to the product they're looking for. People can be very lazy when searching online, if they click a link expecting a product and they are not met with it, they can find it much easier to click the back button and move onto a different website instead of navigating their way through yours, which can mean both a missed customer and a wasted budget.

You'll then be asked to provide keywords for your PPC advert. This is pretty straightforward, but can require a bit of creative thinking; this is when you need to enter the words you'd like your advert to be found for. If you run a car leasing business your keywords might include; 'car lease', 'car leasing', 'business lease', 'business car lease', 'low cost business car lease'. The more precise keywords tend to be cheaper.

Google will tell you approximately what your cost per click needs to be in order for your advertisement to be seen for a certain keyword. Some keywords are extremely competitive and will require a maximum cost per click of £5 to £10+ whilst others can be very cheap, sometimes as low as £0.15 per click. There may be certain keywords or phrases that you want to be found on, so it's worth thinking about increasing your maximum cost per click for these keywords alone. If you increase your maximum cost per click for a certain keyword it'll not increase your maximum cost per click for the campaign as a whole.

Keep checking what is and isn't working when your campaign is running. Certain keywords can provide you with great results whilst others can be very poor; keep an eye on it and make changes when necessary to ensure you're getting the most from your budget.

Negative keywords can also be added to ensure that you're not wasting your budget on phrases you do not wish to be found for. For example if a financial advisor was using Google Adwords to increase enquiries, but they didn't offer mortgage advice then neg- ative keywords would be 'mortgage' and 'mortgage advice'.

Without entering this negative keyword the financial advisor may have their advert show up if someone searched for "independent financial advisor for mortgages" if one of their keyword phrases was "independent financial advisor". Without negative keywords you'll probably spend money unnecessarily so in addition to think- ing about the keywords you want to be found for in your sector, take the time to have a think about the keywords and phrases you don't wish to be found for.

WRITING YOUR ADVERT

Finally, you need to write your advert. If you rush this you're likely to miss out on potential customers. You need to grab the attention of those using the search engine and make them want to click your advert over your competitors. We like to run a few searches using our keywords and see what our competitors are up to, we may get inspiration from them or do something completely different.

It can be very frustrating that you're limited in the amount of char- acters you can use per line so you may need to get a thesaurus to get the most out of the amount of characters at your disposal. Ensure you have a call-to-action. Give people a reason to click on your advertisement. If you're running a special offer, promotion, discount of some sort then include it in the advert. When you've completed your ad put under review to ensure you haven't put any- thing naughty in there. Google have a number of policies regarding

PPC advertising such as not allowing use of excessive punctuation such as "Amazing Deal!!!!!!!!" There are many more and too many to list, but overall they're common sense and aimed to stop those trying to do something dishonest. The full list of policies is available on the Google Adwords website.

ADVERTISING SCHEDULING

Your advert will be live and showing up when people are searching for a product or service that matches yours. Think about your potential customers and your business, do you want your adverts to be showing at 2am or on a Sunday afternoon when no one is in the office to answer an enquiry? If you're running an online retail business with customers making orders 24/7 it won't be an issue. However, if you run an accountancy firm it could be wasted budget. Think about your business and when the most effective times and days for your advert to be seen will be. If you decide to have adverts running 24/7 think about what strategies you can have in place that can still allow a potential client to get in touch and enable you to answer questions that they may have.

PPC advertising is still very new and seems to be constantly evolving, but when used correctly could have significant impact upon your business. The main advice we have for those looking to venture in to PPC for the first time is to consistently analyse how much you're spending against the results you're seeing and making changes accordingly. Don't make the mistake we hear often of creating a PPC advertising campaign, leaving it to run and then logging back in a few months later annoyed at seeing poor results and having spent hundreds, maybe even thousands of pounds. When things are going well, accelerate it, or poorly, resolve it. Identify new opportunities and keep testing.

WEBSITE ANALYTICS

You need to know how well your website is performing. This can be done by using the free and incredible tool called Google Analytics. Using this free tool you can not only see how many visitors you get each day but also where they come from, what pages they look at, how long they stay for and much more.

To create an Analytics account visit www.google.co.uk/analytics and sign up for a new account if you don't have one already. Find a good Google Analytics plugin to install on WordPress, when this plugin is installed you'll be given a choice of which tracking information you need to get from your Google Analytics account. This is a very simple thing to get, all you need to do is login to your Analytics account and click 'Add a new account/site' then fill in the boxes with the details of your website. When completed you'll be given a tracking code to enter into the WordPress plugin. If this doesn't make sense watch an instructional video on how to find the Google Analytics tracking code, or how to set up Google Analytics.

When analytics is installed it'll take a while before you get any data and for that data to mean anything such as when your busy times are. Sometimes people install Google Analytics and wonder why it's not telling them any information right away. Once it's installed it then needs time to collect the data which can only happen over a period of time. Google Analytics could be a book in itself, and there's a wealth of information available. To get started it is a good idea to understand:

- How many visitors you get a day, week and month. As time goes on is your traffic level going lower, staying the same or increasing? If it's not increasing you need to find out why and work to make your traffic increase over time.
- **Bounce rate** - if it's higher than 60% then you need to make changes to your website as too many people are clicking away from it. If you can get your bounce rate to 40% or lower then you'll be doing great work.
- **Engagement** - how long people stay on your site, if the vast majority are staying for less than ten seconds then you know you need to work to make your site more interesting and engaging.
- **Acquisition** - where your visitors are coming from, whether it's visiting directly, social media or search engines you can get an idea of what advertising strategies are and aren't working for you.
- **Location** - this'll depend on your business but if you know the vast majority of your visitors are coming from a certain location there may be changes you can make to increase the conversion rate of visitors coming from this area.
- **Find out what people are looking at on your website** - Google Analytics will show you which pages of your website have had the most traffic, this is great as you can identify what's good about these particular pages and implement changes onto the pages that aren't performing so well.
- **Exit pages** - shows which pages have the highest number of visitors leaving your website. This is important, if you have pages that are turning people away from your website it's time to look at the pages in question and make changes.
- **Conversions** - Whether you want people to complete a contact form, sign up for a newsletter or make a purchase, set-

ting up a 'Goal' in Conversions can help you identify what percentage of visitors are doing what you wish and where they're coming from. If a conversion score is low, it's a great incentive to make your website better and monitor the conversion rate for improvements.

When you first log in to Google Analytics it can be quite overwhelming with lots of graphs and charts. Watching one of the excellent YouTube videos that Google has created will explain the Analytics admin area and show what you need to be looking at as a website owner.

Google Analytics is something that you'll learn more from through interaction. Now that you know what bounce rates, acquisitions and exit pages are, you can get to work on finding out how successfully your website is operating and work to make improvements.

AFFILIATION MARKETING

Affiliation marketing, in simple terms, is when someone else promotes your product on their website in return for a commission. There are four factors involved to make affiliation marketing work:

- Advertiser - The advertiser is the person or company who is selling the goods. They are the ones who pay the commission to the other people who are promoting the goods on their website.
- Publisher - A publisher is a person or company that promotes the goods of the advertiser in exchange for commission. Publishers have a contractual agreement to work with an advertiser who provides the publisher with links, banners, text ads or a unique phone number so that the publisher can add them to their website.
- Consumer - The consumer is the person who sees the advert on the publisher's website, clicks the link and makes a purchase. Therefore, earning the advertiser a sale and making the publisher some commission.
- Affiliate Network - You'll need to use an affiliate network who acts as the intermediary between the advertiser and the publisher.

HOW AFFILIATION MARKETING WORKS

So how does affiliation marketing actually work? Have you heard of cookies? No, not the delicious treat, but the computer version. "A cookie is a simple text file that is stored on your computer or mobile device by a website's server, and only that server will be able to retrieve or read the contents of that cookie. Each cookie is unique to your web browser." (BBC, n.d).

Have you ever searched for something like a holiday or a car, then suddenly you start seeing banner ads for holidays or cars on other websites? These adverts appear because cookies have stored your user preferences. Cookies are how affiliate marketing works. When a consumer clicks an advertiser's advert on the publisher's website, the consumer's browser receives a tracking cookie that identifies the advertiser, the publisher, the specific advert and commission amount.

Let's have an example. Imagine you sell your own branded cosmetics and in order to reach more consumers you join an affiliate network. Publishers who are interested in cosmetics and have cosmetic-related websites such as blogs will work with you to promote your cosmetics for a commission. Readers of these blogs will see your adverts on the blog and hopefully click the link and make a purchase.

The affiliate network provides the advertiser and the publisher with the technology for this to work. The affiliate network also provides you with other services such as providing the advertiser access to publishers. They'll also give you a portal to manage your commission percentages and monitor your sales activity with dashboards, charts, graphs and metrics. Affiliate marketing isn't cheap for the advertiser as you'll have to pay a setup fee and likely pay monthly management fees.

MANAGING PUBLISHERS

One of the advantages of affiliation marketing is that you only pay commission if your publisher achieves a sale, or a registration depending on what your goal is. You also get to set the commission amount. Your commission strategy is important, because you'll be competing against other advertisers possibly selling the same goods as you. If you offer lower commission than your competitors then you'll find it difficult to attract publishers. You may also want to consider basing commission on volume sales, to encourage publishers to sell more.

Good publishers are invaluable to your business, so ensure that you look after them as you would with your internal employees. Take care of them by giving them the opportunity to win rewards, prizes and other incentives for achieving good sales. Also keep publishers up-to-date with all your news, promotions and anything else they might need to make more commission (Smith, 2011).

An important point is not to spam the inbox of your consumers with marketing emails, especially if they've come from your publishers' websites. The consumers will have bought your goods via a trusted recommendation from your publisher's website, so in irritating the consumer you'll also irritate the publishers.

AFFILIATION MARKETING SUMMARY

Depending on what you're trying to achieve and what your business model is, you may want to be an advertiser or a publisher. If you've created your own product then you're more likely to want to be an advertiser and have publishers promote your product. However, a publisher is also an entrepreneur and your whole business model could be about promoting other companies' goods in return for commission. Whatever your strategy is, affiliate marketing can be a great way of increasing your sales figures.

ONLINE MARKETPLACES

An online marketplace, also known as an ecommerce marketplace, is an ecommerce website where products and services are available for purchase by a variety of third parties, but the transactions are processed by the marketplace operator. Some examples include Amazon and eBay. Many people don't realise that with websites like Amazon, while Amazon sell goods through their website, so do third parties.

In this chapter we're going to cover two of the most popular online marketplaces, eBay and Amazon. We'll be looking at the opportunities these platforms provide to business owners, and their drawbacks. This chapter will primarily focus on businesses that sell a physical product. However, we still suggest reading it if you run a service business. There's scope for service-based businesses to retail point of sale (POS) and other products than can help you to promote your brand.

The History of Online Marketplaces

eBay started in 1995 in Pierre Omidyar's living room, it was a simple idea but one that had not been implemented on a large scale, to give individuals an opportunity to buy and sell products online. It's grown enormously and is now an internationally recognisable brand. eBay gives business owners the opportunity to showcase their products to a worldwide audience on a platform that gets millions of unique visitors every month.

Similar to eBay, Amazon was founded around the same time, in 1994 by Jeff Bezos in his garage. Amazon has grown into one of the greatest ecommerce sites of all time, selling everything from books to clothing. Amazon now offers business owners the opportunity to sell their products on their website, which can be an incredible opportunity for online retailers.

BENEFITS OF ONLINE MARKETPLACES

Sales - In today's World, one of the major challenges is acquiring customers in such an overcrowded market both offline and online. Search engine optimisation, pay per click advertising, social media management, offline advertising and more is required to drive customers to your website. However, with platforms such as eBay and Amazon, these online retailers already enjoy huge levels of traffic due to their long trading history and popularity. Taking advantage of their high traffic by selling your goods through these websites makes it more likely for people to view your products and make an order. Note that if your business is offline and you don't have an ecommerce website then using online marketplaces will give you access to a greater market of customers.

Consumer Confidence - eBay and Amazon are highly trusted brands that have millions of online users around the world who have the confidence to use their payment methods. Online retail stores can have low conversion rates due to a lack of confidence. This can be due to it being a new business and or visitors not being willing to provide payment details in order for payments to be processed. Listing products on platforms such as eBay and Amazon allows business owners to promote and sell their products on the websites of some of the most recognisable brands on the planet.

Repeat Business - although eBay and Amazon have strict rules on how users can market their business to customers they acquire, there is the opportunity for repeat business from customers. As a former eBay seller, we had a number of loyal customers who purchased goods from us through eBay as opposed to using other sellers as they favoured our customer service and dispatch time.

Quickly Sell Slow-Moving Stock - poor cash flow is a serious problem, so money tied up in stock that isn't selling will have a real impact on a business. Using platforms such as eBay and Amazon can help quickly sell slow-moving products if the RRP (recommended retail price) is reduced.

Presence on Search Engines - businesses listing items on eBay and Amazon get to enjoy the backing of two major corporations that put significant resources into online marketing and paid advertising. Products listed on eBay and Amazon can frequently show up highly in search engine results. However, be aware that customers, when shopping for specific goods, tend to go direct to online marketplaces rather than general search engines. Another reason to utilise the potential of online marketplaces

Overseas Customers - eBay and Amazon are platforms that are used around the world, meaning businesses have the opportunity to gain clients from outside their usual territory. This is great news for online retailers as it opens up their potential customer base exponentially. For those selling their own brand of goods it's close to an absolute must.

NEGATIVES OF ONLINE MARKETPLACES

Selling fees - with eBay it costs money every time you list a product for sale, they also take a percentage of any sale, if you have an *eBay Store* there is also a monthly fee involved.

On Amazon, retailers can choose between having a 'PRO' account with a monthly charge and a fee every time a sale is made. For those looking for a more basic package, there is an option to only be charged a fee when a sale is made, although this does not come with as many features. We've not listed the exact costs as they are subject to change, all costs are available on each website.

Rules - acquiring a new customer is great, it means you have the opportunity to promote your business to them in the future, if they opt in to receive communications from you. Unfortunately both eBay and Amazon have strict rules on how sellers can communicate with buyers. In short, sellers are not allowed to act in a way that encourages taking the buyer away from the eBay and Amazon platforms. Adding eBay and Amazon customers to an email marketing list or attempting to promote your business away from your seller account is strictly forbidden.

Stock Levels - managing stock levels can be a time-consuming task. The more platforms you have, the more challenging keeping an accurate record becomes. If you sell a product on your own website, eBay and Amazon there is the potential to run out of stock whilst still having the product listed for sale.

We feel that if you're a retailer, both offline and online, the benefits of selling your goods through online marketplaces far outweigh the disadvantages.

USING ONLINE MARKETPLACES

Whether these platforms are right for you will depend on your business model and profit margins. It's common to have fees of over 10 percent of the sale price, so make sure you research and understand the cost of listing an item and the final value fees associated with making a sale.

If you're able to sell your items at a profit on these platforms then it can be a worthwhile activity for business owners. eBay and Amazon will open your business up to a huge number of potential customers around the world; this opportunity isn't otherwise available without investing a huge amount in online advertising.

If you decide to retail your products on platforms such as eBay and Amazon it's a good idea to analyse which items to list and how you can effectively promote your business. Here are some of our pointers:

- You don't have to list every product you offer. It's a good idea to trial a handful of products on new platforms and grow the number of products available when you're confident. Opening your products to a worldwide audience can result in increased sales and enquiries so you need to ensure you have the strategies and time available to deal with a potential influx.
- Promotional items such as t-shirts, pens, stickers or mouse mats, for example, with your company logo on can either be listed for sale if you run a service business, or given away as a free gift with orders.
- If you're listing fast-moving items, make sure you factor in the time it'll take to package and post all of your orders. Selling dozens of a product with a very low profit margin could result in you or a member of staff spending half a day or more packaging the items and not making very much money.

If you'd like to start selling on these platforms there are a number of great instructional videos available on YouTube that'll show you step-by-step how to setup an account and list products. While we could show you the steps in this book the instructions would become instantly out-of-date as these platforms change and evolve constantly.

Other online market places you could consider include:

- Play
- Priceminister
- Etsy
- Sears
- Rakuten

Summary

We both wanted to thank you very much for purchasing this book. We hope you've been able to find what you've been looking for and that it'll be a source of information for you when you need it.

We would take great pleasure in knowing if you've found the book useful. We welcome any improvements, suggestions, war stories, or if you just simply want to get in touch, please, feel free to contact us on:

Email: sayhello@businesshacks.tips

Website: www.businesshacks.tips

Twitter: @RiceandLeong

We both handle the email address personally and we'll reply to all emails.

There's a huge amount of information to take in here, so to get the best out of this book we recommend that you read it more than once and refer back to it whenever you face challenges.

Best wishes,

Jamie Rice and Andrew Leong

REFERENCES & BIBLIOGRAPHY

Andrew. A, Thisismoney.co.uk. 2013. *How start-ups can tap cash from ordinary people and give the prospect of huge profits in return... What is crowdfunding and how does it work?* [Online] Available at: http://www.thisismoney.co.uk/money/smallbusiness/article-2333399/Crowdfunding-does-work.html

BBC. N.d., *What is a cookie?* [Online] Available at: http://www.bbc.co.uk/privacy/cookies/about

Bianchini, D., 2011. *10 Stats to Justify SEO.* searchenginejournal.com, [blog] 21 November. Available at: http://www.searchenginejournal.com/10-stats-to-justify-seo/36762/

Brown. Carolyn M. inc.com (2011). *10 Pros and Cons of Using Groupon.* [online] Available at: http://www.inc.com/guides/201104/10-pros-cons-for-using-groupon.html

Gove.co.uk. 2014. *Making it easier to set up and grow a business.* [Online] Available at:

https://www.gov.uk/government/policies/making-it-easier-to-set-up-and-grow-a-business—6/supporting-pages/getting-banks-lending

HubSpot. n.d. Search Engine Optimization Stats. [online] Available at: http://www.hubspot.com/marketing-statistics

Hubspot. n.d. *The Ultimate List of Marketing Statistics.* [Online] Available at: http://www.hubspot.com/marketing-statistics

Lazazzera, R., n.d. How *To Find a Manufacturer or Supplier for Your Product Idea.* shopify.co.uk [blog]. Available at: <www.shopify.co.uk/blog/13975985-how-to-find-a-manufacturer-or-supplier-for-your-product-idea>

Lewy, A., 2012. *Made In The UK? The Pros And Cons Of Outsourcing Clothing Manufacture Overseas,* enterprisenation.com [blog] 10 October. Available at: <https://www.enterprisenation.com/blog/posts/made-in-the-uk-the-pros-and-cons-of-outsourcing-clothing-manufacture-overseas>

newsroom.fb.com. n.d. *Our History.* [online] Available at: http://newsroom.fb.com/company-info/

Matt., 2012. *14 Ways To Perform Supplier Due Diligence Like A Pro.* dhlguide.co.uk [blog] June 7. Available at: <http://dhlguide.co.uk/14-ways-perform-supplier-due-diligence-pro/> Accessed [15 January 2015]

Parks. S, 2005. *Start Your Business Week by Week.* Harlow: Pearson Education

Shopify - Ecommerce University., n.d. *Finding and Working With Suppliers.* [Online] Available at: https://ecommerce.shopify.com/guides/dropshipping/finding-suppliers

Shopify - Ecommerce University., n.d. *Understanding Dropshipping.* [Online] Available at: https://ecommerce.shopify.com/guides/dropshipping/understanding-dropshipping

Shopify - Ecommerce University., n.d. *Picking Products To Dropship.* [Online] Available at: https://ecommerce.shopify.com/guides/dropshipping/picking-products-to-dropship

Smith. J., 2011. *Start an Online Business.* Warwickshire: In Easy Steps.

Tara. n.d. ideasuploaded.com. *How to Make an Invention Prototype Cheaply.* [Online] Available at: http://ideasuploaded.com/how-to-make-an-invention-prototype-cheaply/.

The Charted Institute of Marketing. 2010. *Cost of customer acquisition vs customer retention.* Available at: http://www.camfoundation.com/PDF/Cost-of-customer-acquisition-vs-customer-retention.

Printed in Great Britain
by Amazon